LIBERTINE STRATEGIES

Contemporary illustration for Cyrano's *Voyage dans la lune*, from *Les Oeuvres libertines de Cyrano de Bergerac*, ed. Ferdinand Lachevre (Paris: Champion, 1921). Courtesy of the Yale University Library.

LIBERTINE STRATEGIES

Freedom and the Novel in

Seventeenth-Century

France

Joan DeJean

OHIO STATE UNIVERSITY PRESS : COLUMBUS

Library of Congress Cataloguing in Publication Data

DeJean, Joan E.
  Libertine strategies.

  Bibliography: p.
  Includes index.
   1.   French fiction—17th century—History and criticism.   2.   Lib-
ertines (French philosophers).
I.   Title.
PQ645.D37   843′.4′091   81-38431
ISBN 0-8142-0325-6   AACR2

For Charlie

TABLE OF CONTENTS

Preface   ix

ONE
The Other *Grand Siècle*   3

TWO
"Theme of the Traitor and the Hero"   33

THREE
Fragments of a Philosophical Discourse   77

FOUR
Camera Lucida   101

FIVE
The Other in the *Grand Siècle*   157

Appendix: Neighboring Trends   203

Bibliography   209

Index   219

PREFACE

It has become something of a commonplace to note that Antoine Adam's *Romanciers du dix-septième siècle* has sparked a renewed concern with French seventeenth-century fiction. The energy of this revival is far from spent, and the near future will certainly bring new histories of trends in the early novel. The present study both is and is not such a history. It does deal with a group of novels similar enough to be examined under a common heading, and it suggests relationships, even relationships of influence, among them. Yet it does not aspire to the comprehensiveness of previous volumes on the seventeenth-century novel. Some may argue that its scope is not vast enough. Certainly there are contemporary novels related in important ways to the novels considered here. For example, Scarron's *Roman comique* could have played an interesting role in the chapter on narrative structures.[1] Such parallelisms do not shatter the unity of my corpus. The novels I refer to as libertine profit in a special way from the type of reading proposed here. Had I chosen to explore every point of comparison with novels outside this small group, I would have obtained thoroughness at the expense of detail.

It is in the domain of what might be termed intimacy that this study differs most clearly from traditional histories of the novel. Categories such as "comic novel" or "realistic novel" produce corpuses too vast for anything but generalized examination. As long as all the seventeenth-century's non-"heroic" texts are considered as a package deal, they will receive only sketchy treatment. The assumption appears to be that the majority of these texts are not rich enough to sustain more rigorous analysis. A critic can easily devote an entire book to a text considered first-rate, but he must deal with many more third-rate works to fill the same number of pages. Enough is known by now about the broad lines of the seventeenth-century novel's evolution to allow critics to begin the exploration of its lesser trends and of their elective affinities, to compose aesthetic rather than factual histories. The type of analyses I propose here could not have been worked out for a larger body of texts. I hope this concentration has enabled me to convey some sense of the uniqueness of these libertine novels.

In the following pages, I often express concern over the critical neglect from which the writers I call libertine have suffered and continue to suffer. Happily, that situation is now beginning to change, at least with regard to some of them. Since I started to write about libertine strategies, one lengthy new contribution, Jean Serroy's *thèse d'état, L'Art romanesque dans les histoires comiques du dix-septième siècle* (not yet published), has come to my attention. Although I have not been able to consult Serroy's study, I do know that the majority of the writers I am concerned with here find a place in it. And there is surely other work in progress, or perhaps even completed, of which I am not yet aware. I do not intend to suggest that these coincidences are in any way unusual; books on similar subjects frequently appear simultaneously. But as an author certain to form part of one such coincidence, I cannot but express my interest in the current pattern of critical inquiry.

Before turning to the strategies I will refer to as libertine, a few words are in order on my own strategies in the following chapters. When I look over my initial prospectus for this book, much of what I finally wrote seems predictable. But the finished product contains many surprises, deviations from my original plan that I not only did not predict but could not have predicted, since they resulted from what I view as an important change in my motivation for writing the book. When I began working on this project, I was essentially motivated by my conviction that these novels are striking precursors of our own literary modernity. I would have described my task as one of making them more accessible to a contemporary public, of finding a broader audience for them. As my work progressed, however, it became increasingly evident to me that the single aspect of this project that I found most fascinating—indeed, almost obsessively so—was the complex bond between the libertine writer and persecution.

"Persecution" is a key term for this study. It may therefore seem surprising that what I mean by persecution is never very precisely defined. With the benefit of hindsight, it is easy for me to explain this vagueness. I was quite simply a victim of those whose victimization I have portrayed in these pages. If I was unable in most cases to set limits to my use of "persecution," to say how, why, to what extent, and above all by whom the libertines were oppressed, it is because I was originally too trusting a reader of libertine texts. The libertine novelist and the libertine hero alike speak obsessively about their victimization. I took the writers' obsession at face value, and did not sort out the very real efforts by the libertines' mostly unnamed adversaries to limit both their physical and their literary freedom from their mythologizing of such efforts. I came to realize that these works had been relegated to a marginal status, not only because of the verdict of some arbitrary historical force or forces over which their authors had no control, but mainly because the libertine novelists consciously chose, and indeed at times militated for, such a position. They *wanted* to present themselves as underdogs, as victims of persecution, because their favorite mode of writing was defensive.

What is most interesting to me about this defensiveness is that it is contagious. The libertine novelist invites his readers (and critics) to identify with him, to pity his persecution, and ultimately to write from the victim's position, to write defensively. At times, I became concerned that, by sympathizing with their defensive posture, I was perhaps making these writers less accessible rather than more so. By the end of the book, I even refuse to grant the libertines the position of influence previously accorded them by some critics. But it is also possible that the libertine defensiveness is not foreign to our modernity, and that, therefore, my own process of understanding was an essential part of my initial project.

It was only after completing this book that I discovered Leo Strauss's *Persecution and the Art of Writing*, in which he refers to defensive literary techniques as "writing between the lines." "The influence of persecution on literature is precisely that it compels all writers who hold heterodox views to develop a peculiar technique of writing, the technique we have in mind when speaking of writing between the lines." By "writing between the lines," Strauss designates the means by which a writer can "perform the miracle of speaking in a publication to a minority, while being silent to the

majority of his readers."[2] I am by no means a convert to Straus-
sianism, but some of its terminology finds parallels in my work.
For example, by "libertine strategies" I mean the techniques of
"writing between the lines" practiced by the seventeenth-century
French novelists I call libertine: Théophile de Viau, Charles Sorel,
Tristan L'Hermite, Cyrano de Bergerac, Chapelle, and D'Assoucy. Each of the following chapters examines one of the techniques of indirection by means of which these writers write "libertinely," that is, transmit their message of intellectual and narrative freedom in a devious manner that serves to camouflage that
message.

   The initial chapter of *Libertine Strategies* defines the problem
and the corpus to be examined and traces the history of libertine
fiction in and after the seventeenth century. I begin the chapter *in
medias res* with the discussion of a problem that acts as a *mise en
abyme* of the entire libertine enterprise and serves, therefore, as a
model for the pages to follow. The major libertine writers are
known by their first names alone: Théophile, Tristan,[3] Cyrano.
The origin of these names and the story of their use present some
of the central questions for *Libertine Strategies*: the importance
of the act of naming for the libertine enterprise, the libertine penchant for fictionalizing history, and the peculiar libertine relationship to persecution. The critical indirection I favor in the first
chapter is repeated in subsequent ones where I introduce a problem of particular importance for the libertine texts before turning
to the passages in the texts I feel are illuminated by the initial
discussion. Thus, chapter two opens with the question of the limits of autobiography, chapter three initially traces the limits of the
novel's territory, and chapter five begins by juxtaposing two theories of periodization and epistemological crisis, those of Bakhtin
and Foucault. This structure seems appropriately libertine: my
critical moves follow the swerve of libertine obliqueness. Actually, I chose this roundabout presentation in an attempt to awaken
the reader's curiosity by associating the libertine texts from the
start with questions more familiar to him than these novels that
have long suffered from critical neglect.

   Early readers of this manuscript suggested that I conclude with
a chapter on the successors of these libertine writers, Rousseau
and Sade, for example. Such a section could have served to place

this study in a context of wider critical interest. I originally decided against writing such a conclusion because I felt the libertines should stand on their own. I was concerned that their works might be overshadowed by those of their more illustrious eighteenth-century "heirs." Now I also know that I did not write this conclusion because I sensed that a chapter would not be sufficient to trace the parallels I wished to explore. I am currently about to embark on what will be in some sense a sequel to this project, a book on the defensive strategies of Rousseau, Laclos, and Sade.

Libertine Strategies was written during the tenure of a fellowship sponsored by the National Endowment for the Humanities. The University of Pennsylvania released me from my teaching duties and facilitated my work in every way. I would like to thank all those who helped me obtain and use this grant, especially Vartan Gregorian. I would also like to thank the colleagues who read this manuscript in its early stages: Jean Alter, Clifton Cherpack, and Georges May. They argued with me, criticized me, even praised me—managed to keep me both going and on my toes. Maurice Laugaa provided encouragement in the crucial last phase of its composition. English Showalter's thoughtful and generous criticism of the completed manuscript helped guide me through its revisions. My debt to Charlie Bernheimer is impossible to measure. He, too, argued with me, criticized me, and yes, even praised me—and he also poured over every word of this manuscript with more attention than I had ever dreamed it would receive.

New Haven, Connecticut
June, 1980

1. In an appendix, I discuss certain novels with affinities to the libertine tradition.

2. Strauss, pp. 24, 25. For most works, complete references are provided in the Bibliography. References that cannot be easily traced in this matter are included in the notes.

3. "Tristan" is sometimes considered a surname, but Tristan himself played with it as if it were a given name.

LIBERTINE STRATEGIES

Euclid's world is very simple and Einstein's world is very difficult; nevertheless it is now impossible to return to Euclid's. No revolution, no heresy is comfortable and easy. Because it is a leap, it is a rupture of the smooth revolutionary curve, and a rupture is a wound, a pain. But it is a necessary wound. Most people suffer from hereditary sleeping sickness, and those who are sick with this ailment (entropy) must not be allowed to sleep or they will go to their last sleep, the sleep of death.—Evgeny Zamiatin

THE OTHER *GRAND SIECLE*

On m'a chassé de la cour, où je n'avais que faire; si on me presse encore à sortir de France, quelque part de l'Europe où je veuille aller, mon nom m'y a fait des connoissances. Je me sais facilement accommoder à toute diversité de vivres et d'habillements; les climats et les hommes me sont indifférents.—Théophile (de Viau)

Ceci est de l'histoire et ne nous regarde plus, simple biographe littéraire, humble critique cherchant quelques perles dans le fumier des écrivains de second ordre.—Théophile (Gautier)

I. THE TWO THEOPHILES

Avant d'avoir lu un seul de ses vers je lui portais déjà un tendre intérêt à cause de son nom de Théophile, qui est le mien. . . . C'est peut-être une puérilité, mais je vous avoue que tout le mal que l'on disait de Théophile de Viau me semblait adressé à moi, Théophile Gautier. Théophile est un nom comme un autre, . . . mais ce nom obscur, . . . je l'aime dans moi et dans les autres. . . .

Voyez come la marraine de Théophile a eu une idée triomphante de l'appeler ainsi et pas autrement! Car il est certain que, si elle lui eut donné pour nom Christophe ou Barthélemy, je ne m'en serais pas occupé le moins du monde.[1]

Two men named Théophile were leaders of what could be considered parallel intellectual and artistic revolutions. A little over two centuries passed after one Théophile was hanged in effigy and imprisoned before the first individual outside his immediate circle of friends took up his defense: the other Théophile. As Gautier admits, he originally noticed his kindred spirit only because of the

3

first name they share, a name otherwise rare in the French literary tradition. Nevertheless, this curious onomastic recurrence is not nearly so interesting as the onomastic difference that sets these writers apart. Their baptismal certificates show that they began life with both a Christian and a family name, yet while history has chosen to employ this double name when speaking of the nineteenth-century French author, an exceptional practice has become current in the case of his predecessor. Gautier was the first to remark that the seventeenth-century man of letters has traditionally been referred to simply as "Théophile." "Sur le titre de ses oeuvres, Théophile, je ne sais pourquoi, n'est désigné que par son prénom." The question should not be dropped with Gautier's casual "je ne sais pourquoi."

The proper name is the only sign with a unique referent. "Théophile de Viau" designates the individual Théophile de Viau and no one but Théophile de Viau. The first name, however, presents special problems within the category of the proper name.[2] When unmarked by deictics, "Théophile" is merely a Christian name with an infinite number of possible referents, referents that become clear only with the addition of a family name: Théophile de Viau, Théophile Gautier, Théophile Un Tel. To suppress "de Viau" and leave only "Théophile" is to destroy the specificity of the functioning of this proper name. When referred to simply as "Théophile," Théophile de Viau loses his identity, becomes one Théophile among countless others. This name fails to fulfill properly its basic function of marking off his personal territory. Were his case unique in the history of seventeenth-century French literature, it would be less significant. There are, however, two other contemporary writers who share Théophile's fate and are known in literary history by their first names alone: Cyrano and Tristan. Such appellations cause obvious confusion. For example, the individual who announces his intention of reading the works of one of these authors may encounter the same eminently logical question: "Which Théophile?" "Which Tristan?"—even, "Which Cyrano?" On a more practical level, the critic trying to track down scholarly references can never be certain of their place in alphabetical classifications. Will Cyrano be listed under "C" for "Cyrano" or "B" for "Bergerac?"[3]

The twentieth-century scholar's bibliographic dilemma is only a largely inconsequential by-product of a phenomenon with much larger implications. The suppression of family names not only produces inconsistencies among indexes, it also reflects a loss of status in literary history. Whereas the inconsistencies are accidental, the loss of status is not. It is the result of a desire to obliterate, along with their names, the values represented by these writers and by many of the works they produced. In their day, Théophile de Viau, Cyrano de Bergerac, and Tristan L'Hermite, to return their full names to them for once, were known as libertines, freethinkers whose flamboyant life styles, dangerous ideas, and attacks on the ruling order(s) threw suspicion on their literary productions. They created daring, unusual novels at a time when partisans of literary codification were beginning their attempts to destroy all that did not conform to their carefully laid out rules.

Using three essential strategies, the *grand siècle* eliminated the blemish of the libertine writer from the otherwise flawless surface it was contriving even then to leave for posterity. First, it created a climate hostile to the publication and the distribution of works by authors of unorthodox philosophical stance. Although the repressive conditions for publication in the seventeenth century often have been exaggerated, certain facts give testimony to the difficulties encountered by the novelists under consideration here. A mere three copies of the first edition of Théophile's *Fragments d'une histoire comique* have survived.[4] Only one copy of the first edition of Tristan's *Le Page disgracié* is known to exist.[5] As for Cyrano's novels, the only text of *L'Autre Monde*[6] available until the publication of the Paris manuscript at the beginning of this century was mutilated by the cutting of his friend Le Bret, and no manuscript of *Les Estats et empires du soleil* has ever been found to rehabilitate the second imaginary voyage. Second, these unwelcome authors were eased out of the literary mainstream by a general disparagement of their talents. From the Père Garasse's diatribes against Théophile in his *Doctrine curieuse des beaux esprits de ce temps ou prétendus tels* (1623) to the scornful evaluation of Cyrano's sometime friend Ménage, "Je crois que, quand il fit son *Voyage dans la lune* il en avait déjà le premier quartier dans la tête,"[7] no efforts were spared to undermine their importance. They became known as second-, if not third-, rate authors of small, outlandish books. Finally, to finish them off, the *grand siècle* removed their last names, the mark of father, family, and heritage. A new onomastic category in modern literary history was created for them—to be closed with their passing and re-opened but twice more, in a gesture of two later centuries' conde-scending sympathy for their own mad writers, Jean-Jacques and Gérard.[8] Madmen, like children and the stars of the day, need only a first name.[9]

Nor is this the end of libertine name games. With the exception of "Théophile," even the first names by which these men are known present problems. In the most extreme case, that of Cyra-no de Bergerac, "Cyrano" is the only component of this name acquired at birth. The future libertine was baptized Savinien de Cyrano, but he apparently tired quickly of this name. At the age of twenty, he had already begun to indulge in flamboyant ono-mastic transformations. He abandoned his baptismal name, "Sa-vinien," changed his family name to a first name, and completed this creation with the addition of "Bergerac," the name of an es-tate that had once been owned by his grandfather[10] and that had belonged in the sixteenth century to a family named de Bergerac. This is the name he continued to use most often, the name by which he was known to his contemporaries, and the name posteri-ty would continue to adopt, and abbreviate, when referring to him. But Cyrano's fascination with naming did not end there. Soon after the adoption of "Cyrano de Bergerac," his nominal creativity led him to appropriate at random the following signa-tures: "de Bergerac Cyrano," "de Cyrano de Bergerac," "Alexan-dre de Cyrano Bergerac," "Hercule de Bergerac," even occasion-ally the anagram "Dyrcona," and variants employing it, such as "Savinien Bergerac Dyrcona." In the ensuing confusion, he was taken at his word, and "de Bergerac" was generally accepted as his family name. The ironic result of his incessant twists is that the so-called first name, "Cyrano," pejoratively used as his only name, is his actual family name. But "Cyrano," as a result of its bearer's own manipulations, no longer functions as a family name but rather as a given name too vague to be sufficient for the identi-fication of a human being. Hence the possibility of the question "Which Cyrano?", even though "Cyrano" as a Christian name is unique in its class.

Cyrano shares the will to shape his own onomastic destiny with his friend Tristan. The latter was baptized François L'Hermite, but near the age of twenty he exchanged his prosaic baptismal name for "Tristan." He probably made this change to give himself legendary airs and certainly to establish an association with a famous previous bearer of the name "Tristan L'Hermite," the *grand prévôt de l'hôtel de France* during the reign of Louis XI. Tristan was also continuing a family tradition, for his entire family, and especially his younger brother Jean-Baptiste, was constantly engaged in complicated genealogical maneuvers in the hope of annexing glorious ancestors, such as Pierre L'Hermite and Tristan L'Hermite.[11] In Tristan's case, when his contemporaries began the practice of referring to him by an adopted first name alone, all links with his actual family heritage disappeared, leaving only a connection with a fairy-tale past of his own invention.[12]

Before examining the implications of this desire to shape grandiose names for oneself, I would like to mention briefly a related case, that of a writer linked with the same libertine circle as Cyrano and Tristan, a writer best known as the "Emperor of the Burlesque": D'Assoucy. As his birth certificate attests, he was baptized with a simple name, Charles Coyppeau, suitable for a lawyer's son. Unfortunately, so few historians of literature have concerned themselves with the dark areas of his highly complicated biography that the age at which he chose to adopt a new name has not yet been established, much less the resonances this name may have had for him. All that seems clear according to his only modern editor, Emile Colombey, is that "D'Assoucy" is a false name of his own invention, selected to replace his family name in accordance with the glorious literary ambitions of an individual who would later exult in his title as the emperor of the most carefree of genres. So complete is the mystery surrounding this name, in fact, that even today, when the orthography of most other family names of the period has been standardized, this one remains uncertain. It may be found written "D'Assoucy," "d'Assoucy," or "Dassoucy."[13]

The three instances I have described were not, of course, the only nominal duplicities that occurred in seventeenth-century France. The practice of annexing "de" in the hope of usurping nobility was current at the period. Actors, and at least one actor-playwright, assumed new names to protect their families from contamination. But examples such as these of writers indulging in willfully creative nominal transformations are unheard of outside the milieu with which I am concerned.

Tristan, Cyrano, and D'Assoucy manipulate their names as a political sign associating them with the libertine movement. In the years following Théophile's trial, a writer who did nothing to hide his allegiance to this milieu would surely have been ostracized by official circles. Rather than waiting to have judgment passed on them, these young writers took over the organization of their own fates by wiping out their original heritage. In the process, they appropriated for themselves a new family and a new heritage. They revealed themselves to be subversive individuals by destroying the importance of a possession treasured by a society where it could open or close doors, the name. They rejected the name and all it stands for: paternal authority, family obligations, a fixed social status.[14] As a replacement for the name, they adopted onomastic masks that give none of the information normally conveyed by names. These pseudo names branded their users with their chosen vocations, as though they were members of a religious order. They were no longer L'Hermites, or Cyranos, or Coyppeaus, but libertines, members of a family they freely accepted and that accepted them freely, a family that replaced traditional responsibilities with intellectual ones, a family destined for promulgation rather than propagation.[15] By calling attention to themselves in such a flamboyant way, they provided, before having set pen to paper, the initial impetus in the process of their own ostracism.

The obscurity of their prose works would have been enough in itself to bar the libertines from great literary success. The official disfavor they encouraged guaranteed their virtual elimination. From the very beginning, all but their immediate circle greeted them with scorn. Since the French critical tradition almost always has respected the seventeenth century's vision of itself, the image of these authors handed down from generation to generation has remained as immobile as they themselves were changing. Any attempt at an exhaustive survey of these dismissals would require at least a chapter in itself. To illustrate the extent to which these writers have been underestimated, one need only look at the most important studies accorded them before the last decade.

Gautier's *Les Grotesques* (1844) inaugurates the "rediscovery" of Théophile and Cyrano,[16] but the title of his volume reflects the peculiar critical slant from which he views them. In the preface to his "collection de têtes grimaçantes," Gautier explains his interest in these "auteurs de troisième ordre, dédaignés ou tombés en désuétude," these "pauvres diables," in terms of a fascination with "difformités littéraires," and "déviations poétiques."[17] Remarks such as these reduce these authors to mere literary curiosities, to be read with any degree of seriousness only by a few maniac bibliophiles, and to be treated simply as a source of amusing anecdotes (Cyrano's nose and such) by a more general public. The same disparaging attitude is evident in Victor Fournel's study of lesser-known writers of the seventeenth century, *La Littérature indépendante et les écrivains oubliés*, which contains chapters on authors associated with the libertine milieu—"des auteurs d'un ordre inférieur, comme Cyrano, . . . Dassoucy."[18]

Literary historians of the early twentieth century generally concern themselves with these writers not because of their artistic merits, but rather because they were part of a group whose religious beliefs they either defend or disparage. The two men responsible for editing and publishing their works, for establishing their bibliographies, and for reconstructing the history of their literary activities, Antoine Adam and Frédéric Lachèvre, are ideal representatives of these opposing stands. Even Adam, the great defender of libertine rights, is not always capable of taking these writers seriously. He refers to Cyrano and D'Assoucy, for example, as "les extravagants."[19] Lachèvre is far more outraged by their excesses, and even as he publishes volume after volume of the series *Le Libertinage en France au dix-septième siècle*, he cannot hide his growing antipathy for the men to whom he is devoting his life's work:

> Plus nous avançons dans la monographie des libertins du dix-septième siècle et dans la publication de leurs oeuvres, plus se précise notre définition du libertin: un faible d'esprit incapable de maîtriser ses passions, en d'autres termes un homme rétif à toute discipline intellectuelle volontairement consentie et ayant perdu le sens des réalités; un déséquilibré chez qui la sensation l'emporte sur la raison.[20]

It is easy to understand from even this brief survey why such writers, studied only for their eccentric behavior or their untimely

religious convictions, could not be granted a place in the grand
fresco of the seventeenth century that was to be passed on to generations of French schoolchildren as the ultimate proof of the
greatness of their national literature. As F. T. Perrens reasons in
Les Libertins en France au dix-septième siècle:

> Ce parti pris, cette partialité optimiste viennent du point de vue
> pédagogique où l'éducation de la jeunesse nous conduit à nous
> placer. Voulant former les coeurs et les esprits, tâche sacrée, nous
> enfermons nos enfants dans l'étude des plus beaux modèles que
> fournissent notre langue et notre littérature, nous ne leur mon-
> trons du dix-septième siècle que tout ce qu'il a de pur, de beau,
> d'admirable, moisson si riche que nous pouvons négliger le reste.[21]

Opinion after opinion confirmed what the contemporaries of
these writers knew from the start: there was little reason to pay
attention to the bizarre texts of slightly mad authors. Today, of
the novels already discussed here, only Cyrano's *L'Autre Monde*
exists in an easily obtainable edition,[22] and volumes of the last
editions of Tristan's *Page disgracié* and D'Assoucy's *Avantures*
and *Avantures d'Italie* are difficult to find, even in major libraries.
The scarcity of texts could continue to confine these works to the
marginal status conferred upon them by a historical period threatened by their difference. Thus, I believe that a serious reevaluation of both their merits and their relationships to each other is
called for.

2. THE EVOLUTION OF A GENRE

René Pintard's definitive study, *Le Libertinage érudit dans la
première moitié du dix-septième siècle*, maps out well the activities of the small group of freethinkers who discreetly gathered
around the so-called Tétrade of their intellectual leaders, Pierre
Gassendi, François de La Mothe Le Vayer, Gabriel Naudé, and
Diodati. In such friendly homes as that of the Dupuy brothers
(the *académie putéane*), they discussed the most important contemporary trends in philosophy and science. Their intellectual in-
vestigations reached a peak in the years immediately following
what both Pintard and J. S. Spink agree is a major dividing line in
seventeenth-century French intellectual history—referred to by
Spink as "the crisis of 1619–25"[23]—that is, the crusade of atheist-
hunting that spanned the years between the burning of Vanini at

the stake for charges of atheism and Théophile's banishment. This was clearly not a period conducive to any form of activity that might attract attention. Propagandizing was unthinkable, as well as out of character, for such reserved philosophers as Gassendi. As a result, the movement of *libertinage érudit* produced relatively few testimonies to its activities and its discussions and almost no followers. In Pintard's description:

> Telle est l'étrange situation de ces "esprits forts:" ils veulent rester eux-mêmes, mais ils redoutent d'être imités; ils souhaitent quelques confidents, mais le moins possible de disciples. Etonnants fouilleurs qui se hâtent d'enterrer de nouveau la moitié de leurs trouvailles; Prométhées honteux de leur audace qui éteignent, avant de la transmettre aux hommes, l'étincelle qu'ils ont dérobée aux dieux.[24]

This was, then, an underground movement for a handful of initiates. They helped keep free thought alive in France during a difficult period, but they carefully avoided the risk of public exposure that might have brought wider attention their way. The movement was also short-lived, virtually extinct after Gassendi's death in 1655.

Gassendi's philosophy did leave its mark on one group of individuals destined to produce important chronicles of libertine life and thought. When he arrived in Paris in 1628, Gassendi carried with him a letter from Peiresc for the Dupuy brothers. In this milieu, friendship was sacred, and the chosen few were always passed from friend to friend, so it was natural that the Dupuys in turn introduced Gassendi to François Luillier, the rich patron of the arts and protector of freethinkers. Luillier offered him the position of tutor for his illegitimate son, Chapelle.[25] Gassendi's decision to accept Luillier's proposal may well be described as one of the major turning points in the evolution of the French novel, since the philosopher's influence in this role was not limited to his pupil alone. It also extended to a group of Chapelle's close friends, most of whom were later to convey their sense of shared experience in unusual novels that altered the limits of the genre as they were then perceived. Until recently, it was generally believed that Gassendi held formal lectures in philosophy for his young students, but Michaud and Pintard have worked to change this view: "Des sortes de conférences familières ont fort bien pu s'y tenir, des conversations amicales, en tout cas, y ont eu lieu."[26]

The list of those who attended these sessions with Gassendi is an impressive one indeed. Chapelle met Cyrano, who introduced him to D'Assoucy, and so, in typical libertine fashion, the band was formed. It finally included Tristan, Bernier, Scarron, and possibly even Molière. Exposure of one type or another to Gassendi meant that, no matter what the philosophical orientation of his discussions with them, these young thinkers had access to a variety of texts and ideas rarely available in France at that time. I do not intend to enter the debate on the religious convictions, or lack of them, of the various members of this group. Chapelle, Cyrano, and D'Assoucy are always classified as atheists—largely on the basis either of their own testimony or of their later attempts at blackening each other's reputations. Opinions on Tristan's atheism run the gamut from the unconditionally affirmative (Adam, Guillumette), to the somewhat hesitant affirmative or negative (Perrens, Arland) to the scandalized denial (Lachèvre)—leaving room in between for what seems most likely: that he was an atheist in his youth, but modified his stand in later years (Dietrich).[27] There certainly is no last word on the inner convictions of each member of the band, but it is important to remember that this group of writers shared two common bonds. They were in some sense students of Gassendi and, through him, were linked with other members of the circle of *libertins érudits*. Because of this alliance, they came to share an ideology based on the defense of philosophical and scientific open-mindedness and were led to defend all the great men associated with this ideology. In short, they subscribed to Sorbière's profession of faith: "Je tiens pour Galilée et Gassendi et j'estime qu'à la longue ils emporteront par dessus Hobbes et Descartes, encore que les bricoles de ceux-là se fassent davantage admirer sur l'adresse des autres."[28]

Certain among them share a final common bond, one that establishes beyond any doubt the importance of the first two. Tristan, Cyrano, Chapelle, and D'Assoucy all left documents—strange novels whose similarities will provide the focal point of this study, testimonies that can be used, with the annexation of two earlier texts, to tell the story of the rise and fall of the libertine movement in seventeenth-century France. The two additional novels indispensable for any discussion of the literature associated with the libertinism of the period are, first, Théophile's *Frag-*

ments d'une histoire comique, "l'autobiographie du libertin triomphant," in Démoris's terms,[29] and Sorel's *Francion* (both 1623).[30] Adam maintains that Sorel's novel is a description of Théophile's youth and its title character a barely disguised double for the real-life libertine hero.[31] But even for a critic who rejects that thesis, it is clear that Francion's surprising adventures, as well as the novel's intellectual and formal audacity, would make this text a prototype for young writers aspiring to find a type of narrative flexible enough to transmit a libertine message. These two novels, Sorel's fictionalized eulogy of libertine youth and its aspirations and Théophile's all too brief but decisive libertine manifesto, can be read together as a description of a first flash of glory and power, of total belief in the transforming potential of a libertine ideology.

Tristan's *Page disgracié* (1643) and Cyrano's *L'Autre Monde* and *Les Estats et empires du soleil*[32] mark the arrival of a new generation, one characterized by its lack of optimism and illusions. The almost carefree bravado of earlier libertine heroes is conspicuously absent here, no longer possible after the years 1619–25. These novels may be said to represent different moments of a grave crisis of pessimism, a crisis reflected in the mode of retreat chosen by each of them: Tristan's "softened" treatment of dangerous themes, and Cyrano's decision not to publish his manuscript. Despite their pessimistic overtones, Cyrano and Tristan's texts remain marked by a spirit of struggle that expresses continued conviction: neither the page nor Dyrcona is broken at the end of his adventures.

During the final period in the evolution of the fiction produced by Gassendi's students, even this hope for an eventual solution is lost. Chapelle's *Voyage à Encausse* (written with Bachaumont, 1663) and D'Assoucy's *Avantures* and *Avantures d'Italie* (1677) merit a separate classification for several reasons. Not only are they characterized by the absence of the traditional libertine notion of struggle, but the optimism and conviction conveyed by earlier texts are replaced by a pervasive sense of the failure and collapse of a movement. The libertine cooperation and camaraderie has broken down into a stream of ugly and potentially damning accusations. Even the once sacred master, Gassendi, is implicated in these outpourings of bile. As Pintard points out, this is

the ultimate sign of the complete disintegration of all the values of
the past:

> Quand les compères, brouillés les uns avec les autres, étaleront les
> souvenirs de leurs débauches et de leur gueuserie, de plagiat, de
> maladies honteuses, de vices dégradants, d'irréligion, quand toute
> la lie de leur temps d'amitié remontera à la surface, l'ombre du
> philosophe se trouvera mêlée à ces évocations fâcheuses (p. 331).

In the relation of these accusations, the personal invades the
fictional to such an extent that these texts begin to strain the
boundaries of the novel.[33] Previous criticism of these works seriously underestimates their content when it stresses their "playfulness," or speaks of D'Assoucy's "lightness" (Fritz Neubert), or
classifies Chapelle and Bachaumont's *Voyage* as a "charmante
satire littéraire" (Sainte-Beuve), or invents the following comparison to describe the *Voyage*: "l'équivalent littéraire des 'Porzellan-
figürchen,' des figurines de porcelaine, de ces biscuits de Sèvres
(ou de Saxes. .) si caractéristiques d'une époque" (Laufer).[34] Of
these critics, only Sainte-Beuve even brushes up against the implications of Chapelle's *Voyage* when, near the end of his *Causerie*,
he remarks casually: "Il est dommage cependant que le tout se
termine par cette histoire désagréable et indécente de d'Assoucy,
sur laquelle l'auteur revient encore plus loin et insiste avant de
finir."[35] A pity, perhaps; disagreeable, certainly—yet such brutal
attacks are not to be avoided in this less than glorious end to the
libertine saga. They may shock, surprise, even disgust, but these
reactions are an integral part of the package. These "adventure"
novels are anything but porcelain figurines. They retain the frost-
ing of Epicurean delights associated with the seventeenth-century
libertine tradition, but they are hollow and bitter at the center:
hollow because their authors can no longer fight the good fight
and defend the ideals and idols of a generation, and bitter because
they are all too conscious of having replaced this ideology with
useless bickering. D'Assoucy and Chapelle had the misfortune of
living long enough to witness, and bear witness to, the end of an
era.

Chronologically, the evolution of this literary trend more or
less coincides with that of the purely intellectual current of *libertinage érudit*. Its moment of euphoria is over by 1625; its breakdown is contemporary with the period of the Fronde. Just as the
libertinage érudit receives its *coup fatal* at the moment of political

upheaval associated with the split into pro- and anti-Mazarin forces, as Pintard remarks (pp. 433–34), so the young writers who banded together around Gassendi in the post-Théophile years also lost their solidarity at this point. Whether dissent first crept in over political issues or over personal ones cannot be established. The fact remains that the most forceful document attesting to the beginning of the final crisis, Cyrano's *Lettre contre les frondeurs* (1651), is essentially a political manifesto. With this text, Cyrano, formerly the prolific author of such caustic *Mazarinades* as the *Ministre d'Etat flambé*, takes on the role of the defender of absolute monarchy. Hand in hand with his political about-face comes the break with the friends remaining on the side of the anti-Mazarin forces, Chapelle and D'Assoucy.

Such chronological parallels, however, do not necessarily indicate frequent interminglings of the *libertins érudits* and the novelists. After an initial period of more or less frequent contact, while Gassendi served as Chapelle's tutor, the two circles moved farther and farther apart. After all, no prudent philosopher or scholar would wish to be too closely linked with writers who, through their increasingly flamboyant behavior and publications, were becoming more and more likely targets for official reprisal. Such ties would involve a sharing of the risks that were surely higher for a writer who chose to make his work public than for a philosopher who talked within the confines of a salon. As Howard Harvey points out, charges of madness were leveled only against literary figures such as Cyrano and not against their more cautious masters, the Descartes and the Gassendis.[36] The *libertins érudits* avoided not only disparaging accusations but also physical penalties. Spink makes a distinction between the two groups based on their attitude toward political authority. There were, on the one hand, "the professional erudites . . . holding stable positions in society" and, on the other, "the wanderers, the irregulars, the independents, resentful of authority, unsubmissive in spirit. It was the members of this latter group who ran a real risk of the galleys and the stake."[37] The danger was evident. As late as 1662, Claude Le Petit was condemned to be strangled and then burned for the alleged libertine content of his works.

3. THE LIBERTINE BOND

Since the *libertins érudits* considered themselves free men in the midst of an enslaved world, they were particularly conscious of the importance of a united front. Friendship was the most sacred of all values for those fortunate enough to be among the initiate, and the hospitality of this friendship was freely extended to all individuals persecuted because of their intellectual beliefs. By reason of this persecution alone, they won admission to the inner circle. Campanella, fleeing the Inquisition, was immediately taken in by Peiresc, who introduced him to Gassendi, who in turn brought him to the Dupuy brothers. They gave him shelter, even though, as Pintard describes them, "la métaphysique, à vrai dire, n'est pas le propre des 'frères Putéans' et de leurs intimes, et ils se soucient assez peu d'approuver ou d'improuver les théories du moine calabrais. . . . Mais qu'importe? Il est persécuté, cela leur suffit" (p. 97).

This sense of brotherhood was even more pronounced among the literary figures connected with this movement, perhaps because of the common danger they confronted. For them, persecution was a sign of personal merit. The most virtuous men were those who were most strongly persecuted. As Lidame's aunt in Edinburgh explains to Tristan's *page disgracié*: "Vous n'êtes pas le premier qu'on a persécuté sans raison, et vous n'en êtes pas moins digne d'être servi, puisque ce n'est qu'une marque de votre vertu."[38] The libertine writers had no homes in which to offer refuge to those fleeing persecution, but they could give written defenses in their works to those they perceived to be their illustrious predecessors in misfortune. Their novels contain startling, anti-novelistic lists of individuals imprisoned, exiled, or forced to wander because of the daring of their ideas. These lists are made up of a rather bizarre jumble of philosophers, scientists, alchemists, and charlatans of all countries and all periods, thrown together in a common melting pot as a result of shared experience.

For example, in the *Page disgracié* there is a passage devoted to Jean-Baptiste Porta and his *Magie naturelle* (pp. 84-85), then a cluster of names: Jacques Coeur, Raymond Lulle, Arnauld de Villeneuve, Nicholas Flamel, and Bragadino (p. 96). Cyrano's *L'Autre Monde* marks the summit of such naming: Pythagorus, Epicurus, Democritus, Copernicus, Kepler, Cardano, Corneille Agrippa de Nettesheim, Jean Trithème, Jean Faust, Guy de la Brosse, the adventurer César, the knights of the Rosy Cross,

Campanella, La Mothe Le Vayer, Gassendi—all find their way into its lists. His *Estats et empires du soleil* contains additional references to Corneille Agrippa and especially to Campanella. The Calabrian monk is elevated from his status as name in a list to that of an actual character, serving as guide and interlocutor for Dyrcona during an important phase of his solar sojourn.[39]

Previous critics of these novels maintain that they function as *romans à clef*.[40] However, decipherment is unnecessary when reading them, since the names to be stressed are plainly inscribed in the text. To suggest as Pintard does that the demon of Socrates in *L'Autre Monde* represents Gassendi and that the *fils de l'hôte* in the same work can be identified with Chapelle is to fail to understand the way Cyrano integrates references to those he sees as his brothers-in-arms.[41] If he had wanted to make an additional allusion to Gassendi or to include one to Chapelle, he would have done so directly and without cover-up. This is no society game of guessing who's who, but a reaffirmation of oneness in alienation. These writers reject the *à clef* mask in favor of a more explicit union with the past.

For example, when Tristan names the alchemist encountered by the page "le nouvel Artefius" (pp. 97, 162, 212), he does so in order to establish a link between the character of his invention and a pattern of occult relationships. Tristan's alchemist gains thereby a share in the identity of the twelfth-century hermetic philosopher, author of a treatise on *The Art of Prolonging Life*, who claimed to have lived for a thousand years through the secrets of his art—and whose contemporaries further extended his grasp on the past by contending that he had known a previous existence as Apollonius of Tyana. Tristan's alchemist is a reincarnation of Artefius, just as Artefius was himself a reincarnation of Apollonius.

The libertine novelists continue their practice of being more daring than their intellectual mentors. The *libertins érudits*, realizing how suspicious their activities were to others, always took the precaution of using a tight system of self-censorship to protect their freedom of expression. They consistently avoided the use of all proper names connected in any way with libertine concerns, replacing them with a carefully constructed code of Greek pseudonyms, a code Pintard describes in these terms:

> De là [i.e., from their desire for self-protection] dès qu'ils livrent quelqu'une de leurs confidences, le souci de la voiler sous des noms empruntés et des allusions obscures; de là encore l'habitude, et bientôt la manie des pseudonymes. . . . Avec un mélange d'inquiétude et de plaisir, ils tissent autour de toutes leurs actions une trame transparente aux initiés; mais qui trompera les profanes. Ils s'accoutument à s'entendre à demi-mot, à parler un language intelligible à eux seuls, à multiplier entre eux les liens d'une sorte de complicité (p. 176).

This brand of self-censorship is supposedly active, for example, in such works as La Mothe Le Vayer's *Dialogues d'Orasius Tubero*, in which, according to Pintard's interpretation, the initiated reader was to identify the members of the Tétrade and their immediate circle behind the various interlocutors.

The libertine novelists' rejection of the *à clef* formula as practiced by the *libertins érudits* constitutes the first of a series of unifying traits that define the peculiar character of their works. They clearly wished to set their novels apart from the libertine philosophical dialogue or treatise, perhaps because they sensed that its veiled references could never be properly understood outside a small secret society, and, furthermore, that any impact thus obtained would be very short-lived. Here the libertines' awareness of the importance of posterity that motivates their manipulation of their own names is important once again. These writers crafted appellations for themselves that reflect their rejection of their own heritage and their adoption of a libertine one. When they openly name the names of their persecuted "forefathers," they do so in order to inscribe the notion of persecution in their texts and to flaunt their own real and imagined tribulations (Théophile's and Tristan's exiles and D'Assoucy's imprisonment; Cyrano's conviction that the Jesuits were seeking his death).[42]

In their works, these young writers traced a libertine family tree. In addition, they showed that the family was still alive and flourishing by making various references to each other. This mutual referentiality further established their identity as a band of renegades. When an important work by one of them appeared, it would sometimes be introduced by a series of prefatory poems by other members of the group as a sign of libertine solidarity. This tradition was inaugurated in 1648 with the appearance of D'Assoucy's *Jugement de Pâris*, ornamented with *pièces liminaires* singing its praises and those of its author signed by Chapelle, Tristan, and Cyrano—who, as was occasionally his practice, marks only his initials, or one set of them at least, "C.D." For this occasion, Cyrano also contributed an *épître-préface* "Au sot Lecteur et non au sage," a tour de force of the insulting burlesque style more frequently associated with D'Assoucy himself. Two years later, D'Assoucy's next burlesque epic poem, *L'Ovide en belle humeur*, was once again accompanied by prefatory verses by Tristan and Cyrano. The era of the joys of friendship was already nearing its end, however, and when Cyrano in turn was able to publish a collection of his works in 1654, the absence of prefatory sonnets, epistles, and other marks of participation by a circle of friends is striking.

The most memorable inscription of libertine solidarity is Cyrano's eulogy of his friend Tristan, pronounced by the character who often serves as the author's *porte-parole* in *L'Autre Monde*, the demon of Socrates:

> Pour abréger son panégyrique, il est tout esprit, il est tout coeur, et si donner à quelqu'un toutes ces deux qualités dont une jadis suffisait à marquer un héros n'était dire Tristan L'Hermite, je me serais bien gardé de le nommer, car je suis assuré qu'il ne me pardonnera point cette méprise; mais comme je n'attends pas de retourner jamais en votre monde, je veux rendre à la verité ce témoignage de ma conscience. . . . Enfin je ne puis rien ajouter à l'éloge de ce grand homme, si ce n'est que c'est le seul poète, le seul philosophe et le seul homme libre que vous ayez (p. 57).

Here, Cyrano underlines the potential risk involved in the evocation of a fellow renegade: "Je me serais bien gardé de le nommer." There is no such thing as casual name-dropping in a work by a known libertine, and Cyrano realizes that by inscribing Tristan's name in his text at the end of an extensive list of ancestors (from Corneille Agrippa to Gassendi), he identifies Tristan with this tradition. Tristan's link with freethinkers past and present is firmly established for anyone who knows how to interpret the weight of the proper name in the libertine text. As Adam points out: "Pour qui connaît Cyrano, cela ne peut laisser aucun doute. . . . Cyrano le loue dans les mêmes termes qu'il donnerait à Théophile si Théophile était vivant."[43] The simple presence of the name is equivalent to saying, "He is a libertine," or "He is one of us."

But if such inscriptions are far more explicit than the opaque veils of the *roman à clef*, they also constitute a new form of self-censorship. The name is present with no cover-up, yet the metaphorical implications are not clearly spelled out. The simple fact of never saying "Tristan *is like* Campanella" provides a minimal form of protection. This type of metonymical juxtaposition makes plain the conclusions to be drawn, but carefully avoids taking the ultimate step of drawing them.

Libertine listings with their discreet use of names are characteristic only of the novels of Tristan and Cyrano and are no longer found in those following the *Fronde*. Cyrano destroys all libertine unity, first with his politically based attacks in "Contre les frondeurs," then with subsequent *lettres publiques* such as "Contre Chapelle, brigand de pensées" and "Satire contre Soucidas,"[44] both containing a wild vision of former friends as plagiarists. Afterward, discretion is thrown to the winds, and Chapelle and D'Assoucy respond by going beyond the mere naming of libertine names to make the implications of such a gesture explicit.[45] In the *Voyage* and the *Avantures*, the proper name is always accompanied by accusations capable of wounding both personally and politically the coworker become adversary.

Chapelle launches the assault by turning his acid pen, not against the more logical target, Cyrano, but against D'Assoucy. Two passages of the *Voyage* are devoted to what can only be viewed as a savage and gratuitous attack on the already sullied remains of D'Assoucy's reputation. They recount parallel meetings with a bedraggled Emperor of the Burlesque, no longer welcomed by his admirers but obliged to flee like a criminal before the angry crowds pursuing him. Chapelle leaves the first and most dramatic vignette deliberately vague and inconclusive. The women of Montpellier are rioting *en masse* against D'Assoucy— "Elles avoient déjà déchiré deux ou trois personnes"—so Chapelle and Bachaumont decide it would be prudent for them to leave. On their way out, they encounter D'Assoucy. If he is able to elucidate the mystery of the riot, this information is not passed on to the reader, who is left with only two clues that hint at the source of Chapelle's mockery: the description of the women of Montpellier raging as though D'Assoucy "les auroit toutes violées. Et cependant il ne leur avoit jamais rien fait"; and the insistance on the shadowy figure accompanying D'Assoucy, "un petit page assez joli."[46] Chapelle finally reveals his hand with his account of his subsequent nocturnal conversation with "ce malheureux," obliged by then to hide his face in the edge of his long cape, but still followed by "ce petit garçon." The accusation of homosexuality that follows and on which he chooses to end his text must surely have been one of the most scandalous literary bombshells of the period (pp. 97–98).

D'Assoucy's response to the accumulated insults of his former friends Cyrano and Chapelle is, understandably enough, compounded of amazement, rage, and desire for revenge. He pretends to seek an explanation for Cyrano's bitterness, and decides that it must have had its source in an incident in which D'Assoucy hid a freshly roasted capon under Cyrano's bed, leaving only its aroma to tantalize the hungry "Démon de la bravoure" (pp. 192–93). Perhaps D'Assoucy felt free to burlesque psychology because Cyrano was already dead at the time of the composition of the *Avantures*. It was too late to do anything more than continue to thwart the mystified outsider by dressing up a ridiculous anecdote as an explanation. When D'Assoucy turns his energies to Chapelle, however, any such delicacy is cast aside.

> Car il faut par necessité
> Parer le coup qu'il m'a porté:
> C'est un destin inévitable.
>
> (P. 188)

The resulting accumulation of insulting accusations becomes staggering. In addition to repeated descriptions of his alcoholism (e.g., pp. 184, 201) and cowardice (p. 197), Chapelle is called a plagiarist (p. 198), in somewhat veiled terms an atheist (p. 189), and in the chapter entitled "ample réponse de Dassoucy au Voyage de Monsieur Chapelle," D'Assoucy finally turns the accusation of homosexuality made against him back at Chapelle himself (p. 201). Looming large behind all these blows is the awareness of what is obviously for D'Assoucy the greatest of Chapelle's sins, that of disloyalty. The naming that served for Cyrano and Tristan as a sign of libertine recognition and a positive force in their works is used for the last time clouded with the sadness of an old man who has seen the end of an era. D'Assoucy retraces the history of their friendship, as he cries out against the ultimate betrayal, the simultaneous betrayal of the bonds of friendship and of those of a literary and ideological tradition:

> Pourquoi donc, après tant de témoignages reciproques d'amitié, l'avez-vous pû traitter ainsi, ce pauvre Dassoucy qui ne vous fit jamais rien, et qui seroit bien marry de vous avoir fait quelque chose? . . . Est-ce ainsi que vous traittez vos amis, vous qui, du temps que vous recherchâtes ma connoissance, n'estiez encore qu'un Ecollier, et qui . . . n'avez point eu d'autre guide que moy? . . . Est-ce là le progrès que vous avez fait, marchant dessus mes traces et suivant le chemin que je vous ay frayé? Indigne fils des Filles de la Mémoire (p. 179).

4. THE MEANING OF LIBERTINE

Other critics have already proposed that the texts I am examining here be grouped together as not-so-strange bedfellows. In surveys of the novel in France in the seventeenth century, most of these novels are found under the same heading, the title of which varies according to critical bias or interpretation. Fournel includes them in a chapter entitled "Du roman comique, satirique et bourgeois." For Reynier, they are members of the class "roman réaliste," established in opposition to the "roman sentimental." In Adam's system, their place is with either the "tradition réaliste" or the "romans satiriques et comiques." Coulet uses the term "roman personnel" to characterize them.[47] All these categories, however, share the defects of being neither exclusive nor particularly illuminating. Works are included in them either because of surface similarities or because they fit in no other classification. Hence these novels may be discussed in the same breath with, for example, the *Roman bourgeois* and the *Roman comique*, with which they have little in common, simply because they are all very definitely not *romans héroïques*. The creation of systems of classification may not provide an adequate rationale for a critic's existence, but it does constitute a first step in the direction of a potential reevaluation of a body of works.

Although this study does not claim to be the badly needed updating of Reynier's survey of seventeenth-century prose fiction, my hope is to provide at least a reasonably appropriate framework for the examination of a group of novels whose importance has been largely underestimated until now. I propose to adopt the term *libertine* to characterize this tradition of French seventeenth-century prose narrative for three reasons: the texts to be discussed here were produced by men associated with the circle of *libertins érudits*; it is possible to trace through them the evolution of that movement; and their authors are freethinkers not only in the domain of philosophy but in that of literature as well.

It is immediately obvious that my use of *libertine* has little in common with the manner in which it has been adopted with regard to the eighteenth-century French novel—in recent studies by Herbert Josephs, Jacqueline Marchand, and Ernest Sturm, to cite but a few examples—and, by extension, although more rarely, with regard to the seventeenth-century novel as well—as in Barry Ivker's *Anthology of Seventeenth and Eighteenth-Century French Libertine Fiction*.[48] At least part of this recent trend originates, as Ivker demonstrates, in Sade's search for his literary ancestors in the third version of *Justine*. Hence the tradition of libertine fiction is currently defined by a blending of eroticism and rationalism, with the accent generally placed on the erotic. The adjective "libertine" has thus come to be more or less synonymous with "titillating" or "pornographic," and its implications of ideological freethinking are often relegated to the domain covered by "philosophical." Seekers of libertine fiction in this sense of the term certainly have a vast terrain to explore in the novels produced in France in the eighteenth century, but when this meaning of the adjective is extended to the seventeenth century, its boundaries are greatly restrained. The student of seventeenth-century erotic libertine fiction is restricted to texts of quite limited interest, such as Millot's *L'Escole des filles* (1655), Chorier's *Le Meursius français ou L'Académie des dames* (1680), or Barrin's *Vénus dans le cloître ou la religieuse en chemise* (1683). To attempt to revive interest in these novels seems to me a fruitless critical venture. "Libertine" as a stand-in for "erotic," with or without a modicum of rationalism, is simply not a flourishing concept in the seventeenth century. Ivker's assertion that the history and definition of seventeenth-century libertine literature are more clearly established than those of the eighteenth century is based on a forced and erroneous analogy between Pintard's use of "libertine" and that accepted by *dix-huitièmistes*.[49] If any claim is to be made for the existence of a libertine novel in the seventeenth century, a

definition of the adjective that corroborates the research of Pintard, Lachèvre, and Adam should first be agreed upon.

Lachèvre's most concise and least scornful formulation of his
conception of the seventeenth-century libertine writer—"un esprit fort doublé d'un débauché"[50]—serves as an excellent spring-
board, especially when viewed in the light of definitions in dictionaries of the period.[51] The notion of the "esprit fort" is a
complex one, comprising a refusal to conform to the laws of both
civil and ecclesiastical authority, as expressed in the only definition of the adjective found in both Furetière and Richelet: "qui
hait la contrainte." The purely religious aspect of "libertin," clearly the most threatening to all defenders of the faith from Garasse
to Lachèvre, is formulated, interestingly enough, only in Furetière: "se dit principalement à l'égard de la Religion, de ceux qui
n'ont pas assez de veneration pour ses mysteres, ou d'obeïssance
pour ses décisions." For Lachèvre, the "esprit fort" is always a
"débauché," and the vision of the debauched libertine is also
prominent among Richelet's definitions. However, the seventeenth-
century excesses must be carefully distinguished from the eighteenth-century dissipations with which they too readily invite
comparison. Eroticism, veiled or explicit, is totally absent from
all of these texts but *Francion*. Aside from the problematic, but
totally nonerotic, homosexual allusions, their wildest debauchery
involves gastronomic indulgence (from D'Assoucy's capons to
Chapelle's partridges) and gambling sprees (the source of problems for D'Assoucy and the page's undoing on several occasions).
Wine and song, maybe, but never women.

"Libertine" in this context is applicable above all to the defense
of liberty and liberation against any form of restraint. These novels are dedicated to a glorification of freedom in all possible
forms, from the freedom to carouse in bands and frequent ca-
barets to the freedom to believe in, and defend, the teachings of a
Cardano or a Galileo. They all trace the path from nonconformity
to the alienation it seems inevitably to create. Even though none
but *L'Autre Monde* can be said to constitute an attempt at un-
dermining officially sanctioned systems of belief, all are characterized by an underlying spirit of questioning. For this reason, the
adjective "libertine" finds in them an application worthy of its
seventeenth-century connotations.

The term *novel*, given that it suggests an (almost completely) fictionalized content, is often inadequate to describe these texts. Because of the exceptional mixture of unveiled fact and fiction found in them, they could more accurately be referred to as "life-novels."[52] This blending places them in a no-man's-land between novel and memoir, although somewhere closer to the novel's border, and bestows on them a status unique in their century, and perhaps in any but the twentieth. This unusual blurring of fact and fiction, of which the libertine naming already discussed constitutes but one component, is the first of a number of shared similarities that serve to link these texts in a group meriting study under the same name. Such resemblances are anything but accidental. They originate in a common desire to express the libertine experience with the greatest degree of freedom possible, and to express it through the self-censored reading they impose on their own texts. When Gassendi worried that he would be unable to find a language to convey messages of consolation to Galileo in prison, Peiresc advised him: "Je vous conseillerois bien de les concevoir en termes si reservez et si ajustez, qu'il y ayt moyen d'entendre une bonne partie de voz intentions sans que le littéral y soit si preciz."[53]

The effort to "adjust their terms" leads the libertines to locate their writing in the middle ground between autobiography and novel. The various libertine novels—with the exception of the frame narrative of *Francion*—are all written in the first person. This constitutes a break with the dominant comtemporary tradition of the *roman héroïque*, always narrated in the third person, as befits the self-proclaimed heir of the epic tradition.[54] As Démoris points out, this switch in person is one of the principal "signatures" of the libertine novel.[55] These texts are also united by the structure of their narration. With the exception once again of *Francion*, they are all divided either into chapters or into another type of clearly independent, short sections, substituting tens of pages for the hundreds that constituted the basic units of the *roman héroïque*. These narrative fragments are also organized in a characteristic manner: the brief compositional units do not so much build to a conclusion as they juxtapose episodes of equal weight for varying effects. Fragmentation may even include an alternation between prose passages and verse interludes, a reminder of what is an essential tradition for all these authors, Menippean satire. The final narrative characteristic of the libertine novel is its open-endedness. In these texts, conclusions are never drawn, and there is no final word to be pronounced. Furthermore, the notions of fragmentation and open-endedness are intimately linked to a number of almost obsessional recurring themes: magic, madness, and dream. The desire to inscribe the taboo in their works and their remarkably similar vision of the taboo also unite the libertine writers. Their *récit* centers around a vision of alienation with a basic and inevitable thematic unity.

The similarities among these libertine novels are conscious, the result of a sense of tradition unique in their time and rare in the history of the novel in general. The ever-present weight of this libertine tradition with its system of reminders and references to other moments creates a type of intertextual play that generates a first level of dialogue among these texts. In addition, they explore the "other" logic of the various themes of alienation with which they are concerned, a logic that is perpetually dialogic. Their sense of tradition is, finally, linked to the notion of self-consciousness—the problem of the *histoire comique* goes beyond the subtitle three of them share and permeates the texts. These three related questions—intertextuality, exploration of the logic of the "other," and self-consciousness—make the libertine novels the most completely dialogic works of seventeenth-century French literature and ensure their special status in seventeenth-century prose fiction.[56]

The libertine novel is perhaps the most interesting current of the seventeenth-century novel, and one that has the potential today of attracting the readers it has often lacked at other periods. After all, topics such as autobiography, madness, fragmentation, and dialogue are among the most intense preoccupations of students of literature in the twentieth century. This rather amazing conjunction could be explained by a parallelism in intellectual revolutions. To characterize a recent *bouleversement*, Evgeny Zamiatin wrote, "Euclid's world is very simple and Einstein's world is very difficult," and "When Lobachevsky crumbles with his book the walls of the millenial non-Euclidean space, that is revolution."[57] In his formulation, the name of Aristotle could be substituted for that of Euclid and Galileo for those of Einstein and Lobachevsky without producing significant distortion. Surely those living in the wake of these two uneasy, threatening revolutions share an enormous intellectual heritage. Modernity is constantly in the process of reevaluating itself, and occasionally it manages to come up with the same answers twice.

1. Théophile Gautier, *Les Grotesques*, pp. 64–65.

2. The *Grammaire générale et raisonnée* describes the peculiarities of the first name in this way: "Ce n'est pas qu'il n'arrive souvent que le nom propre ne convienne à plusieurs, comme *Pierre, Jean*, etc., mais ce n'est que par accident, parce que plusieurs ont pris un mesme nom. Et alors il faut y ajouter d'autres noms qui le déterminent, et qui le font rentrer dans la qualité de nom propre, comme le nom de *Louis* qui convient à plusieurs, est propre au Roy qui regne aujourd'huy, en disant *Louis quatorzieme*. Souvent mesme il n'est pas necessaire de rien adjouter, parce que les circonstances du discours font assez voir de qui l'on parle" (p. 36).

3. To give but one example of inconsistent classification, in vol. 1 of Antoine Adam's *Histoire de la littérature française au dix-septième siècle*, the "index des noms cités" contains a listing for "Bergerac, Cyrano de." In vol. 2, however, the page references are found under the heading "Cyrano de Bergerac."

4. Maurice Lever, *La Fiction narrative en prose au dix-septième siècle*; F. Lachèvre, *Le Libertinage devant le Parlement de Paris*. The *Fragments d'une histoire comique* constitutes the *première journée* of *Les Oeuvres du sieur Théophile, seconde partie*.

5. Amédée Carriat, *Bibliographie des oeuvres de Tristan L'Hermite*. N. M. Bernardin believes that the first edition received little interest at the time of its publication because the public's attention was completely diverted by the complexities of the political situation (the execution of Cinq-Mars and De Thou, etc.): "Qui pouvait alors, à la cour et même à la ville, se soucier beaucoup d'un roman, quelque agréable qu'il fût?" (*Un Précurseur de Racine, Tristan L'Hermite*, p. 227). This answer could be used to explain in various ways the disappearance of the first edition: either few copies were sold or the novel attracted no public, so copies were not preserved. Any such reasoning, however, remains suspiciously facile. A work's success is not often determined by the political situation at the time of its publication—unless it is written, like the *Mazarinades*, to capitalize on that situation. The events of 1642 were not grave enough to hinder the success of all novels published in their wake—La Calprenède's *Cassandre*, for example. Besides, the lack of contemporary interest in the *Page* must also be viewed in the light of the fate suffered by other novels whose authors frequented libertine circles.

6. I use this title when referring to the first part of Cyrano's imaginary voyage in conformity with current critical tradition (Laugaa, Démoris, etc.). The Bibliothèque Nationale manuscript bears on its spine *L'Autre Monde ou Les Estats et Empires de la Lune*. The work has, however, always been referred to by a wide variety of titles. To give but a few examples, first among Cyrano's contemporaries: Ménage speaks of the *Voyage de la lune*, Jean Royer de Prade of the *Estats et*

empires de la lune, not to mention Le Bret's choice of *Histoire comique*. For his edition, Lachèvre groups both voyages under the title *L'Autre Monde*, even though he maintains that Cyrano reserved this title only for the voyage to the moon. Georges Mongrédien refers in his biography of Cyrano to the *Voyage aux estats et empires de la lune*, and the author of the most recent study of Cyrano's novels, Jacques Prévot, returns to Royer de Prade's *Estats et empires de la lune*. This selection far from exhausts the range of possibilities, but my purpose is merely to illustrate once again the extent to which naming—or rather, the absence of stability in this area—is a problematic issue when dealing with these authors.

7. *Menagiana*, pp. 238–39.

8. In *Rousseau juge de Jean-Jacques*, Rousseau demonstrates his fear that the loss of his family name would be permanent: "J'ai pris la liberté de reprendre dans ces entretiens mon nom de famille que le public a jugé à propos de m'ôter, et je me suis désigné en tiers à son exemple par celui de baptême auquel il lui a plu de me réduire" (*Oeuvres complètes*, 1:663).

9. On the other hand, first names are generally judged to be superfluous for great authors. One finds editions of their works marked simply "Racine," "Corneille," "Freud," without "Jean," "Pierre," or "Sigmund," as though they had no kin. This onomastic system is not universally valid. In Italy, for example, it was common for great figures to be known by their given names. "Galileo" is a late example of this custom. Perhaps Garasse had this Italian model in mind when he described the fact that Théophile de Viau was known by his first name alone as a sign of libertine egotism. He believed that Théophile chose to give up his family name because he believed himself to be so well known that he could be identified without it (*Doctrine curieuse*, p. 1023).

10. Cyrano's grandfather was the "Savinien" for whom he was named. By adopting "Bergerac," Cyrano re-created in his own fashion the onomastic link originally forged for him by his family.

11. Cyrano and other members of his family also enjoyed appropriating titles and fake coats of arms. The Cyranos were fined several times during the seventeenth century for "usurpation de noblesse." Jean-Baptiste L'Hermite appears to have been so jealous of Tristan's genealogical *coup* that he also decided to adopt the same famous name from their alleged ancestry. In the signatures of his various genealogical treatises, three variants of his signature involving "Tristan" appear: "J.-B. L'Hermite, dit Tristan," "J.-B. Tristan L'Hermite," and "Tristan L'Hermite de Solier." In similar fashion, the title of one of his works indicates that Théophile's brother either took on his better-known sibling's first name or was given it by editors who assumed that "Théophile" was a family name: *Le Sacrifice des muses à M. le Prince et à Mme. la Princesse de Condé par le sieur H. Thèophile, Frère du défunt S. Théophile* (J. Guillemot, 1627). Since the brother's name was Paul, it is hard to imagine what the letters "H" and "S" stand for.

12. The first edition of the *Page disgracié* complicates matters even further by identifying the work's author as "Mr. *de* Tristan" (Toussainct Quinet, 1643).

13. The orthography of D'Assoucy's family name also varies. In addition to the common hesitation between "Coippeau" (used by Emile Colombey) and "Coyppeau" (Lever, Bibliothèque Nationale catalogue), it is sometimes written "Couppeau" (Adam)—and even "Coypeau" by D'Assoucy himself (*Avantures,*

ed. Emile Colombey, p. 154; all subsequent references to the *Avantures* and the *Avantures d'Italie* are to this edition, and will be given as page numbers in parentheses—a practice I will follow with all works from which I quote frequently).

14. In Cyrano's case, his rejection of paternal authority culminated in his behavior at the time of his father's terminal illness. Cyrano's biographers interpret the dying man's testimony to mean that Cyrano and his brother Abel took advantage of their father's helplessness to pillage his house before his very eyes: "On a forcé les serrures des armoires et coffres où étaient lesdites choses et attendu qu'il sait par quelles personnes lesdites choses lui ont été soustraites, les noms desquelles il ne veut être exprimés par certaines considérations, il en décharge entièrement ladite Descourtieux et tous autres." The onomastic rejection seems mutual. Even in his accusation, Cyrano's father joins in the suppression of his son's name.

15. The existence of a libertine "family" was noted by Théophile's archenemy, Garasse. In his *Doctrine curieuse*, he traces the libertine genealogical tree and calls attention to the libertine penchant for onomastic deviousness: "Entre mille coquins qui ont déclaré la guerre à Jésus-Christ, et sont sortis de son Eglise pour faire bande à part, ou d'Heresie, ou de Schisme, ou de Libertinage, ou d'A-theisme, il y en a neuf cens cinquante qui ont changé de nom" (p. 1018).

16. Gautier refers to the latter as "Cyrano Bergerac," thereby adding still another variant.

17. Gautier, pp. v, vi, viii.

18. Fournel, *La Littérature indépendante et les écrivains oubliés*, p. v.

19. *Histoire*, 2:117.

20. Frédéric Lachèvre, *Les Successeurs de Cyrano de Bergerac* (H. Champion, 1922), *avant-propos*, n. p.

21. F. T. Perrens, *Les Libertins en France au dix-septième siècle*, p. 2.

22. *Voyage dans la lune*, ed. M. Laugaa.

23. *French Free-Thought from Gassendi to Voltaire*, p. 6.

24. *Le Libertinage érudit*, p. 564.

25. The origin and the spelling of "Chapelle" also present problems. In the preface to his edition of the *Voyage*, Nodier explains: "On a écrit partout que Claude-Emmanuel Luillier . . . naquit en 1626 au village de la Chapelle. . . . Le nom de Chapelle ou La Chapelle lui resta, et il s'en est si peu soucié de son vivant, qu'on ne sait pas quel est celuy qu'il a préféré" (p. xix). On the title page of Maurice Souriau's edition of the *Voyage à Encausse*, the only edition based on a contemporary manuscript copy, Chapelle's name is written "Chappelle."

26. G. Michaud, *La Jeunesse de Molière*; Pintard, p. 624.

27. Adam, *Théophile de Viau et la libre pensée française en 1620*, p. 124; Doris Guillumette, *La Libre Pensée dans l'oeuvre de Tristan L'Hermite*, p. 72. Perrens, p. 273; Marcel Arland, ed., *Le Page disgracié*, preface, p. 41. Lachèvre, *Une Réparation posthume due au "Précurseur de Racine."* In his introduction, Lachèvre unveils the origin of his zeal when he states that he has prepared the volume in response to "l'injuste accusation d'athéisme qu'il n'a jamais meritée" made by Adam. Auguste Dietrich, ed., *Le Page disgracié*, preface, pp. xxii–xxiii.

28. *Sorberiana*, p. 104.

29. René Démoris, *Le Roman à la première personne*, p. 43.

30. Charles Sorel's life, as Adam admits, "est obscure. Ses biographes n'en disent pas grandchose, et en savent moins qu'ils n'en disent" (*Histoire*, 1:142). His close ties with Théophile and others associated with the libertine movement can be established by citing two cases of literary collaboration. In 1623, Sorel joined forces with Théophile and others to compose the ballet *Les Baccanales*, and he later (pub. 1650) coauthored with François de La Mothe Le Vayer a novel, *Le Parasite Mormon, histoire comique*.

31. "Il existe un roman de cette epoque qui ne s'explique pas sans l'existence du mouvement libertin. . . . Le héros de son roman fait plus d'une fois penser à Théophile, et l'oeuvre a été écrite pour développer certaines thèses essentielles des libertins" (*Les Libertins au dix-septième siècle*, p. 61). Adam also explains the changes between the first and second editions of *Francion* as due to Sorel's fear after Théophile's imprisonment and trial (*Histoire*, 1:154).

32. It is impossible to determine the date of the composition of Cyrano's novels. *L'Autre Monde* was probably written in the late 1640s, at any rate before 1650. *L'Autre Monde* was first published in 1657 under the title *Histoire comique*, and *Les Estats et empires du soleil* in 1662.

33. Indeed, in Lever's bibliography, which stresses in its preface its attempts to eliminate nonfiction texts previously classified as novels from its listings, D'Assoucy's two works find a place, but not Chapelle's *Voyage*.

34. Fritz Neubert, *Die französischen Versprosa-Reisebrieferzählungen und der Kleine Reiseroman des 17. und 18. Jahrhunderts*, pp. 47, 39; Sainte-Beuve, *Causeries du lundi*, 2:45; Roger Laufer, *Style rococo, style des "Lumières,"* pp. 9–10.

35. *Causeries du lundi*, 2:50.

36. "Cyrano de Bergerac and the Question of Human Liberties," p. 122.

37. Spink, p. 12.

38. *Le Page disgracié*. ed. M. Arland, p. 196.

39. *L'Autre Monde*, ed. M. Laugaa, p. 31. *Les Estats et empires*, ed. F. Lachèvre (Champion, 1921), pp. 104, 181, and passim.

40. The first section of chapter two of this study is devoted to the relationship between the *roman à clef* and libertine fiction.

41. Pintard, pp. 625–26. Pintard's identifications have recently been defended by Jacques Prévot, who extends the limits of the game to suggest that the Spaniard on the moon represents Campanella, despite the fact that Campanella actually appears in the *Estats et empires*: "*L'Autre Monde* prend place dans notre littérature romanesque comme un *Grand Cyrus* du Libertinage" (*Cyrano de Bergerac romancier*, p. 105).

42. Earlier libertine men of letters inaugurated this practice of openly naming their predecessors. Cardano, for example, is constantly aware of parallel situations and influences and mentions both the sad end of Corneille Agrippa and the importance of Artefius's treatises of divination for his own (*Les Livres de H. Cardanus medecin Milannois intitulez de la Subtilité, et subtiles inventions, ensemble les causes occultes, et raisons d'icelles*, pp. 441b, 452).

43. *Théophile de Viau*, p. 125. Because of the presence of "méprise" in this passage, Madeleine Alcover rejects a reading of it as a eulogy (*L'Autre Monde*, preface, p. 68). I would argue that "méprise" simply indicates the demon's aware-

ness that his speech is an "error" or "fault" because of the dangerous consequences it could have for Tristan.

44. For Cyrano, the rejection of the proper name in favor of the anagram is appropriate only in the context of the letter of insult.

45. D'Assoucy's counterattack probably also included a posthumously published satirical pamphlet attributed to him, the *Combat de Cirano* [*sic*] *de Bergerac avec le singe de Brioché au bout du Pont-neuf*. The pamphlet recounts an anecdote that can be described as a burlesque version of Cyrano's exploits as the *Démon de la bravoure* (Cyrano singlehandedly routing a hundred men at the *porte de Nesles*, etc.). i.e., Cyrano's fight to the death with the "presqu'homme des marionnettes," a monkey dressed as a *laquais*.

46. *Oeuvres de Chapelle et Bachaumont*, pp. 84–85. I follow the "libertine" practice (D'Assoucy's references in the *Avantures*, for example) of naming Chapelle alone as author of the work.

47. Fournel, *La Littérature indépendante*; Gustave Reynier, *Le Roman réaliste au dix-septième siècle*; Adam, *Histoire*; Henri Coulet, *Le Roman jusqu'à la révolution* (vol. 1).

48. H. Josephs, "Diderot's *La Religieuse*: Libertinism and the Dark Cave of the Soul"; J. Marchand, *Les Romanciers libertins du dix-huitième siècle*; E. Sturm, *Crébillon fils et le libertinage au dix-huitième siècle*.

49. "Towards a Definition of Libertinism in Eighteenth-Century French Fiction," p. 221. This article constitutes an attempt to annex ancestors for the eighteenth-century tradition culminating in Sade.

50. *Le Libertinage devant le Parlement de Paris*, p. 147.

51. For a survey of definitions found in seventeenth-century dictionaries, see Walter Lemke's " 'Libertin': From Calvin to Cyrano."

52. I borrow the term *lebensroman* from Fritz Neubert (*Die Französischen Versprosa Reisebrieferzählungen*, p. 40). Neubert uses it to describe D'Assoucy's *Avantures*.

53. Nicolas-Claude Fabri de Peiresc, *Lettres*, 4:410. Pintard's description of libertine self-censorship is quite similar: "Tous, s'ils écrivent, sont condamnés à feindre plus ou moins les opinions ordinaires, ou à poser les questions de biais, et, par une démarche oblique, à approcher des points brûlants sans les toucher. . . . Si variées que puissent être leurs dispositions intimes, leurs indépendances utilisent les mêmes détours et revêtent des apparences analogues; ils forment une famille d'esprits; cruellement marquée des stigmates de la contrainte, mais à qui ces stigmates mêmes confèrent une curieuse originalité" (p. 566).

54. On this point, see Jean Rousset's discussion in *Narcisse romancier* (p. 53 and passim) of Madeleine de Scudéry's difficulties with the problem of the hero's *récit*, where she delegates authority to secondary characters, thereby avoiding the use of the first person.

55. "Les récits à la première personne sont, de façon fort claire, reliés aux écrivains qui, en ce début du dix-septième siècle, constituent la tradition libertine, même si, comme Tristan et Sorel, ils ont été amenés plus tard à s'en écarter" (*Le Roman à la première personne*, p. 54).

56. A discussion of seventeenth-century novels resembling libertine works is included as an appendix.

57. Quoted in Marc Slonim, *Soviet Russian Literature* (New York: Oxford University Press, 1967), p. 84.

CHAPTER TWO

"THEME OF THE TRAITOR
AND THE HERO"

*In Nolan's work, the passages imitated from Shakespeare are the
least dramatic; Ryan suspects that the author interpolated them
so that one person, in the future, might realize the truth. He un-
derstands that he, too, forms part of Nolan's plan. . . .*

*At the end of some tenacious caviling, he resolves to keep silent
his discovery. He publishes a book dedicated to the glory of the
hero; this, too, no doubt was foreseen.*—Jorge Luis Borges

1. FOR A NEW AUTOBIOGRAPHY

Libertine novels have had a hard time establishing their *titres de
fiction*. Their commentators and editors generally find themselves in agreement on at least one point: these texts must be situated in the domain of autobiographical literature, since most of
the events they recount actually took place. When Gautier uses
fragments of the *Fragments* to reconstruct the life of the young
Théophile,[1] he inaugurates a type of mixed reading that will continue to hamper the reception of these texts. Following in Gautier's footsteps are all subsequent biographers not only of Théophile but more especially of Tristan, whose life seems to exert a
particular fascination on historians of literature. Such a fascination is difficult to explain. So few documents concerning Tristan's
life have survived that his biographers can do little more than
repeat the story told by the *Page*, which they accept as the scenario of the early years, and follow with a rapid survey of the meager
evidence available on the page/Tristan grown up. Without his
novel, Tristan's existence could hardly be described as a rich ter-

rain inviting exploration. Little wonder then that the great majority of those who direct their attention to the *Page* do not hesitate
to accept its content as autobiographical. Dietrich's proclamation, "Le *Page* . . . est avant tout . . . une autobiographie véritable et sincère," is echoed, for example, in statements by
Perrens, Savarin, and Grisé.[2] In view of their far more overtly
personal statements, it is even less surprising that Chapelle's
Voyage and D'Assoucy's *Avantures* are both read as consistently
autobiographical texts. Referring to the *Voyage*, one of its
nineteenth-century editors affirms that "la personnalité des deux
auteurs se confond avec leur principal ouvrage. Parler de l'ouvrage, ce sera parler des auteurs."[3] Emile Colombey demonstrates
a similar attitude when he presents the *Avantures* as "l'autobiographie de D'Assoucy."[4]

An especially evident problem avoided by such a reading of
these texts is that of the proper name. The section of my first
chapter concerned with the integration of proper names as a form
of libertine recognition may suggest that names are to be found in
some abundance in libertine texts. In fact, nothing could be farther from the truth. I chose to dwell upon the listings of libertine
precursors because the very mention of their names should be
regarded as a risky venture. But it is important for my present
argument to note that proper names, except for their function as
referents to the historical past, are rarely encountered in these
texts. Actually, the authors consistently avoid naming the individuals evoked in connection with their stories. Persons merely
talked about are identified, but characters who play an active role
in the narrative remain anonymous. So, whereas names of historical figures (Gassendi and such) may be mentioned in the course
of discussions, the characters whose lives are unfolding are usually unidentified. Such an absence of proper names would be
worthy of note in even a purely fictional work. In one that is to be
regarded as autobiographical, it is an ever-present source of embarrassment. If the reader accepts the editor's advance warning
that the text he is about to begin is historically accurate, he must
be equipped with the skills of a first-rate sleuth in order to participate in the autobiographical experience with any degree of satisfaction and conviction. Instead of a certain number of identified,
or at least identifiable, proper names, he is given as "clues" only

such intentionally vague appellations as "mon aïeule maternelle" or "ma maîtresse."

If the task of an editor can be considered largely one of removing potential obstacles to a smooth reading of a work, then these texts provide an editorial paradise. Indeed, in the infrequent cases when libertine novels are rewarded with critical editions, easy explanations are adopted for the absence of precision in references to the individuals encountered: "Quant à l'omission totale de noms propres que l'on y regrette, . . . elle s'explique d'une façon toute naturelle. D'une part, plusieurs des personnages que Tristan met an scène ou vivaient encore, ou avaient laissé des descendants, et l'auteur était, en conséquence, tenu à une grande circonspection à l'égard de ceux-ci comme de ceux-là."[5] The editor feels permitted to immerse his reader in a sea of identifications designed to fill in the undesirable silences and ambiguities of the text: "Tristan, en ne donnant . . . aucun nom propre dans son ouvrage, en avait rendu la lecture moins amusante et même difficile pour le grand public."[6]

The *Fragments* and the *Voyage*, probably because they are so short, have never had the benefit of this type of editorial scrutiny. Editors of *Francion* are quick to decide that Sorel is either telling his own life story or that of Théophile. However, because the first-person narration in the final 1633 edition is limited to one-third of the text and is, as Démoris describes it, "partielle, fragmentée and encadrée,"[7] they generally save their footnotes for the transmission of other types of information.[8] The complex web of inventions, fantasies, and theories in Cyrano's voyages has enjoyed priority with his editors over questions of character identification.[9] But D'Assoucy and Tristan have certainly attracted their fair share of footnotes, and since Tristan's commentators are faced with the most complex case, their efforts can serve as a particularly illuminating illustration of a type of textual "bending."

Only in its original edition may the *Page* be read as Tristan intended; that is, studded with purposeful ambiguities created by the absence of proper names. With the appearance of the second edition in 1667, the transformation of Tristan's hybrid into a showcase for editorial ingenuity begins. Whereas the 1643 edition is published by the well-known Toussainct Quinet, the text of 1667 is "signed" in the place reserved for the name of the *libraire* by the less-known A. Boutonné.[10] This Boutonné is responsible for the preface, "Le libraire au lecteur," in which he explains the nature and purpose of the additions with which he has taken the liberty of endowing the text established by Tristan: "Pour rendre cette lecture plus intelligible, j'ai encore ajouté la clef et les annotations qui servent à l'éclaircissement de quelques noms propres et autres passages obscurs, que l'auteur avait ainsi fait imprimer pour des considérations qui me sont inconnues et qui cachaient une partie des beautés de ce roman" (p. 47).

"Boutonné" is traditionally identified as Jean-Baptiste L'Hermite, Tristan's younger brother and would-be borrower of his name and glory.[11] But the *Page*'s first editor chooses to mask his *clef* to the novel's characters behind a second *clef*: he wants to reveal other names, but at the same time to hide his own. Such an identification would therefore seem unfounded, a mere result of critical tradition, were it not for the fact that Jean-Baptiste shows his hand with the style he adopts in his notes. As I have already mentioned, J.-B. L'Hermite, in his attempt to surpass his brother's efforts in at least one domain, developed Tristan's genealogical tricks into a true genealogical obsession in his interminable treatises. His mania overflows in a most astonishing fashion in the pages he devotes to "remedying" his brother's lack of genealogical conscientiousness in the *Page*. Jean-Baptiste, alias Boutonné, goes so far beyond the discreet cover-up implied by his name[12] that he surpasses the level of fervor expected from even the most zealous editor. To give but one example, a simple reference by the page to "mon aïeule maternelle" is overburdened in a note by Jean-Baptiste that is closer to an entry in the international social register he certainly dreamed of composing than a "clarification" of the text: "Denise de s.-Prés, Dame de saint Prés les Chartes, fille de Jean de saint-Prés, dit Gros Jean, renommé és guerres d'Italie, où il commandoit la Compagnie de Gendarmes de Monseigneur Yves d'Alegres; sa mere Anne de Château-Chalons tiroit son commencement des anciens Ducs et Comtes de Bourgogne."[13]

Jean-Baptiste adds footnotes whenever he believes he has the knowledge necessary to bridge a "gap" in the *Page*. Stamped with the weight of brotherly authority and thereby legitimated to an unusual extent, his critical reading represents an impressive burden for subsequent editors. Indeed, none of the modern editors of the *Page* manages to escape Jean-Baptiste's influence, and only Dietrich is able to blend the fraternal commentary with his own erudition in a manner that clearly establishes the boundaries between the two. He relegates the genealogical meanderings of L'Hermite de Solier to an appendix, and limits his own contributions to simple "identifications." "Mon aïeule maternelle," in Dietrich's judgment, calls for a minimal footnote: "Denise de Saint-Prest."

Editors less wary of the extent of the fraternal presence (Arland, for example) build confusion into their work by maintaining the anonymity of the author of the prologue and by pillaging his *clef* without reproducing it in its entirety. The reader unaware of the editorial past of this text is thus faced with a nearly hopeless muddle. Logically, he has no choice but to attribute all the notes to the only editorial voice assuming responsibility for them, that of the "libraire Boutonné." He quickly realizes, however, that certain notes (linguistic commentaries, for example) cannot be contemporary with the text and can only be the product of a more modern editorial instinct. He may read as carefully as he likes, but he will never be entirely certain of the identity of the voice assuring him that "mon aïeule maternelle" is/was Denise de Saint-Prest. He may eventually begin to suspect some sort of editorial joke along the lines of the "Préface-Annexe" to *La Religieuse*. At least one thing is certain: such a critical edition cannot explain or clarify the interpretive problems posed by the *Page* for contemporary readers.

Tristan created a work in which the absence of proper names is a striking feature. If he had wanted it to be viewed in the light of the added precision names can provide, he could either have inserted them into the text or have provided his own *clef*. His brother, a maniac for names and the links among them, sensing the opportunity to show off his genealogical capabilities (and perhaps at the same time to breathe new life into what he probably viewed as a washed-out text), decided to fill in the blank each time Tristan chose to replace the specific with the general, and all subsequent editors follow suit. Why?

"Boutonné" explains that his annotations will "improve" the text because, without them, some of its "beauties" are hidden and some of its passages are "obscure." He simply wants to make it "more intelligible." Bernardin agrees with this opinion and contends that the *clef* makes the novel more "amusing" and less "difficult." Dietrich justifies his own increased efforts in this domain by stressing the deficiencies of even Jean-Baptiste's complex work. He stresses "l'omission totale de noms propres . . . à laquelle la *Clef* de Jean-Baptiste L'Hermite est loin de suppléer suffisamment."

None of these explanations, however, seems legitimate. It has never been adequately demonstrated, or indeed demonstrated at all, that the *Page* in its original version is an obscure text. For whom, then, is it being made more comprehensible? Questions of intelligibility have little or nothing to do with the true motivation of these various *clefs*—witness the example of Arland's "mixed" text. The editors of the *Page* seek to do much more than merely "sharpen" the contours of the reading proposed by Tristan for his work, as they claim. They are attempting instead to give his text an entirely different type of reading, one in which a somewhat simplistic vision of reality and of reference is prized as much as, or more than, the novel itself. They assume that the facts of a life can be counted and measured, like the ingredients in a recipe. Consequently, they do not recognize that (auto)biography is a creative art. Their glosses represent an attempt to explain the "sources" of the text, as though there could be no doubt that the page's "aïeule maternelle" was also Tristan's. They are attempting to decipher a text that does not ask to be decoded in a literal, or so-called normal, manner but otherwise. And because the interpretations they strive to impose on this text, far from being natural to it, are explicitly rejected by it, editors are inevitably confronted with absences or silences behind which they cannot discover the "truth." At these times when the *Page* throws off all attempts to read it literally as "straight" autobiography, its editors usually write off such aberrant behavior as momentary frivolity, insisting all the while that they know best how to calm this text that dares to fight back: "*Le Page disgracié* est une autobiographie, nous le savons, mais une autobiographie empreinte, çà et là, d'un cachet un peu romanesque, et il ne faut donc pas prendre à la lettre cette affirmation de notre auteur."[14]

Sometimes, they simply skim over unexplainable passages,

passages for which there exists no *clef*, in silence. Thus, Arland, faced with the "nouvel Artefius" chapters, makes no attempt either to guess at the identity of the philosopher or to speculate on the validity of this episode, of such central importance for the *Page*. His notes in this section are limited to such matters as unusual grammatical constructions or the identification of those historical figures the page evokes to describe the alchemist, such as Jacques Coeur. This example illustrates the principal weakness of all such attempts to construct a *clef* for Tristan's text. Only secondary figures, those mentioned in passing references, have been given names. Despite the best efforts of those determined to reveal the *Page*'s secrets, its main characters retain their original anonymity. The very silence the editors are obliged to maintain with regard to them serves to proclaim the fictionality of the text.

The blind commitment to reality that guides these readings of the *Page* reflects, in addition to attitudes about the nature of biography, autobiography, and critical editions, a widely prevalent attitude toward seventeenth-century fiction: that it can be appreciated only as a strange sort of historical document. This point of view was encouraged by seventeenth-century readers, who provided in abundance the first *clefs* to contemporary novels, and it was nurtured and repeated by subsequent generations of readers and critics. Thus, Dietrich's second explanation for the absence of proper names in the *Page* ("Il s'est conformé tout simplement à la mode de son temps. Tous les récits de l'époque, en effet, à part les mémoires proprement dits, sont des récits à clef.")[15] echoes the prevailing ideas of his day, as expressed in articles by Nodier and others.[16]

The culminating monument to this critical fascination with *clefs* is Fernand Drujon's three-volume compilation, *Les Livres à clef*. Drujon's commentary on his collection of *clefs* is characterized by a conviction of its indispensability and at the same time by a fear that it lacks foundation: a conviction that these novels can only find readers when accompanied by their *clefs*, and a fear that all of the "information" he is publishing is of a highly dubious nature. "Cet ouvrage n'offre aucun intérêt maintenant, il ne serait utile à lire que si l'on en retrouvait la clef." "Le malheur est que toutes les attributions de ces clefs sembleraient n'être pas très exactement fondées."[17] The obsessive need to find *clefs* for the libertine novels establishes the affirmation of historical or autobiographical content in seventeenth-century novels as still another manifestation of the overwhelming desire on the part of subsequent periods to treat these novels as *jeux de société* or curiosities for bibliophiles.

Amazingly enough, to date no critics have pointed out that this application of autobiography is actually anti-autobiographical,[18] and few even mention the fact that these texts, when taken to be the factual accounts of the story of a life, present, as Adam phrases it, occasional "invraisemblances." Adam admits that, when seeking parallels between Tristan and his novel, "c'est se risquer fort que de prétendre tirer de cette oeuvre romanesque une histoire exacte de ses premières années."[19] Such an appraisal, however, simply replaces one point of view with its opposite, and fails to contribute to an understanding of what it is in the text that makes this type of reading possible. Admittedly, certain of Madeleine de Scudéry's novels overtly beg to be included in Drujon's lists and to have their not-so-secret secret codes drawn up at great length. I hope to have demonstrated that such is not the case with Tristan's text, yet a question remains: Is the *Page* totally innocent of responsibility for these explanations? Only Démoris hints at a certain complicity on Tristan's part: "L'allusion à la réalité a pu contribuer à induire un mode de lecture légèrement différent de celui qui s'appliquait ordinairement aux romans."[20] But there is no need for hesitation on this issue. The *Page* "beguiles" its reader, "induces" him to believe that its strange world cannot be accounted for in purely novelistic terms. It simultaneously invites and rejects allegiance to the world of "autobiography," not only because it calls for the type of "mixed" reading advocated by Adam, Démoris, and occasionally even Arland, but more importantly because the reality it integrates is a reality consciously rearranged according to the peculiar specifications of the libertine author.

To find a writer altering and disguising personal experience for presentation in a fictional work is no more unusual than to discover that certain events may be demonstrated to have been cloaked in a robe of fictionality when presented by a novelist in an autobiographical context—hence the "purist" belief that man can never know himself and that true autobiography is impossible, advanced in the mid-seventeenth century by, among others, La

Rochefoucauld, Nicole, and Pascal. Neither of these tendencies can be equated, however, with the transformations effectuated by Tristan and the other libertine novelists. They in a sense have no choice but to present events with a simultaneous existence in the realms of reality and fiction. They can create a special brand of literary autobiography because they have already succeeded in the creation of an unusual mode of existential autobiography. They "handle" their own existences as though these existences were equivalent to those of a character in a work of their own creation.

"Je suis le Heros veritable de mon Roman" (p. 9), says D'Assoucy in the first sentence of the *Avantures*, as if heroes were real and life were a novel. These libertines maintain a distance from the events of their lives that allows them to mingle what actually took place and what they imagine as having taken place (what they would have liked to take place?), so that in the long run all notions of true and false become inoperative. For them, the reality of an event is less important than the presentation of that event as real. Their passion for control over events, like their obsession with onomastic autonomy, makes them entirely responsible for their lives. They attain their goal, that of molding lives like no others in their day.

What are the facts about Cyrano's legendary dueling skills: did he really chase Montfleury from the stage, rout a hundred men at the Porte de Nesles? Was D'Assoucy actually burned in effigy in Montpellier? Did Tristan, alias the *page disgracié*, really meet a magician?[21] Under the guidance of libertine manipulations, all such questions become illegitimate. According to D'Assoucy's conclusion:

> Chapelle t'en a bien conté,
> Dassoucy t'en fait le semblable:
> Mais pour dire la verité,
> L'un et l'autre de son costé
> N'a rien écrit de véritable;
> Croy, Lecteur, que c'est une fable
> Et que le tour est inventé.
>
> (P. 188)

The libertine novelist's way of handling his existence invalidates the assumption advanced by all composers of *clefs* and footnotes that the composition of (auto)biography is somehow less artistic than that of literary texts. By making operative a theatrical conception of reality, he transforms himself into a living carnival, what Démoris calls, in reference to the hero of a contemporary comic novel not without thematic links to the libertine tradition, *Le Gascon extravagant*, a "fou conscient . . . spectateur d'une société où il se trouve déclassé, mais . . . aussi un acteur conscient d'être un spectacle."[22] In their personal existences, Théophile, Tristan, Cyrano, Chapelle, and D'Assoucy act out the myth of the writer larger than life. They dramatize themselves and forge their own destinies, arranging and shaping occurrences in a literary way, according to literary models. A far cry from the passive, almost accidental mingling of fiction and reality found, or at least suspected, in much contemporary personal literature, this represents a conscious project to make reality imitate the fictional. The would-be libertine biographer who becomes aware of such deformations must come to the conclusion that he cannot verify the events described, but can only trace the contours of their legends. Such a realization is strangely similar to that which enlightens Ryan, the hero of the Borges story from which, in an attempt to be faithful to the spirit of these authors by keeping my own critical reality within boundaries already set by literature, I borrow the title and the epigraph for this chapter. This is a chapter *of* quotations, but also *about* a particular brand of quotation, illustrated best in Borges's allegory.

Ryan's attempt to write an autobiography of his great-grandfather, Fergus Kilpatrick, a political hero and victim of assassination, is hindered by his discovery of an unthinkable number of parallels between his ancestor's last days and those of Julius Caesar. He postulates the existence of a "secret pattern in time, a drawing in which the lines repeat themselves," until he realizes that part of a reported conversation with Kilpatrick on the day of his death had already been pronounced in *Macbeth*. "That history should have imitated history was already sufficiently marvelous; that history should imitate literature is inconceivable." When Ryan pieces together the "truth" of Kilpatrick's death, he discovers that the patriot was in fact a traitor who chose to be executed according to a prearranged script borrowed from the two Shakespeare plays in order to provide the hero needed by the Irish rebellion. None of those who participated as unwitting actors in the drama staged by Kilpatrick and his former friends suspected the prepackaged and plagiarized nature of its scenario; they saw only the tragic and heroic death of a great leader. Ryan himself decides not to betray the legend, but to publish "a book dedicated to the glory of the hero."

Borges's story shows that literature is or can be more real than life, more believable and certainly more gripping. More precisely, it can provide, as Borges's Irish rebel and our group of French ones illustrate, a model for a world view that enables its followers to laugh in the face of traditional norms and categories of behavior, and thereby free themselves from them. By forging for themselves lives "based on the techniques of art," they gain the distance from the events they are living described by Viktor Shklovsky in his own autobiographical novel, *Zoo*: "We play the fool in this world in order to be free. Routine we transform into anecdotes. Between the world and ourselves, we build our own little menagerie worlds."[23] The libertines choose to adopt neither the role of hero nor that of traitor, but the more ambiguous status of the doubtful hero, playing out a series of not always heroic acts in a spirit of grandiose, and borrowed, glory. They thereby change their autobiographies into literary material, into the biographies of heroes in a novel. They become in real life ready-made characters, deliberately setting themselves apart and demanding consideration, not as ordinary human beings, but as superhuman mixtures of fact and fiction. As a consequence of this irreverent playfulness, the fact they mingle into their works generally cannot be treated as ordinary fact, and is destined to defy interpretation in footnotes. An event in such a life is already a bit of literary material, and to make reference to it is therefore to indulge in nothing less than a striking form of citation. It can be said that any autobiography incorporates or in a sense "quotes" material already in existence, but its libertine variant takes this notion one step further, since the act of citation involves the real already made fictional, and as such constitutes a true text within a text.

Thus, when the lack of proper names is compensated for by what would seem the ultimate in realistic naming, the presence of the author's name in his own text, the function of such an evocation is far from clear. It is certainly not sufficient to conclude quickly that, because the narrator of Cyrano's utopias bears the anagram Dyrcona, or because D'Assoucy's name is omnipresent in the chapter titles and in the text of the *Avantures*, the identity among author, narrator, and main character is confirmed. The first indication of the complexity of this presence is given by the fact that Cyrano chooses for his narrator what is perhaps the most bizarre of the long list of signatures he employs, one he did not use to take possession of a literary work, one outside his plural replacements for the normally unique *nom d'auteur*.

"Dyrcona" is an anagram, a type of name usually associated with hiding or self-protection. This is its function when used, for example, by an author either to refer to himself in a daring context or to a target for ridicule in a satire or a *roman à clef*. This latter context is one familiar to Cyrano, who turns to anagrams to "cover up" his most ferocious satirical letters: "Contre Ronscar," "Contre Soucidas." The anagram's enigma is that it usually provides the barest minimum—indeed, an almost nonexistent—cover. Any secrecy obtained by an anagram is fragile. If the word from which it is composed remains unknown, then the anagram maintains its incognito—"Voltaire," for example. In the case of the great majority of anagrams, nothing is involved but the pretense of a game, the innest of in-jokes for the initiate so bored that he wants to be given the illusion of working to decode, whereas the task is, in fact, effortless. The anagram pretends to hide something that it really unveils. It is the ultimate in onomastic titillation, libertine in the other sense of the word. In describing "Dyrcona" 's function in naming Cyrano's narrator, Jean Serroy, the only critic to have directed his attention to the problem of this anagram, concludes too quickly that, just as the moon is "le monde autre, le monde à l'envers, . . . il n'est pas jusqu'au nom même de Cyrano qui ne soit inversé."[24] Dyrcona is not, however, allowed to assume his twisted name until he has left the land of reversals (where he remains nameless) and has returned to earth at the beginning of the *Estats et empires*. Furthermore "Dyrcona," unlike Cyrano's other examples of the art of anagramming, "Soucidas" and "Ronscar," is not based simply on inversion—here, the juggling is more complex.

Generally speaking, the subclass of the proper name that is the author's name has no place within the literary text. It can be found inscribed in only two types of works. In self-conscious fiction, *Don Quixote*, for example, the man holding the pen sometimes includes a signature within his creation,[25] the ultimate in what Jean Rousset has so aptly named "fenêtres indûment ouvertes sur le dehors,"[26] invasions of fiction by reality that succeed in blurring the boundaries between the two. In the autobiographical work, the appearance of the author's name is a reassuring one, a unifying presence, and a guarantee of authenticity. The inscription of the author's name in the libertine life-novel provides an important indication of its status somewhere on the frontier between these two types of narrative, independent, yet dipping into the territory of each. Cyrano's use of "Dyrcona" partakes of some of the shock value much prized by self-conscious writers. If "Cyrano" is already a complex signature for the author of *L'Autre Monde* and the *Estats et empires*, "Dyrcona" is no more than a travesty of a travesty—a false name so obviously false that Cyrano does not use it to sign his literary productions.

In the case of "Dyrcona," the reader is confronted with a linguistic entity in a playful relationship to the connotations of the *nom d'auteur* as these are described by Foucault:

> Un nom d'auteur assure une fonction classificatoire; un tel nom permet de regrouper un certain nombre de textes, d'en exclure quelques-uns, de les opposer à d'autres. . . . Le nom d'auteur ne va pas comme le nom propre de l'intérieur d'un discours à l'individu réel et extérieur qui l'a produit. . . . Le nom d'auteur n'est pas situé dans l'état civil des hommes, il n'est pas non plus situé dans la fiction de l'oeuvre, il est situé dans la rupture qui instaure un certain groupe de discours et son mode d'être singulier.[27]

The proper name exists as *nom d'auteur* only with regard to a body of works, and cannot begin to exercise this function until at least one of these works is in circulation. The *nom d'auteur* is not a *nom d'auteur* unless the reader, seeing it, can say: "Oh, yes, he wrote_____." "Peut-être n'est-on véritablement auteur qu'à partir d'un second livre, quand le nom propre inscrit en couverture devient le 'facteur commun' d'au moins deux textes différents."[28]

Cyrano manages to short-circuit the functioning of the *nom d'auteur*. He does so first of all by refusing to standardize his name, to present a stable name to be associated with his collected literary production. Second, he chooses to inscribe in the *Estats et empires* a variant of his name without literary connotations. "Dyrcona" is neither a *nom d'auteur* nor really even a proper name—at least, it does not look like what would be accepted as a "normal" proper name in French. It is a game, a formation of shifted letters that points to only an individual protected by a series of masks, neither completely author nor nonauthor, grounded principally neither in reality nor in fiction. That someone could transform himself according to artistic techniques, that history could be made to imitate literature, is in a sense, as Ryan concludes, "inconceivable," so the critic, biographer, and reader of Cyrano all come away baffled. "Dyrcona" may have a foundation in reality, but it functions in Cyrano's text not as a *nom d'auteur* but as a *nom de personnage*.

D'Assoucy continues the problematic raised by Cyrano by "doubling" his own name in the *Avantures*. From the dichotomy he maintains, it would seem that there was a private individual (Coypeau) whose existence was cut off by the birth of the literary persona (D'Assoucy). The first ceases to exist when the second gains recognition. On the unique occasion when D'Assoucy seeks to evoke the past and the man outside literature, the family name is used. The encounter with his "cousin de Carpentras"[29] is an acceptance, even though accidental, of origin. The pseudo cousin approaches D'Assoucy and pushes him to pronounce for the first time the name that links him to his past: "Ma foy, luy dis-je, j'ay eu autre fois un oncle, qu'on appeloit Coypeau" (p. 154). It is then the cousin's turn to reconfer the abandoned name: "Je vous appelleray mon cousin Coypeau" (p. 155). Indeed, the entire scene takes place under the banner of the forgotten "Coypeau," a sign mentioned no fewer than seven times in the course of two pages. The meeting and evocation of his past does not seem painful for D'Assoucy—"Je m'en rejoüis, luy dis-je" (p. 154). He, nevertheless, does not seek, and fails to find, occasion to repeat it. "Coypeau" is never mentioned again in the *Avantures*.

The proper name most in evidence in the text is the name chosen to replace "Coypeau," the stage name, "D'Assoucy." Attention is called to the "falseness" or "literariness" of this title through the integration of a moment of onomastic playfulness. When the people of Montpellier want to attack him, "au lieu de

Soucy Musicien, ils . . . m'appellassent Sorcier et Musicien."[30]
An unmistakable indication of the center of interest in the text is
the fact that all but three of the chapter titles in the *Avantures* and
the *Avantures d'Italie* contain "D'Assoucy," and they almost always begin with this name: "Dassoucy, partant de Paris pour aller
servir leurs A. R. de Savoye, rencontre un Filou," and so on. In
addition, on the three other occasions in the *Avantures* on which
the narrator is named by someone else, whether in the course of
being robbed [31] or being saved from robbery, he is always ad-
dressed as "D'Assoucy."

The preference for this name expressed in the *Avantures* would
seem at first glance to be a clear case of reference to a *nom d'auteur* in Foucault's sense. The "monsieur Dassoucy" mentioned
during the three name-assuming encounters is always, in fact,
D'Assoucy, poet and author of numerous collections of verse:
"Vous souvenez-vous de cette chanson à boire que vous fistes, et
que tout le monde chantoit à la Cour?" (p. 24); "Je luy présentay
tous mes ouvrages burlesques dans trois livres differens, bien re-
liez et bien dorez" (p. 46); "et luy . . . me riposta autant de fois,
en disant à la santé du Grand Dassoucy, Prince des Poëtes Burlesques" (p. 86). A well-known literary name, but the story it
evokes is past and concluded. The composition of songs was accomplished in a bygone era. The books have ceased to roll off the
presses. The only eulogy in the present tense is made by Philippot,
a "poëte du Pont neuf," and therefore hardly an appropriate
judge of genius. In short, the man of letters who tells his story in
the *Avantures* is a has-been, and the name "D'Assoucy" has become more and more readily associated with the scandalous life
of the composer of the poems and the travelogue. The initial
break with the past destroys the family name; the second leaves
the *nom d'auteur* behind.

2. FOR A NEW NOVEL

The preceding pages may be read as an attempt to do the impossible: to simultaneously affirm and deny the presence of autobiography in the libertine text. I want to deny the possibility of an
autobiographical interpretation that could be termed traditional
in any sense of the word and to affirm the existence of a conception of autobiography particular to the libertine novel.

These texts can be read neither as *romans à clef*, nor as historical documents, nor as precursors of the texts generally accepted today as the first manifestations of modern autobiography. Their case is exceptional, not, however, because the conditions for modern autobiography were absent in the seventeenth century, as perhaps they were in earlier periods.[32] It is exceptional because they tantalize by inviting, yet escaping, assimilation in any of the traditions of the "prehistory" of autobiography discerned by Lejeune or others. To describe the libertine texts, it is necessary to step outside the norms and the terminology developed from and for less malleable texts, and to stumble about in a blurred and not quite definable space. When Jean Fabre, for example, raises the question of the existence of an "autobiographie 'libertine,' " extending from Cardano to Rousseau, in which the libertines "dévoilaient à dessein, aggressivement, leurs secrètes pensées et les scandales de leur vie,"[33] even this "home" must be denied the libertine novelists. If (and the point is certainly open to debate) Rousseau can be traced to Cardano, the seventeenth-century libertines cannot be easily used to complete the chain. The very conditions for autobiography affirmed by modern theoreticians on the basis of such texts as the *Confessions* exist for seventeenth-century freethinkers only to be partially rejected, and for this reason, if for no other, the filiation cannot be neatly traced. I have attempted to describe their particular conception of autobiography and the implications it had for the conduct of their lives. I would now like to examine the effect of this attitude on their novels, to trace the imprint of the libertine vision of personal history on them. It will be necessary at times to reopen questions raised in the first part of this chapter in order to provide as complete a picture as possible of the specific qualities of libertine narrative. By measuring the technical distance that separates these *autobiographies romancées* from autobiographies, I hope to arrive at a more complete description of the libertine sensibility.

As Lejeune conveys in his now-famous formula, "le pacte autobiographique," autobiography originates in the asking. I, the author, make explicit in some way and at some point in my text my desire to have this text read as the most accurate account I can possibly give of my psychological and factual existence(s). The libertine writers seem at times to be making this request. The

Page opens with a cry from the heart to a certain "cher Thirinte": "La fable ne fera point éclater ici ses ornements avec pompe; la vérité s'y présentera seulement si mal habillée qu'on pourra dire qu'elle est toute nue. On ne verra point ici une peinture qui soit flattée, c'est une fidèle copie d'un lamentable original; c'est comme une réflexion de miroir" (p. 50). This rivals La Rochefoucauld's confrontation with the mirror in its pretense of sincerity. But the *Page* is part fiction, Thirinte entirely so, and there is no truth to tell anyway. The libertines are aware of the fact that their protestations of accuracy are clouded by a primordial drive toward fable. The resulting notion of "pact" is best expressed in D'Assoucy's warning to the reader not to believe a word of what he reads (p. 188).

How could there be a pact of fidelity in texts that systematically reject initiation and development and indeed all factors of autobiographical "stability"? Such notions are central to most current theories of early autobiography, Georges Gusdorf's, for example: "Toute autobiographie digne de ce nom présente ce caractère d'une expérience initiatique, d'une recherche du centre." The importance Gusdorf places on this new "quête du Graal" is derived from a conversion experience of "un christianisme à la première personne" that he feels is inextricably linked to the formation of the genre.[34] In this light, the libertine texts can be described as the record of anti-Christian and anti-conversion experiences. They continue the liberation from the divine made by the humanistic autobiographies of the Renaissance, but differ from them in their refusal to see an evolution in what they view as a shifting *moi*.

All libertine narrative takes place under the sign of what Starobinski, speaking of the picaresque, has called "le temps faible": "le temps des faiblesses, de l'erreur, de l'errance, des humiliations."[35] The libertine narrator is even more static than his picaresque counterpart. By this I mean that, even though he is constantly on the move, he never moves out of "le temps faible." Whereas the picaro's *récit* is told from the vantage point of a present characterized by rest from turmoil and folly, by some sort of peaceful comprehension of past weaknesses, even by integration into the society that sought to humiliate him, the libertine's (with the exception of *Francion*) unfolds against a backdrop of continuing upheaval, both social and intellectual. The present repeats the story of the past, and the unseen future can only bring more of the same, in a world in which there is no salvation—religious, intellectual, or social—and therefore no possibility of conversion. The libertine hero can neither develop nor unfold in the course of a series of adventures. The only integration of difference left open to him is absolute change, stripped of explanation and blatant in its simplicity. Thus, he may defend a certain belief at one point, its opposite at another, like Dyrcona, who makes the switch from Catholic to atheist without even the minimal signal of the drop of a hat.

Little wonder, then, that in the accumulations of follies, past, present, and certainly to come, there seem to be no limits in the domains of both feasibility and complexity. Even if there is initially something of the identity among author, narrator, and hero that all theoreticians of autobiography, from Starobinski to Lejeune, believe to be essential, this conformity is quickly lost, and the narrator/hero often embarks on a separate course of adventure possible only in the novelist's imagination. The context of the libertine story may vary from author to author, even while retaining the same basic mixture of what can be attributed to the domain of authentic and accurate autobiographical description and what is evidently part of the fantastic portrait. On this question, the *Page* provides a good point of departure, since the spectrum of events it contains ranges from the verifiable, the measurable (Tristan and his hero both have early "careers" as pages; both travel extensively), to the credible, if not yet verified, or indeed not verifiable (the circumstances of first loves, the itinerary of their voyages), to the completely improbable (Tristan's sharing of his page's encounter with someone able not only to make gold before him but also to offer him a selection of magic potions). The events belonging to the last category often contribute the most striking points of comparison among the various libertine texts.

Théophile's *Fragments* provides the best example for a detailed analysis because the shortness of the text permits a complete listing of the events it describes. To begin with, almost all the tidbits of information that can be gleaned about the narrator of the *Fragments* can be assigned without hesitation to one of the first two categories described above. For the most part, they fall under the heading of the historically verifiable in terms of Théophile's biography: Théophile and the narrator both are literary "moderns"; both are exiled; both are well-known figures; both are polyglots; and, most strikingly, both are poets. In the second category belongs the outline of a psychological portrait provided by the *Fragments*: the mood of the narrator/hero, and quite possibly of Théophile as well, is influenced by the weather; for him/them, it is necessary to feel passions simultaneously in several domains; and he/they dislike overly formal social situations.

These two listings omit only two indications about the narrator's life, both intimately linked to the status of the *Fragments* as a libertine text. The narrator describes in some detail the scene in which he is responsible for unmasking a "démoniaque" who, with the assistance of a priest and an old woman, had succeeded in convincing the public that she was possessed. This scene is a central one, not only for its humor and its striking topicality, but also because it borders on the impossible—the likelihood of Théophile's indulging personally in such a flamboyant exposure of the abuses of organized religion and then boasting of it in a public confession seems slim.[36] Moreover, this gesture is in open contradiction to the other problematic event in the *Fragments*, the narrator's own "unmasking" when he is discovered to be a Huguenot. At this time, his first reaction is to defend himself, not from condemnation by fellow libertines for his open statement of religious belief, but rather from condemnation by Catholics who might be outraged by any gesture of support for such a heretical group. He protests: "Dieu ne m'avoit pas fait encore la grace de me recevoir au giron de son Eglise,"[37] thereby negating the potentially dangerous affiliation by affirming his subsequent conversion to the one, true faith and his entry into a state of grace.

With this seemingly innocent sentence, Théophile plunges his reader into the problem of autobiographical interpretation. The narrator's profession of religious orthodoxy functions as a trick to catch the unwary reader. Near the end of a text filled with similarities and points of identification between its narrator and its author, the narrator slips in an affirmation that even a reader who does not believe Garasse's slanders and the evidence accumulated by his persecutors cannot accept as true. There is no information to support the assertion that Théophile was a willing convert to Catholicism at an adult age roughly contemporaneous with the composition of the *Fragments*. The very presence of this line in his work solicits a protective reading for it, but one that is also false and troubling. How can Démoris's interpretation of the *Fragments* as "l'autobiographie du libertin triomphant" be wholeheartedly defended in the face of such a statement? Théophile's narrator certainly dwells at times on moments of libertine glory—the strident literary polemic of the first chapter is proof enough of his confidence—but as long as the freethinker feels obliged to hide behind a mask of beliefs, he is far from completely *triomphant*. Keeping in mind Théophile's refusal to stand up and be counted as a libertine, it becomes impossible to accept Démoris's attractive explanation for the unfinished state of the text: "Théophile n'écrira pas son roman autobiographique, dont l'esquisse est motivée sans doute comme réponse au fait de l'exil. Le libertin heureux a sa vie: il n'a pas besoin de son histoire."[38] To a large extent, the *Fragments* describes the fun and games of a happy libertine, but of one, nevertheless, deprived of intellectual freedom, and therefore perhaps of the desire to complete a story that can only have an unhappy ending. The hesitant autobiographical mode fathered by Théophile in the *Fragments* and adopted by the libertines puts any classification of their works into question.

The life stories traced by these works are all partial, both chronologically and experientially. There is no claim to totality in the libertine text, no attempt to account for the fullness of a life, an aim generally deemed essential to autobiography. *Francion* clearly presents the most complete treatment, taking its hero from birth up to marriage (in the third edition), yet even here it is obvious that the reader has not arrived at the end of the tale. There must be something to life that does not end with marriage, even for a libertine super-hero. The *Fragments* contains the account of a small slice of adulthood, lasting no more than a few days, with a unique excursion into the near past for the story of the "démoniaque." The *Page* makes no attempt to extend its horizons beyond youth and adolescence; when we leave its hero, he is only nineteen. Chapelle's tale has the smallest scope of all, no more than that of a short-distance voyage with a few brief encounters. And though the attention devoted by D'Assoucy to his family background and to episodes from his childhood cannot be underestimated, his *Avantures* and *Avantures d'Italie* remain essentially the story of another voyage, even though a longer and more complex one than Chapelle's outing. As for the life story covered by Cyrano's two utopias, it could hardly be less complete. In fact, even to speak of autobiography with regard to a text that tells the story of voyages in strange vehicles to and from the moon and the sun and describes the even stranger group of individuals found in these worlds seems uncalled for, if not laughable.

But it is precisely the type of autobiographical revelations contained in *L'Autre Monde* and the *Estats et empires* that is most characteristic of libertine texts. For them, the life story is, or can be made, important, but it is not essential. Rather than the stories of facts, dates, and events, these are intellectual autobiographies. Thus, external events are secondary to attitudes toward them and the philosophies developed or borrowed to deal with them. Plot is subordinated to sensation and belief. What is important in these texts is not what the heroes do, but how and in what spirit they do it.

More radically than the previous writers of intellectual autobiography (Cardano, for example), they do away with any attempt at seeking chronology and causes. After all, how could these beings who subvert names, genealogy, and all other forms of authority and control over their existences devote their energies to a search for origins? They are, not because—. They simply are. They do not believe such and such because—. They simply believe. The portrait ultimately assembled may not seem complete when judged by the standards of cause-effect logic, but it succeeds in transmitting an image of intellectual distress in the face of a world determined to keep those who dare ask questions in a position of alienation. Théophile's narrator and Dyrcona are obliged to perform intellectual about-faces. The page and D'Assoucy are able to distance themselves from their disgraces, but they cannot escape them. Events are present only to confirm the ultimate intellectual sensation of aporia.

These heroes live their adventures in a spirit faithful to the libertine attitude toward personal history. The belief in "literary" detachment is handed down from author to narrator. The page, Dyrcona, and the other narrators are auctorial reflections essentially because of their visions of themselves. Like their creators, they see themselves as characters, so they play out continuously the role with which they identify. The confusion between life and reality evident in D'Assoucy's opening formula, "Je suis le Heros veritable de mon Roman," also permeates the tone in which his narrative unfolds. The detachment with which D'Assoucy in his role of "Don Quichotte moderne" narrates his adventures is so thoroughly burlesque that, were it not for the predominance of prose, the *Avantures* could be described as one of the epic poems characteristic of that genre. D'Assoucy is wrong to apologize, even in jest, for the time robbed from his poetry for this text: "J'eusse bien mieux fait de continuer à composer des vers . . . que d'aller, comme un Don Guichot [*sic*]; chercher des avantures étranges par le monde" (p. 7). All libertine compositions, in life as well as in fiction, have essentially the same status, a point made clear by Boutonné's remark: "Entre ses oeuvres je n'ai pas estimé que le roman de sa vie fût des moins achevés" (p. 47).

These narrators who simultaneously affirm that their stories are "véritables," based on real life, and that they are defined according to literary terms and thereby consumed from within, demonstrate a carefree attitude toward chronological and factual precision that reveals the fiction of their accuracy. Thus, D'Assoucy's attempt to situate the starting point of his journey is limited to a hesitant "Je ne sçay si ce fut l'an mil six cens cinquante quatre ou cinquante cinq." (His editor Colombey feels obliged to "clear up" the matter with a note explaining that it was actually neither 1654, nor 1655, but 1653 [p. 11]). In a similar manner, the page closes his narrative by remarking to his "cher Thirinte" that he has taken him up to the point "où finit le dix-huit ou dix-neuvième an de ma vie" (p. 317).[39]

Texts that are "véritables" may transmit doubtful information, but they rarely admit to doing so, or at least stop short of flaunting the fact. The libertine text reveals a kinship with the burlesque in this domain, a kinship reinforced by a certain hesitancy with regard to basic narrative problems. Who, for example, is the hero of D'Assoucy's text? D'Assoucy seems to have forgotten that he has provided the most logical answer to this question by affirming that he is himself the true hero of his novel when he later echoes his striking opening formula with no explanation for either the change of mind or the change of word order: "Pierrotin, le Heros de mon veritable Roman" (p. 71). This is precisely the kind of seemingly offhand comment with which any burlesque narrator worthy of the name delights in teasing his reader—witness the *Roman comique*'s "hero intervention": "Le Comedien la Rancune, un des principaux Heros de nostre romant, car il n'y aura pas pour un dans ce livre-icy; et puisqu'il n'y a rien de plus parfait qu'un Heros de livre, demy-douzaine de Heros ou soy-disant tels feront plus d'honneur au mien qu'un seul." [40] D'Assoucy's wavering is not as overtly self-conscious as Scarron's, but it ultimately serves the same purpose of casting doubt on the exclusiveness of the notion of the hero.

As a result of their double life on the frontier of life and literature, these narrators share the psychological blindness of the original self-conscious hero and D'Assoucy's model, Don Quixote. The switch to the first person from the third person used to narrate the Don's adventures gives them no additional insights, as is shown when the page presents a choice of motivations for his actions. Here, the doubt used by self-conscious narrators to mark the distance between them and their creations is found in a first-person account of a former self, indicating that this self has been so completely objectified into third-person status that the appropriate emotions can no longer be re-created: "Je me retirai dans une hôtellerie assez écartée, où je soupai peu, *soit* par lassitude *ou* par tristesse" (p. 94; italics mine). In a different vein, but with a similar effect, D'Assoucy's psychology remains completely burlesque. He revels in such non-explanations of his actions and cavalier treatments of his personality as his attribution of the origin of the quarrel with Cyrano to the theft of a capon. He claims that he fled to Italy and began living his *Avantures* simply because he had seen Cyrano carrying a gun—even though he knew that he was only taking it to be repaired.

In any but the libertine text, such reasoning would seem an affront to a reader's intelligence. In these novels, where character is static, constructed through parataxis rather than the result of causal progression, its mysteries cannot be explained, but only recorded. Instead of including the evolution leading to a crucial moment, an evolution normally associated with a work of philosophical or psychological initiation, these texts are simply structured around the seemingly infinite repetition of a key situation, the situation responsible for the posture assumed in their narration. Francion outwits Valentin in the novel's opening scene and continues to be victorious in every round of the never-ending battle of wits that eventually leads him to the satisfaction of all his desires: social status and wealth, as well as friendship and love. The narrator of the *Fragments* is as victorious in showing up other representatives of intellectual dishonesty, bad poets, and pedants, as he is at unmasking the possessed woman. Both are eternally faithful to the "franchise" Francion bears inscribed in his name, the honesty and directness that expose the imposter.

In the *Page*, this invariability of characterization is even more evident, as well as more brutal, because of the totally pessimistic vision of the libertine fate the novel introduces. The reader begins with the conclusive judgment provided by the work's title: the "I" of the narrative voice is always already a *page disgracié*. Evidently, the older page responsible for the existence of the text chooses this title. While he was living the events that compose the story of his life, the young page could not yet have known that all mobility was forever to be denied him. Because of the work's title, in the reader's mind he remains frozen in the initial position selected for him. As Démoris points out, this is one case in which the fact that an autobiography is incomplete is of no consequence: "L'important est que le lecteur sache que cette suite absente ne doit rien changer au sens des premières expériences."[41] The page moves from disgrace to disgrace in the existing volumes of his adventures. An additional volume is announced in the last pages of the text, and held out like a carrot by Boutonné to the "good" reader who had the power to make the book a commercial success: "L'auteur a aussi laissé quelques fragments d'un troisième volume qu'il se promettait de faire imprimer . . . que je m'efforcerais d'assembler, si le lecteur paraît satisfait de cet essai" (p. 47). But it certainly would have done nothing to change the page's disgraceful course, and thus would have been completely superfluous.

Dyrcona's wanderings may be described as a continuous free fall from grace, broken by occasional landings. He falls into, as well as out of, paradise, drops back to earth, slams down onto the sun's surface, a cosmic Slinkey condemned to perpetual motion. When the libertine hero finds a good role, he holds onto it, as the example of D'Assoucy confirms. Like the *Page* and *L'Autre Monde*, the *Avantures* is the story of a victim—not just an ordinary victim, but a victim whose victimization takes on gigantic proportions through repetition. He is robbed and swindled by virtually everyone he meets, a perpetual realization of the fable of *Jacques le Fataliste*, every man's dog. The last libertine heroes find themselves sharing the repetitive punishment of a Prometheus, the mythical figure mentioned most often in *L'Autre Monde*.

Unlike the victorious libertine figures who proceed joyfully to unmask every fake in the universe without stopping to ask questions about the origin of their power, their less fortunate successors seem anxious to place the blame for their state on an outside source. Echoing the lamentations of the characters of the *roman héroïque* (who at least have the consolation of finding an end to their trials), they speak of their destiny, of the bad star under which they were born,[42] or they attribute their ability to attract misfortune to the devil's intervention. The page remarks, "Dieu permet que les démons s'en mêlent" (p. 52), thereby transferring to a universal present Dyrcona's explanation for the slip that incurs the wrath of Elie in the *paradis terrestre*: "Le Diable s'en mêla" (p. 53).

The most striking illustration of this use of fate is provided by the adjective the page chooses to describe himself. He is not in a state of grace, either because he has been deprived of grace— pushed, like Dyrcona, out of the paradise that is never really present in the *Page*[43]—or because, like the damned in Jansenist terminology, he simply was never given any to begin with.[44] Moreover, his graceless state seems permanent, given the finality of the work's title. Unlike the narrator of the *Fragments*, he is not destined to receive grace from God.[45] D'Assoucy's humbler equivalent to describe his own fallen state is the adjective whose popularity he helped establish. The *Avantures* and the *Avantures d'Italie* are often grouped together under the title *Avantures burlesques*,[46] a suitable label for a work in which D'Assoucy proves that the Emperor of the Burlesque is a true medieval fool king, master and slave wrapped up in one. With the numerous disgraces he endures, he outstrips even the most famous burlesque hero in prose, the *Roman comique*'s Ragotin, who, like the tattered Emperor, is a human *godenot*, or marionette, constantly made to fall down for the crowd's entertainment.

In this vision of himself, the later libertine hero is indeed an anti-hero, fortune's scapegoat. In the page's terms, "Je trace une histoire déplorable, où je ne parais que comme un objet de pitié et comme un jouet des passions des astres et de la fortune" (p. 50). The key words are "objet," "jouet." Despite his use of the first person, the libertine narrator's experience is apparently a totally passive one. He is a puppet, and fortune is the puppeteer, pulling the strings and playing with him as though he were a mere object to be tossed about. As a result of this predicament, the page and D'Assoucy are unable to assume total responsibility for the sub-jective vision of first-person narration. Thus, although the body of the account is controlled by the first person, third-person nar-rative is not wiped out, as could be expected, but continues to exist in the chapter titles: "L'Enfance et élévation du page disgra-cié," "Comme le Page disgracié faisait la cour à son maître, qui était tombé malade d'une fièvre tierce," "Dassoucy traverse la Bourgogne, et va à pied pour son plaisir; il décrit son crotesque équipage, et fait voir la simplicité de ceux qui se rendent esclaves du sot honneur." These headings maintain the existence of "he" and "his" alongside "I" and "my." "I" chooses to ensure the pres-ence of its object next to itself. The third-person cannot be erased from these texts because the subject continues to see itself, in gambling as in life, as the object of the verb "jouer."

In considering this insistence on the presence of "I" as object and as victim, the fact that the third person is relegated to a sec-ondary status in chapter titles cannot be forgotten. The subjectivi-ty of the first-person vision clearly dominates, and there is an occasional realization that the notion of the self as victim is a role actively assumed. "I" chooses to be viewed as "he," and controls the transmission of this vision. Through that choice and that con-trol, "I" takes on an active role. The libertine hero may lament his fate, but he aggressively works to manipulate it. When outside forces trick him, he is the object, or plaything, of the verb "jouer," but such occurrences do not exhaust the importance of this verb in the libertine text.

Far more often than he is toyed with, the narrator himself leads the game. Thus, D'Assoucy presents a "portrait enjoüé" of his life (p. 7). In the *Page*, role-playing runs rampant, since the hero is always playing at being what he is not. When the need arises, he pretends to be asleep, rich, noble. For his mistress, he re-creates himself and his past, in order to make himself into a hero of the type of love story he feels will impress her: "Je m'étudiai à oublier tout à fait mon nom et à me forger une fausse généalogie et de fausses aventures." He even frees himself so completely from the constraint of his past that he not only acquires the new name that goes with his new genealogy but also stresses the fact that he bestows it on himself: "Je me nommois Ariston" (p. 119). Ever taken in by play, even when he is in charge of it, the page succeeds in disguising himself so well that "je ne me connusse pas moi-même" (pp. 93–94) and in changing his past so thoroughly that "je croyais ces choses-là véritables" (p. 152).

It appears that his play-acting is so well executed that the page can even succeed in shaping his destiny, in actually making his tales come true. With his mistress, for example, when she is afraid he loves her cousin, "j'avais joué le personnage d'innocent accusé" (p. 127)—which he later becomes. When he is accused of having tried to poison his mistress, "j'étais l'innocent persécuté que l'on tenait comme en prison" (p. 172). His desire to conform to his vision of himself forces things to happen as he believes they should with regard to still another episode of the past he crafted for his mistress's benefit. For her, the page pretends to be the son of a merchant (p. 119). Later, in the course of the voyages he undertakes when he is obliged to flee England, his valet buys furs in Norway so they can make a profit from their stay. When faced with *paraître* become *être*, the page comments: "Et de seigneur et de prince imaginaire que j'avais été, je me vis effectivement marchand" (p. 203).

Confronted with this vision of the narrator as the creator of the game of his life, the reader is never entirely convinced that "he / I" accepts the explanations so readily given for his status. The page, for example, clearly feels he should have been more successful, since he was so richly endowed at birth: "et si l'espérance de pouvoir trouver cet homme ne m'eût point longtemps abusé, je me fusse trouvé trop riche du bien de mon patrimoine et des talents qu'il avait plu à Dieu de me donner" (pp. 212–13). He hesitates between *fortune* and *artifice* when it comes to placing the final blame, to giving the ultimate explanation for his status. Is he *disgracié* because he is a victim of the whims of fate, or because he himself creates this fate with the strength of his vision? He wonders "si ce que je croyais être un caprice de la fortune n'eût point été un pur ouvrage de l'artifice" (p. 218).

Nothing illustrates more forcefully the page's indecision than the pair of names he bears in the text. Is he defined by the title adopted by the older narrator and linked to his status as a third-person object, or is he better described by the false name the young page chooses for himself in a gesture of the first-person's subjective artifice: Ariston, the best, upper class?[47] The coexistence of the fate-artifice couple in the *Page* is indicative of a fundamental indecisiveness in its hero's sense of identity, and this indecisiveness is echoed in the special character of the two names he adopts. This reduction of the proper name to a title composed of a common noun and an adjective and to an invented, cardboard name is not incompatible with the absence of proper names in the *Page*. These tags do not really function as names, but are substitutes that fool no one and can do nothing to bridge the gap at the non-center of the work.

In the opening pages of his story, the page uses another third-person title to replace his father's name: "Je ne vous déduirai point toute cette aventure, . . . vouloir la représenter sur ce papier, serait vouloir écrire l'histoire de l'écuyer aventureux, et non pas l'aventure du PAGE DISGRACIE" (p. 51). The strange presence of capital letters only strengthens the impression that the page is aware of the inadequacy of these name objects and wants to call attention to their artificiality. He himself confirms their functioning as mere extensions of his silence about his origins when he admits the existence of a third, supposedly "real," name. Typically, he refuses to reveal this name, despite the pleading of his faithful valet, who before leaving his service begs to be told his name in order to be able to say where he had served (p. 211).

The page's obstinate refusal to lift the veil covering his own name is echoed by his secrecy regarding his mistress's: "Je ne lui dis pas le nom ni la qualité de ma maîtresse, m'étant résolu de ne découvrir jamais à personne un secret si fort important" (p. 230). In most other cases, the names of the characters encountered are revealed only as they are about to disappear from the pages of the novel. For example, the valet who wants so desperately to learn his master's name has a name, Jacob Cerston, which designates

him more appropriately than the vague "l'irlandais" or "mon irlandais" used for him throughout their travels, but it is not passed
on to the reader until after the valet has left the novel. Likewise,
we learn only as the English sojourn is coming to an end that the
woman referred to simply as "la favorite de ma maîtresse" has a
name—of sorts: "Après que Lidame (c'est ainsi que j'appellais la
favorite" [p. 175]). This appropriation of the right to name is
enacted by the page once more in the text when he mentions "ce
petit chasseur de qui j'ai parlé et que je nommerais Gélase" (p.
262).

He thus admits that the proper names assigned to the secondary characters in the *Page* in this offhand, after-the-fact manner
do not really function as they should. They do not indicate origin,
since they are invented by the page in an attempt to create still
another façade in front of the characters in his story, and to subvert the normally trustworthy function of the name in literature.
"Gélase," for example, would be an ideal name for a character in a
novelistic system where "Greek name" equals "character's name."
The normal process of interpretation of such a name in such a
system would involve a simple transcoding through which the
suggestiveness of its meaning in Greek, in this case "he who
laughs," would be properly appreciated. In the *Page*, however,
this type of interpretation is blocked by the intervention of the
narrator's "que je nommerai," which announces a self-consciousness incompatible with a highly codified system and one
which no editor's footnote can eliminate.

The most problematic name in the *Page* shares certain of the
peculiarities of this use of "Gélase." When not considered as a
reference to an actual bearer of the name, "Artefius" tantalizes by
appearing to invite integration into the "Greek or Latin name"
category responsible for "Ariston" and "Gélase." This classification quickly shows itself to be inadequate. All the meaning to be
extracted from "Artefius" is already present in its French homo-
nym, *artifice*. The assimilation Artefius/artifice is generally overlooked, perhaps because it is so obvious, even though it is invited
by the presence of "artifice" only a few lines before the first use of
"Artefius": "je lui rendis celle-là fort adroitement et vis par cet
artifice" (p. 96). It is also encouraged by the unusually high rate of
appearance of this word in the *Page*, in contexts that suggest both

its link to magic and its association with the power of language.[48] "Artefius" is clearly the most important proper name in the *Page*. It must be interpreted both historically and allegorically in order to see that it is at the same time an acceptance of libertine origins and a rejection of all others. The man of artifice can be reincarnated at will, but he remains ultimately the being without center, he who cannot be named.

In parallel, if often less complicated, ways, the other libertine texts continue the reflection on the proper name found in the *Page*. The only real exception to this is *Francion*, where names are never absent. This novel shows off a vast web of names, from Valentin to Laurette, designed mainly to offer a system opposed to that of the heroic novel. In a discussion on libertine naming, only the name of the book's title character has a place. Francion is always frank and always physical, characteristics already inscribed in the two halves of his name, but nevertheless explicated for those who might have missed the obvious.[49] The act of naming occurs frequently in the novel in order to flaunt Francion's fidelity to his destiny. He is named before he appears; he is named by the narrator; he is named by numerous other characters. As soon as his name is mentioned, all present recognize it. When he is called upon to tell his story in the inn, he begins without hesitation: "Sachez donc que je m'appelle Francion" (p. 94). He thus demonstrates libertine immutability with none of the libertine hesitation about making the self public.

In the *Fragments*, on the other hand, this hesitation, this holding back, is present in an interesting manner. The first-person voice assumes responsibility for the narration with a simple "I," an "I" identified only by a certain number of traits, but never by a name. The other characters in the *Fragments* have Greek names ("Sidias," "Clitiphon") of the kind used by the tradition the narrator denounces in the first chapter. Such names seem to ask for a sort of allegorical decipherment in what could be seen either as a gesture of parody or an attempt to point out the simplistic rigidity and limited functioning of the old names next to the freedom of the newly nameless.

Cyrano's *L'Autre Monde* continues the libertine tradition of the unnamed narrator, and goes even further than the *Page* in subverting the reign of the proper name as a means of identifying, and eventually of interpreting the function of, characters. With only one exception, that of M. de Montmagny, viceroy of Canada, the only proper names to be found are those of the numerous mythological, biblical, and historical figures brought up in discussions. It is important to note that the example of "Montmagny" occurs before the narrator leaves for the moon, whose cold light encourages neither procreation nor the ultimate sign of origin, the proper name. This fact is amply illustrated by the appellations chosen for the characters encountered there. The demon of Socrates bears only an almost-name, since it is one that tells the reader nothing about him other than that he once inhabited the individual known as Socrates. Since, however, this demon was not particularly exclusive and also inspired the minds of at least a dozen or so other historical figures, just to count those listed by him in the text, such an appellation does not provide a very complete description.

As in the *Page*, many of the characters in *L'Autre Monde* are referred to by the vaguest identifications possible: "l'Espagnol," "le fils de l'hôte" or "le jeune hôte," "une des demoiselles de la Reine." On the moon, the narrator sometimes even goes so far as to replace names (of kings, rivers, and so on) with musical notations, employing the so-called "idiome des grands" ("celui des grands n'est autre chose qu'une différence de tons non articulés, à peu près semblable à notre musique" [p. 60]). When he eventually returns to earth, while still under the moon's influence (as the howling dogs prove), he continues the page's silence about geographical matters and refuses to identify the Italian city where he is taken by the peasants who find him, replacing it with three dots (p. 117).

It would seem that a voyage to warmer climates loosens the narrator's tongue, for the *Estats et empires* is less hesitant on the subject of names. *L'Autre Monde* insists that the heat of the sun's fire is necessary for generation. The name of Prometheus, who "fut bien autrefois au ciel dérober du feu" (p. 32), is appropriated to designate the male sexual organ: "un membre sans qui nous serions au rang de ce qui n'est pas, le Prométhée de chaque animal" (p. 108). With (t)his fire, procreation is possible, as in the case of crocodiles, who are born "du limon gras de la terre échauffé par le soleil" (p. 87). And with the acceptance of origin comes naming.

Thus, the narrator's two benefactors, the marquis de Colignac and the marquis de Cussan, are allowed the full use of their titles. On the sun, the majority of birds in "l'Histoire des Oiseaux" have names. The magpie who fights to save the narrator, for example, reveals not only her own name but those of her parents as well.

It is, of course, also in the *Estats et empires* that the narrator is identified as Dyrcona.[50] The functioning of this anagram as a kind of now-you-see-it, now-you-don't mask, however, is the first indication that, even at the source of origin, the proper name in a libertine text can only have a problematic existence. Margot, the magpie, tries to make the narrator less objectionable to her fellow birds by replacing his human title with "Guillery l'enrumé,"[51] a formula that clearly fulfills the necessary criteria for a bird name: the partridge bringing suit against him, for example, is known as Guillemette la charnuë. The fact that both "Dyrcona" and "Guillery l'enrumé" are used to refer to the same character makes them in a sense equivalent, and this equivalence attracts attention to the patronymic. "Dyrcona" does not sound right; it simply does not correspond to the image of a family name. In the case of the bird name, the first part is perfectly "normal," but the choice of an adjective as noun for the last name is merely descriptive, and contains no indication of origin. Guillery is referred to as "l'enrumé" because of what he is or seems to the birds to be, not because of his genealogy or what his father was. The double names of the narrator, the one used by others (the name object) and the one he himself answers to, in the long run serve, much like those of the page, to challenge the notion of origin. Also worthy of note is the scene in the *Estats et empires* in which one of the "venerable" members of the Parlement of Toulouse, attempting to arrest Dyrcona for heretical acts, refuses to pronounce the devil's name: "avoir monté à la Lune, cela ne se peut-il sans l'entremise de. . . Je n'oserai nommer la beste" (p. 102). He thereby indicates a parallel between the nameless libertines and the nameless devil, and a moment of parody of the libertine fight against the proper name.

In the travelogues of Chapelle and D'Assoucy, this fight is somewhat mitigated. In addition to the names brought up in the course of conversations, also present in earlier works, the names of many individuals actually encountered are included, especially by Chapelle. D'Assoucy toys with the rejection of identification by his frequent reduction of the name to its initial(s). He hesitates between presence and this form of semi-absence, referring sometimes to Chapelle, for example, with his full name (p. 146) and at others with only a "C." (p. 133). It is true that the name behind this "C." and those represented by most other initials in the *Avantures* may be easily supplied in context, but D'Assoucy's instinctive move against the space normally allowed the proper name in a text continues the libertine tradition.

Linked to the libertines' resistance to naming is a resistance to the consequences of the use of the first person. The choice of the first person is an exceptional one at the period for works with any fictional content, so exceptional in fact that it invites the assimilation of such works into the category of memoir literature. This invitation to a subjective reading is, however, quickly undercut by the distancing with regard to the personal I have been describing here. This combination of presence and absence results in a use of the first person unique in the history of literature with autobiographical intentions, a far cry from the expected "retour du moi sur soi-même."[52] Because of the absence of development in these texts, the choice of the first person may seem strange. Starobinski argues convincingly that, in the case of the narrator of a life without change, "il lui aurait suffi de se peindre lui-même une fois pour toutes, et la seule manière changeante apte à faire l'objet d'un récit serait réduite à la série des événements extérieurs: nous serions alors en présence des conditions de ce que Benveniste nomme *histoire*, et la persistance même d'un narrateur à la première personne n'eût guère été requise."

Starobinski goes on to explain that a text can only be rescued from the attraction of *histoire* by the presence of a dialogue between present and past, between new and old: "En revanche, la transformation intérieure de l'individu—et le caractère exemplaire de cette transformation—offre matière à un discours narratif ayant le *je* pour sujet et pour "objet."[53] The division of "I" into subject and object is a matter of central concern to the libertine text. It succeeds in escaping the monologism inherent in the picaresque narration of a life by opening up the contact between two temporalities ("I" as subject and "I" as object) in a manner without literary precedent. Furthermore, this manner does not

really come into its own, as far as the novel in France is concerned, until the reign of the eighteenth-century memoir novel.

In these less than total accounts, the look to the past does not
go back very far. Childhood plays an uncertain, reduced role,
evoked only in exceptional circumstances.[54] The *moi* with whom
a dialogue is set up is generally a young adolescent in a period of
intellectual formation. The narrator only occasionally practices
dédoublement, and then simply to confirm the destiny his older
self believes was always mapped out for him. This dialogic
movement marks, nevertheless, a first step toward the separation
of voices with such an important future in autobiographical and
pseudo-autobiographical narration. Francion, for example, does
not merely retell his life; he relives its various episodes in order to
find a justification for them and to illustrate the fidelity and uni-
formity of his existence. The narrator looks back at his younger
self to see signs of the future, and occasionally marvels at the
perfection of those he finds. By the time he is old enough to leave
home for lessons with the curé:

> J'avois desja je ne sçay quel instinct qui m'incitoit à hayr les ac-
> tions basses, les paroles sottes, et les façons niaises de mes com-
> pagnons d'escole, qui n'estoient que les enfans des sujets de mon
> père, nourris grossierement sous leurs cases champestres. Je me
> portois jusques à leur remonstrer de quelle façon il faloit qu'ils se
> comportassent . . . ces ames viles ne cognoissants pas le bien que
> je leur voulois . . . me disoient en leur patois . . . mille niaiser-
> ies et impertinences rustiques (p. 169).

Francion stresses the fact that there was already present, in the
child that he was, a clearly developed sense of the separation between the self and others, or at least others of a different social
class—"*leur* patois." All the scorn and condescension of the
would-be "grand seigneur" who will later attend the village marriage simply to make fun of it is foreshadowed here in Francion's
early behavior.

With the *Avantures* and especially the *Page*, the look over the
shoulder becomes more troubled, as the narrator can see in his
past only warnings of the misery that was to follow each action. In
such an atmosphere, premonition reigns. The narrator is unable
to forget the outcome of an event, a forgetting essential to an
objective narration. For example, the older page, the page who is

no longer a page, sees danger where his former self could only have been blind to it. He therefore begins his account of what the page would certainly have presented at the time as a scene of triumph, Artefius's offering of the vials of magic substances, with a description of Pandora's box that concludes: "On ne sut jamais si elle était un mal ou un bien, ou si c'étaient tous les deux ensemble" (p. 102).

On occasion, the relative subtleness of such a warning yields to the more strident voice of the man bitter at the thought of what he has lost, and the narrator cannot stop himself from intervening in his story to anounce its outcome. Even as he is building castles in Spain with his mistress, based on the wealth he is to obtain from the alchemist, the anachronistic voice of pessimism is heard:

> Comme la jeunesse est audacieuse et folle, tenant bien souvent pour des biens solides les biens qu'elle ne possède qu'en espérance, j'osai l'assurer qu'avant qu'il fût trois mois, je la viendrais demander en mariage à ses parents avec un équipage et un éclat qui serait égal à ceux des plus grands d'Angleterre. Et j'étais si simple de me promettre toutes ces prospérités sur la parole de l'alchimiste que je ne revis plus jamais (pp. 139–40).

Like the model "romantic" hero that he is, the page cries out "nevermore" at regular intervals throughout his story, keeping the older self and his subjective interest in the narration alive. And D'Assoucy, more strident still and far less polished, continues to make the cry resound: "O moy misérable! je me réjouïssois approchant de mon Paradis terrestre, tandis que mes destins enragez m'entrainoient tout vivant dans les Enfers" (p. 103).

Concurrently with this subjectivity in moments of premonition, the libertine narrative voice retains comic elements associated with the burlesque tradition. Of these techniques that refute the notion of personal exploration, preterition is the most striking. The page breaks off the story of his passion for his English mistress with an abrupt "Je ne vous dirai point ici des choses qu'on peut mieux ressentir que dire" (p. 150). D'Assoucy cuts short a description of one of his misfortunes with an equally curt "Je ne diray pas à quelle extremité je fus reduit" (p. 97). At these moments, the reader is thrown off guard by this avoidance of emotion in texts often capable of telling all with feeling.

Perhaps the most effective narrative means of by-passing personal involvement is the particular brand of first-person narration chosen by Chapelle and Bachaumont. Their "nous" has nothing to do with the artificial plurality of various noble forms of address and unmistakably contains two separate voices.[55] It therefore restricts the text to the level of experience shared by both members of the couple. Nothing must go beyond the events of the voyage made together. Events are seen not as either one of them would have alone but in a collective vision to which both can affix their signatures, as though the narrators were acting, in Rousset's expression, "en témoin latéral plutôt qu'en sujet central."[56] Personal impressions or reactions to what takes place, links between present and past, anything that does not belong simultaneously and equally to both pairs of eyes, have no place in this narrative model.

This distancing may be interpreted as one more manifestation of the seventeenth-century's distrust of the first person and of subjective narration, a distrust that is given coherent formulation by Madeleine de Scudéry: "Quand on dit soi-même son histoire, tout ce qu'on dit à son avantage est suspect à ceux qui l'écoutent. . . . Il est mille et mille fois plus raisonnable que ce soit une tierce personne qui raconte, que de raconter soi-même."[57] Scudéry's adjective "suspect" may well deserve a broader application than it receives in this passage. When a narrator is telling his own story, he not only becomes aware that an account painting him in a favorable light may seem suspicious to others, but also that a portrayal of himself in a less than favorable position may equally well be viewed with suspicion.

D'Assoucy's pervasive paranoia is aggravated by the announcement of his death in Loret's *Gazette* the year of the composition of the *Avantures*, by Chapelle's attacks, and by countless other incidents, many of which are referred to in his text. It makes the *Avantures* partly a self-justification before public opinion. Hence his frequent references to the "très-sage Lecteur" capable of vindicating him. Any attempt at pleading his case must of necessity delve into unsavory material, however, and the "I" of the *Avantures* realizes, as any "I" admitting a libertine past must, that to be subjective is to invite danger by providing excellent ammunition for one's enemies. For libertine purposes, the only justification or revenge possible has to be sought through an "objective," always distanced subjectivity.

In the light of this problematic, I propose to return for the last time to this chapter's opening discussion of the lack of proper names in these texts. The libertine projects have always (correctly) been assumed to be autobiographical, and this absence in them has been perceived (equally correctly) as anti-autobiographical. The proper name, as Lejeune affirms, is intimately connected with the standard autobiographical project:

> L'autobiographie est le genre littéraire qui . . . marque le mieux la confusion de l'auteur et de la personne. . . . D'où l'espèce de passion du nom propre, qui dépasse la simple "vanité d'auteur," puisque, à travers elle, c'est la personne elle-même qui revendique l'existence. Le sujet profond de l'autobiographie, c'est le nom propre. On songe à ces desseins de Hugo, étalant son propre nom en lettres gigantesques à travers un paysage en clair-obscur.[58]

The self-effacement characteristic of the libertine text is a far cry from Hugo's almost monstrous affirmations of his person. In a world colored not by chiaroscuro but by the less dramatic effects of gray, these authors who destroy the personal in their lives through objectification perform the same operation in their texts. Ultimately, their enterprise takes on a strange resemblance to another vision of autobiography, one with which they would appear to have little in common.

In the section of the *Grammaire de Port-Royal* devoted to pronouns, Arnauld and Lancelot give an explanation of their origin and role:

> Comme les hommes ont esté obligez de parler souvent des mesmes choses dans un mesme discours, et qu'il eust esté importun de repeter toûjours les mesmes noms, ils ont inventé certains mots pour tenir la place de ces noms.
>
> Premierement ils ont reconnu qu'il estoit souvent inutile et de mauvaise grace, de se nommer soy-mesme, et ainsi ils ont introduit le Pronom de la premiere personne.[59]

The grammarians' coolness and scientific spirit allow them to treat this point as though it were of no importance to the complex theological system for which they are spokesmen. Only a single phrase, "de mauvaise grace," evokes the specter of the Jansenist attack against the proper name. The proper name for the grammarians is not only ungraceful but also grace-less, attracting attention to physical presence in a way that is morally wrong. They criticize it according to the reasoning used to attack the theater and painting, other representatives of the all-too-solid human flesh.

Just as Philippe de Champaigne bent his style to suit the demands of Jansenist theory, so the writer of memoirs for the greater glory of Port-Royal was also obliged to make his narration conform to their system if he wished to gain approval. The *Mémoires* of de Pontis, originally composed in the third person, were completely altered to permit the substitution of the first person and thereby avoid the repetition of his name.[60] "Je" is a less noticeable, more transparent replacement. According to the *Logique ou l'art de penser*, "Les personnes sages évitent autant qu'ils peuvent, d'exposer aux yeux des autres, les avantages qu'ils ont; ils fuient . . . de se faire envisager en particulier, et ils tâchent plutôt de se cacher dans la presse, pour n'être pas remarqués."[61]

The ideal Jansenist text would be as personless, as weightless, as possible, in order to allow the self to be dominated by the absolute weight of fatality and the mystery of the *Deus absconditus*. Man without a name loses his sense of place and therefore his ability to defend himself in language and in life: "Rien ne lie mieux un homme au langage que son nom. . . . Cette pauvreté en noms . . . tient, de la façon la plus intime, à l'essence d'un ordre dont les membres vivent sous une loi sans nom, soumis à une fatalité qui répand sur leur monde la pale lumière d'une éclipse solaire."[62] Walter Benjamin describes in this manner another text that seeks to be nameless, the *Elective Affinities*.

The fatality in the libertine text must, of course, be held separate from the Jansenist fatality. Lionel Gossman distinguishes Rousseau's anguish at the world's silence from Pascal's by arguing that Rousseau replaces the *Deus absconditus* with the equally mysterious Other.[63] His distinction is certainly valid in the case of the libertine novelists. Nevertheless, the sense of inevitability shared by the libertine and the Jansenist texts links them in an important way. It is perhaps ironic that stories of conversion and stories of damnation should take the same form. It is less ironic that the dialogues around which they are centered should be the most complete, the most anguished, of their period. These two systems without compromise brand themselves with the same narrative mark.

"Ce n'est pas pour rien que tant de romans personnels sont les histoires des gens sans nom,"[64] remarks Démoris far too casually, for he fails to draw any consequences from his statement. Without a name to identify it and thus anchor it to a system of exchange, "I" becomes a generalized, floating signifier limited only by the information that can be associated with it. The reader wants to use a name to restrict a character's implications, to follow what Barthes terms "la nature économique de Nom—en régime romanesque, c'est un instrument d'échange: il permet de substituer une unité nominale à une collection de traits en posant un rapport d'équivalence entre le signe et la somme."[65]

In every case but that of *Francion*, however, the libertine novelists frustrate the reader's expectations because they want to make it clear that the story narrated by the deliberately unnamed "I" is not only the story of their unnameable, because politically dangerous, authors. The narrator/heroes are also unnameable because their story is not the story of one person to be identified with one name. As in the Borges allegory, literature can repeat history here. It can only do so because history has repeated history—and undoubtedly will continue to do so. The libertine fate is not anchored geographically or chronologically, but is played out again and again by those who dare to question accepted systems. The men who were denied names by their own period created unnamed and unnameable *porte-paroles* to underline the universality of the form of alienation these "characters" endure. "Je" is not only "un autre" but also all those who chose and choose to remain "autre."

---

1. Gautier, pp. 76–77.

2. Dietrich, p. v; Perrens, p. 273; Jacques Savarin, ed., *Le Page disgracié*, p. ix; Catherine Grisé, "Towards a New Biography of Tristan L'Hermite," p. 298. Adam contends that the *Page* also contains another fragment of Théophile's story. He feels that the "poète nouvellement sorti des écoles" whom the page saves from actors (p. 56) is none other than Théophile, and not Alexandre Hardy, as editors generally claim (*Théophile de Viau*, p. 19).

3. Louis Tenant de Latour, preface, p. 8.

4. Colombey, preface, p. xxi.

5. Dietrich, p. xxxvi.

6. Bernardin, p. 227.

7. Démoris, p. 23.

8. The decision to include *Francion* is a discussion of (conceivably) autobiographical texts is questionable, even for proponents of the real-man-behind-the-character theory. I would defend it in two ways. In the first place, the largely, if not completely, fictional nature of the life story told in it is not incompatible with the ideas on autobiography advanced in this chapter. The texts examined here may be considered more or less autobiographical, but they all present similar problems. Furthermore, I plan to limit my discussion of *Francion* to the 1623 edition (books 1–7), partly because, as Adam admits, this is the text "qui fait apparaître les plus belles audaces, le texte primitif du *Francion*" (*Romanciers du dix-septième siècle*, preface, p. 34). I also use the first edition because of the far greater role played by autobiography in it, a fact stressed by Démoris: "Il semble en effet que l'oeuvre se soit constituée *autour* du projet autobiographique, progressivement 'digéré' et réduit à un rôle moins important dans les versions successives, à mesure aussi que le livre perd de son audace et renonce à ce qui pouvait faire scandale" (p. 23). Indeed, if Francion's dream is included as a prologue to his *récit* (justifiable in this context, since it provides a sort of "psychological" autobiography), 59 percent of the 1623 edition is devoted to autobiography. Its share will be reduced to 37 percent in the 1626 text, and to 32 percent in the 1633 edition.

9. To such an extent that surprisingly few critical studies of *L'Autre Monde* and the *Estats et empires* are concerned with literary aspects of the works. Prévot, for example, chooses the title *Cyrano de Bergerac romancier* for his work and then proceeds to devote most of it to a discussion of scientific and philosophical theories, avoiding the question announced by his title, the process by which these ideas are transformed by their presentation in fictional form.

10. It is likely that A. Boutonné was chosen to encourage confusion with Rolet Boutonné, who published novels by Du Bail and others until his death in 1639. For information on R. Boutonné, see H.-J. Martin, *Livre, pouvoirs, et société à Paris au dix-septième siècle*. A. Boutonné has been identified as André Boutonné, but the puzzle of this *libraire*'s complicity with J.-B. L'Hermite has never been clarified.

11. Although no explanations for the attribution are given, it is accepted by Bernardin (p. 14), Dietrich (p. xxxvi), and Carriat: "La dédicace . . . est l'oeuvre probable du frère de Tristan, auteur également de la clé et des notes terminales" (p. 20).

12. If his first initial is included, however, "A. Boutonné" does stress the notion of unveiling.

13. Dietrich, p. 429.

14. Ibid., p. xxxvii.

15. Ibid., p. xxxvii.

16. For example, Nodier's "De quelques livres satiriques et de leurs clefs," *Bulletin du bibliophile*, offprint.

17. Fernand Drujon, *Les Livres à clef: étude de bibliographie*, 1:250–51, 90.

18. As Philippe Lejeune affirms, "L'autobiographie n'est pas un jeu de devinette, c'est même exactement le contraire" (*Le Pacte autobiographique*, pp. 25–26).

19. Adam, *Histoire*, 1:369. For Adam, such a judgment is pejorative. Elsewhere, he chastises the *Page* for being imperfect as an autobiography and therefore unsuitable for the historian's purposes: "C'est un défi à toute méthode de vouloir tirer d'une oeuvre aussi fantaisiste que celle de Tristan une précision de date. Des scènes vraies, le livre en contient, mais librement, et très librement disposées" (*Théophile de Viau*, p. 20).

20. Démoris, p. 42.

21. All these legends, however improbable, ultimately find later-day Rostands to support their factual existence. Bernardin, for example, faced with the unlikelihood of an encounter between Tristan and a real magician, refuses to eliminate the story from the autobiographical category, and quickly translates it into more acceptable terms: "Il a rencontré tout simplement quelque escroc" (p. 59).

22. Démoris, p. 36.

23. Victor Shklovsky, *Zoo*, p. 24.

24. "Le Monstre anthropomorphe," p. 60.

25. "But what is that one next to it?"

"*La Galatea* of Miguel de Cervantes," said the barber.

"Ah, that fellow Cervantes and I have been friends these many years" (*The Ingenious Gentleman Don Quixote de la Mancha*, p. 57. The presence of the author's name in self-conscious fiction seems, in fact, to be much less common that would be expected.

26. Rousset, *Narcisse romancier*, p. 76.

27. Michel Foucault, "Qu'est-ce qu'un auteur?", pp. 82–83. The peculiarities of the junction between proper name and author's name are described in similar terms by Philippe Lejeune in the section of *Le Pacte autobiographique* that deals with the importance of the proper name for the autobiographical text, p. 23.

28. Foucault, p. 83.

29. The "cousin" eventually turns out to be a fake, like most individuals encountered by D'Assoucy in the course of his travels, but that problem does nothing to alter the importance of the exceptional choice of name in this context.

30. This is similar to the moment in the *Combat de Cirano de Bergerac, avec le singe de Brioché* when D'Assoucy speculates on the etymology of "Cirano": "Bergerac soutenoit en plaisantant, que Mage et Roy etoient *unum et idem*, qu'on appelloit un Roy Cir, en françois Sire, et comme ce Mage, ce Roy, ce Cir, pour faire ces enchantemens, se campoit au milieu d'un cercle, c'est-a-dire d'un O, on le nommoit Cir an O" (pp 5–6).

31. Although the robbery is no realer than the cousin, and has actually been staged to enable the Marquis de. . . to bestow his hospitality on D'Assoucy for a time—but this is still another problem. The relationship between the false name and robbery should be linked to the libertine obsession with plagiarism (Cf. chapter 4).

32. See Paul Zumthor's discussion of the absence in the Middle Ages of these conditions (the notion of author, the auto-referential use of the first person in literature) ("Autobiographie au Moyen Age?", pp. 165–80).

33. *RHLF* 75 (1975): 998.

34. "De l'autobiographie initiatique à l'autobiographie genre littéraire," pp. 971, 985.

35. "Le Style de l'autobiographie," p. 264.

36. Théophile is questioned about this incident during the third interrogation of his trial. In his defense, he indicates a blending of fact and fiction in the *Fragments* parallel to those I have been discussing here. Théophile admits to having visited the "démoniaque," but "desnye avoyr parlé à elle ny faict aucun effort en sa personne et qu'il y avoit grand nombre de personnes en la chambre où elle estoit" (Lachèvre, *Le Procès du poète Théophile de Viau*, 1:397).

37. *Oeuvres du Sieur Théophile, seconde partie*, p. 25. I use this edition because it reproduces the same text as the first edition of 1626, but with clearer punctuation.

38. Démoris, pp. 43–44. For a more detailed reading of the role of autobiography in the *Fragments*, see my "The Case of Théophile de Viau: Autobiography on Trial," *Poétique* (forthcoming).

39. As François Rigolot remarks about Renaissance poetry, "La datation est moins une affaire de vérité historique que de convenance poétique" (*Poétique et onomastique*, p. 204). Much of Rigolot's discussion about the relationship between history (autobiography) and Renaissance poetry is pertinent to a treatment of similar problems with regard to libertine fiction.

40. Adam, *Romanciers*, p. 540.

41. Démoris, p. 37.

42. The page provides a graphic illustration of this when he describes in some detail the astrological configuration of the moment of his birth (p. 52).

43. Furetière: *"disgracier: priver quelqu'un de ses bonnes graces,* éloigner quelqu'un de sa présence, lui ôter la faveur, la protection qu'on lui donnoit." *Disgrace* thus can be a synonym for *exile*, another key word in the libertine vocabulary.

44. Furetière: "disgracié: outre la signification de son verbe, on le dit aussi des hommes malfaits de corps ou d'esprit, comme s'ils n'avoient reçu aucunes graces du Ciel ou de la nature."

45. It must be admitted that the state of grace the narrator says will follow his unmasking as a Huguenot ("Dieu ne m'avoit pas fait encore la grace de me recevoir au giron de son Eglise.") cannot have been of long duration, since the beginning of the *Fragments* finds him once again stripped of grace, this time by the exile he describes as "ma disgrace."

46. On the title page of the Colombey edition, for example. Since I can find no earlier reference to it, this title is probably of Colombey's invention.

47. Even as he takes over the power to name, the page is surrounded by this veil of hesitation. The name he appropriates for himself is in direct conflict with the past he chooses at the same time. His name means "upper class," yet he claims to be the son of a merchant: "Je lui dis que je me nommais Ariston, que j'étais fils d'un marchand assez honorable que j'avais perdu depuis un certain temps" (p. 119). Even when he is in complete control over the fiction of his life, the page is unable to erase contradiction.

48. For example, when he turns to storytelling to explain his tears to his mistress's mother: "Sa fille admira mon invention et me sut bon gré de cet artifice" (p. 135).

49. Hortensius's etymology: "Il luy dit qu'il s'appelloit Francion parce qu'il estoit rempli de franchise, et qu'il esoit le plus brave de tous les François" (p. 436). Valentin's: "Vous n'estes venu en terre que pour me faire jouyr d'une douce chose de qui par une rencontre fatale l'on trouve le nom dans celui que vous portez, si on en veut oster un I" (p. 69). Each is able to decipher only the inscription of that "quality" he himself lacks.

50. He is first named by his protector, the marquis de Colignac: "Et vous, dit il, monsieur Dyrcona, quel a esté le vostre?" (p. 106).

51. Dyrcona is named for the second time by a bird dear to burlesque authors because of its proverbial reputation for the gift of gab: "jazer comme une pie (borgne)." But how can a chatterbox with troubled vision make an accurate distribution of descriptive names?

52. Rousset, p. 65.

53. Starobinski, "Le Style de l'autobiographie," p. 261.

54. Only the *Avantures* privileges scenes from childhood in any way. Using a flashback technique, it devotes two central chapters (numbers 10 and 11 out of 19) to an account of youthful persecution.

55. Speaking, interestingly enough, to a pair of addressees, the marquis and count du Broussin, so that the duality is retained in the process of transmission.

56. Rousset, p. 65.

57. *Clélie*, 1:1378; quoted by Rousset, p. 52.

58. Lejeune, p. 33.

59. *Grammaire générale et raisonnée*, p. 59.

60. A phrase in the *avertissement* to the first edition of de Pontis's *Mémoires*, probably by Thomas du Fossé, provides a parallel between the vantage point from which these Jansenist memoirs are written and that of the libertine text. De Pontis, as much as the page, is a disgraced hero. "Il arriva toûjours par je ne sçay quelle disgrace de la fortune . . . qu'il se rencontroit à toute heure de nouveaux obstacles à son établissement dans le monde" (Guillaume Desprez, 1676), pp. 2–3.

61. *Logique*, p. 329.

62. "*Les Affinités électives* de Goethe," in *Mythe et violence*, p. 173.

63. *Men and Masks: A Study of Molière*, p. 273.

64. Démoris, p. 8.

65. Roland Barthes, *S/Z*, pp. 101–2.

CHAPTER THREE

FRAGMENTS OF A
PHILOSOPHICAL DISCOURSE

You see, added Rastelli, after a pause, that our profession wasn't born yesterday and that we have our own story—or at least our stories.—Walter Benjamin

Un auteur paradoxal ne doit jamais dire son mot, mais toujours ses preuves; il doit entrer furtivement dans l'âme de son lecteur et non de vive force. C'est le grand art de Montaigne qui ne veut jamais prouver et qui va toujours prouvant, en me ballotant du blanc au noir, et du noir au blanc.—Denis Diderot

The libertine text may be considered progressive and ahead of its time in terms of the first-person narrative technique it develops. A similar first person, one also enriched from contact with personal literature and its two-timing dialogue, would be associated in the eighteenth century with the birth of what is commonly known as the "modern" novel. In one important way, however, the seventeenth-century works considered here are narratively conservative and archaic; they do not look forward to a literature liberated from the system of codification accepted by contemporary prose fiction but over their shoulders, back to a formal tradition that includes as its conscious and unconscious adherents such figures as Petronius, Menippus, and even the authors associated with the Arabic literary form known as *maqāmāt*.[1] The quality linking the libertine text to these predecessors may be defined, vaguely, as a certain formal bizarreness. As a result of this structural aberration, all these works tend to defy classification.

No literary genre is as successful in avoiding definition as the novel. I choose to adopt Walter Benjamin's image of the "average" novel, not because I subscribe wholeheartedly to it—I am far too aware of its idiosyncracies to do so—but because I find that it enables me to point out the formal peculiarities of the libertine text as I see them. Benjamin's typical novel might seem atypical by other critical standards; but within his system, the libertine text's narrative uniqueness can be situated, so I hope my readers will be willing to overlook their potential disagreements with Benjamin's suppositions. In the definition he elaborates in his brilliant essay "The Storyteller," Benjamin stresses the novel's singleness of purpose. It is dedicated to the "meaning of life," and in particular to the meaning of one, and only one, life: "*one* hero, *one* odyssey, *one* battle."[2] The novel is the archetypal remembrance of things past, the story of a man's life, with the assumption that this life is uniquely important. From this assumption, the novel develops its particular sense of character. The full meaning of life cannot be grasped before its conclusion. The novelist must be prepared, therefore, to provide his readers with a vision of growth, culminating in the hero's "experience of death," at the very least, a "figurative death—the end of the novel—but preferably [his] 'actual one.' "[3]

Although surface resemblances might seem to link the libertine texts to the novel as described by Benjamin, a closer examination reveals that none of the major points stressed in his discussion are applicable to them. They remain finally as distant from this sense of the term "novel" as from "autobiography." A reader can hope to find no "meaning"—of life or of anything else—from their characters, because their lives can come to no end. They will not, or cannot, reach death, either literal or metaphorical, cannot obtain the seal of completion it places on even a literary existence. In a sense, death in literature is comforting. At (long) last those slippery beings, those creatures who give the illusion of possessing a life of their own (especially when they dare to appropriate the first person) can be laid to rest, put in their places, denied any additional emotional encroachments into their readers' hearts. With death, or at least some sort of surrogate closure, the reader, maintained in a state of perpetual victimization by the hero's *peripeteiae*, at last is able to regain his control over the text and over himself. The hero's sense of destiny is usually appreciated in the same way as his death by the reader of a novel. "It is my destiny to

———," say the heroes of the *romans héroïques*, meaning that when their destiny is accomplished, and they win the war and get the girl, they will either die, or be as good as dead.

The principal characters in the libertine texts deny the comfort of mastery to their readers. They may speak in the first person, as the heroes of many eighteenth-century French novels will later do, but this first person is not linked to the developmental, cause/effect narration that is generally considered appropriately novelistic. In his essay, Benjamin opposes the novel to the story. According to the distinction he sets up, the narrative structure of the libertine work appears closer to that of the story. This somewhat paradoxical phenomenon may be explained at least partially by some of the peculiarities of the libertine "I." These authors reject as much as possible the presence of a first-person narrator with limitations of identity. There is no room in their texts for the "I" of a hero with a unique vision, the type of vision deemed essential by Benjamin for the developmental structure characteristic of the novel.

The recounting of uniqueness in its unfolding is characteristic of the "I" of the novelistic narrator, but hardly of either the libertine hero or the storyteller, Scheherazade's doubles, for whom the logic of causality is ultimately as impossible as the logic of uniqueness. For the storyteller, a hero's end is important not as the culminating fulfillment of his personality but for its universal implications, for its role as a moral or parable, as a metaphorical reflection of the human condition. "Enfin je suis un raccourci de la misère humaine," as Scarron says in his burlesque self-portrait.[4] The hero of a story never claims singularity: he is Everyman. Unlike the characters of the *roman héroïque*, this hero is not the stuff dreams are made of. No reader could find in him what is lacking in his own life. This hero is presented to the reader not as larger than life but precisely in terms of his similarities. All storytellers are as inventive as their archetype in the *Arabian Nights*. This means they have the ability to see that one story always leads to another, because all stories are ultimately the same, just waiting for Propp to provide the basic schema that reveals their lack of uniqueness.

Hand in hand with its rejection of uniqueness and its metaphorical use of the hero, the story favors a type of narration that is opposed to traditional notions of logic and explanation. The story's web is at odds with the plausibility or verifiability associated with "information," that form of communication so privileged during the rise of the novel, and described by Benjamin in dark tones as responsible for the destruction of magic in narrative. Information "tells all," is in possession of all the facts and all the answers, in a sense does the reader's work for him. Just the opposite is true of storytelling, and it is certainly the story's holding back, its refusal to take the reader by the hand and lead him from one end of the narration to the other, that is the source of Benjamin's admiration for its charms. The dreams provided by the novel are somehow too facile (too escapist?) for this intellectual Emma Bovary, this Baudelairian aesthete in search of more complex visions. Hence the peculiarities of his description of the nature of storytelling:

> It is half the art of storytelling to keep a story free from explanation as one reproduces it. . . . The most extraordinary things, marvelous things are related with greatest accuracy, but the psychological connection of the events is not forced on the reader. It is left up to him to interpret things the way he understands them, and thus the narrative achieves an amplitude that information lacks.[5]

For Benjamin, the source of storytelling's greatness or "amplitude" is in the ability of its not completely fleshed-out narrative to leave space for its reader to fill with his dreams. Storytelling therefore resembles those paintings Baudelaire described as open to the critic's theorizing because of their lack of explicitness and their distance from the overly realistic charms of that ever-present seducer, the too solid flesh. Benjamin's preference for this type of narrative is certainly linked to his interpretation of another Baudelairian theory, that of the *flâneur*. Just as an individual inhabits his own interior in a special way, so the *flâneur* "tames" a city by living in it, by making it comfortable, and eventually his own. The city and its crowds allow him to transform them. They invite his participation in their creation. They are not closed, but open to his personal contribution. Comparing him to the *flâneur*, Benjamin says of Baudelaire: "he envisioned blank spaces which he filled with his poems";[6] and the same could be said of Benjamin himself, changing his formula to replace "poem" by "criticism."

His admiration for the beauties of storytelling and his predilection for the work with connective gaps are the result of a modernist search for what might be termed a more "poetic" form of narrative.

In order to find a point of comparison with the seemingly incomplete structure of Tristan's text, Arland is forced to make a considerable forward leap chronologically (although an equally considerable backward one would have been just as appropriate): "Si l'on tient à lui découvrir des correspondances, il convient de les chercher peut-être dans les souvenirs de Gérard, dans ceux de Heine ou dans certaines oeuvres de notre temps . . . qui visent à une sorte de vérité poétique."[7] What might otherwise be quickly dismissed as no more than the efforts of writers unable to structure a text properly, or as naïve, somewhat primitive narratives,[8] may in this light be appreciated instead for their powerful integration of the narrative gap, for their weakening of prose's so-called metonymical bonds in favor of an exploration of the riches of storytelling's essentially poetic (metaphoric) narration.[9]

I do not plan to limit my discussion of the structure of the libertine text to a search for aesthetic justifications, but intend to stress the ideological or philosophical roles performed by this lack of cause/effect development. It is important to note that the presence of a paratactical narration in the libertine novels cannot be attributed simply to a desire to maintain the form associated with the dominant prose tradition of the period. The libertine use of this narrative style is both infinitely more complex and more intellectually coherent than that found in the *roman héroïque*, where parataxis is simply the easiest means of integrating even the most farfetched *hors d'oeuvres* and of passing from one thread of a complex intrigue to another with recourse to nothing but a bare minimum of formal organization—more a result of a desire for enormity than an attempt to illustrate a philosophical system.

In addition, it would be difficult to characterize the libertines as mere formal hangers-on, since elsewhere they amply demonstrate their break with contemporary norms. They manage, in fact, to anticipate one of the most far-reaching novelistic revolutions of the late seventeenth century, the change in length that was perhaps the last barrier to drop in the transfer of power from romance to novel. They thus prove to be a major, and generally neglected, exception to the schema advanced by Adam and other theoreticians of the novel:

> Depuis le début de la Régence, la mode allait aux vastes sommes romanesques. Le public avait applaudi *Cassandre* et *Cléopâtre, Cyrus* et *Clélie.* On pouvait croire, vers 1660, que ce goût durerait encore. . . . Puis les lecteurs se lassèrent. S'ils restèrent fidèles aux longs romans d'une réputation consacrée, personne ne songea plus à faire imprimer une histoire en dix volumes. Il fut décidé qu'un roman devait avoir pour première vertu d'être court.[10]

The libertine writers were almost alone in their day in abandoning the narrative freedom exploited by the heroic novelists to ramble on for hundreds, even thousands, of pages, and to continue their stories with only the barest pretense at division into smaller, more easily digestible units. For the immense length of the *roman héroïque*, the libertines, with the obvious exception of Sorel, substitute far shorter, tighter works. And for the most part, they continue their tightening by replacing the standard heroic division into volumes or tomes (each often longer than many a complete libertine text) with chapters or other relatively short compositional units, sometimes only a few pages in length.[11] Such a conception of division demands a completely different type of reading for these novels, a demand that might seem contradicted by the maintenance of parataxis, if the complex new role assigned to this narrative form by the libertine writers is not properly evaluated. They fail to make a break with the narrative disorder of the heroic tradition that seemed essential to the great majority of writers influential in the early evolution of the French novel. In their texts, the libertines not only maintain but privilege the narrative gap, and they do so not simply to indulge in still another manifestation of the rhetoric of absence, of the type associated with their treatment of the proper name. They continue to use this form of narrative silence because it leaves them free to play their complex and often dangerous games.

The first consequence of this antidevelopmental narration is an unusual, shifting type of characterization. The libertine narrator's journeys take him, in the case of the Tristan/D'Assoucy model, from one life experience to a second disturbingly similar experience to a third. In the Théophile/Cyrano variant, they take him from philosophical system to religious discussion to political debate. In every instance, however, the lack of self-analyzing tendencies on the part of the narrator is striking. He draws no conclusions from all he sees and hears. He is apparently unmarked by his travels and experiences. There is no (evident) goal for his journey. Unlike most main characters, the libertine hero does not undergo any form of vertical development—instead, he defies psychological growth and causality by remaining, through repetition, on a strictly horizontal level of characterization.

Only in *L'Autre Monde* can there be observed a libertine hero capable of change, and even here characterization remains resolutely opposed to standard logic, never leaving the domain of the horizontal and paratactical for the generally privileged vertical and developmental. Cyrano performs this seemingly impossible task through the acknowledgment and integration of paradox. Instead of maintaining the immobility of characterization standard in the classical period, Cyrano chooses to place the responsibility for the narration in the hands of an intellectually unstable main character. The narrator's ideas about various phenomena are contrasted with those of a series of interlocutors in the dialogues that constitute the main body of *L'Autre Monde*. His own point of view in these dialogues is shifting; the reader never knows on which side of a particular question the narrator will take a stand. At different moments in the text, he is even capable of defending contradictory positions on the same question. For example, he is forced to leave the Garden of Eden when he makes what Elie considers a profession of atheism: "Abominable, dit-il [Elie] en se reculant, tu as l'impudence de railler sur les choses saintes. . . . Va, impie, hors d'ici, va publier dans ce petit monde et dans l'autre, car tu es prédestiné à y retourner, la haine irréconciliable que Dieu porte aux athées" (p. 53).

The final "return trip" to "l'autre monde" predicted by Elie in this scene will take place only because of a complete about-face in religious matters on the narrator's part. His last conversation is with the young man referred to as "le fils de l'hôte." In the course of their discussion, the latter argues for the mortality of the soul, against the resurrection of the dead, and finally against the existence of God. The narrator, in this dialogue at least, consistently defends the point of view of Catholic orthodoxy against the "opinions diaboliques" of the man he feels may be "l'Antéchrist dont il se parle tant dans notre monde" (p. 116). Through the combined use of innocence—often far blinder than that of the heroes of Voltaire's philosophical tales—irony, and provocation, Cyrano creates the most complex anti-hero in early French fiction.

Since the ultimate libertine hero contains paradox, is capable simultaneously of defending contradictory opinions, of believing and not believing, of understanding and not understanding, it seems logical that his complexities cannot be expressed in terms of cause/effect narration. From the first, texts that current readers would unhesitatingly accept as novels, in Philip Stewart's words, "begin at the beginning," and then "imitate the linear chronology of life itself."[12] Such a developmental chronology is generally associated with the novelistic. "To begin at the beginning" and progress with a series of "as a result of that, this happened" steps, until the most closed-off ending possible is reached, such is the ideal of the novel's "anti-poetical" narrative, based on a logic that refuses the integration of paradox. Ultimately, as Kristeva points out in an article that sets up a typology of the forms of logic in discourse, the rigid causality of such a system demonstrates its acceptance and integration of origin and authority, in the form of submission to such forces as God or history.[13] The paradoxical logic of the libertine text (of the type Kristeva calls "logique corrélationnelle"),[14] however, categorically rejects these notions, just as the libertines themselves fought against them in their own lives.

The libertine text, coming from nowhere and with nowhere to go, unfolds somewhere outside or beyond standard literary chronology. The characters in the *Fragments* go to bed and wake up in the morning, but that temporal distinction seems as artificial and as unmotivated by any force other than a desire to separate chapters as the division of Théophile's collected works into *Journées*. D'Assoucy is terrified of staying in one place, as though, if he turned off the perpetual-motion machine of his travels, there would be no way of filling up his days, and more importantly, no way of providing a chronology for them. Thus, when his Burgundian benefactor tries to shower him with riches, stability, and comfort for even a short time, the Emperor flees this problem-free existence in a panic. He cannot, however, provide the disorder of his adventures with a developmental story line, so the reader soon forgets to distinguish the temporal and geographical setting of each scene of gambling and swindling.

L'Autre Monde is such an extreme case of this defiance of time that its paradoxical chronology is as seemingly impossible as its paradoxical characterization: "Je descendais vers la terre . . . j'y retombai quelque temps après, et à compter l'heure que j'en étais parti, il devait être minuit. Cependant je reconnus que le soleil était alors au plus haut de l'horizon, et qu'il était midi" (p. 33). By means of its narrator's voyages through day and night, over and through the earth's revolutions and its so-called time zones, *L'Autre Monde* provides the clearest demonstration of an essential goal of the libertine text: to serve as a reminder of the artificiality of such notions as calendar time and watch/clock time, and above all, of the fragility of the comfort they provide as a form of control over life. *L'Autre Monde* begins: "La lune était dans son plein, le ciel était découvert, et neuf heures du soir étaient sonnées lorsque nous revenions d'une maison proche de Paris, quatre de mes amis et moi" (p. 31). This beginning adds a remarkable new precision to one of the standard opening formulas for contemporary novels of the comic and heroic traditions alike, the establishment of the time of day at which their first scene takes place. In other novels, the time is indicated only very vaguely,[15] but here it is just after 9 P.M., and the narrator is able to pass on this information with certainty because he has heard the hour "proclaimed" by an official keeper of time. But, as he will soon learn, 9 o'clock at night is at the same time 9 in the morning in Canada and the entire other half of the globe, and who knows what time on the moon (this problem is prudently avoided in *L'Autre Monde*).

For this confusion artificially regulated by convention, the libertines substitute the clarity of a unique time, which might be described as an eternal present, were that term not too suggestive of fullness and completion. Libertine time is rather an eternal about-to-be, an eternal gamblers' time. It resembles the temporality Benjamin describes as "time in hell, the province of those who are not allowed to complete anything they have started."[16] The libertine text is always centered on the next hand, the next round.

This is the domain of the *éternel retour* of Scheherazade and other storytellers who, with their stories, put off death, until they finally become immune to it. They are no more than a voice (or in this case, a pen) telling stories that, because of their place within the vast web of all possible and interrelated stories, acquire a relativity unknown to the novel with its intimations of immortal unrepeatability. Time does not exist for the storyteller, so he cannot grow old. Thus, D'Assoucy fights Loret's proclamation of his death by refusing to admit the possibility of an end. He describes the last years of his life as no other writer of his century did, and largely for the purpose of showing how that life never changed, never developed. Without evolution, how can he age, how can he die? He continues to announce more adventures at the end of every volume.

Temporal relativity is ultimately the result of repeatability, of the ability of a text to seem able to go on forever. Because it continues a tradition of paratactical narration, the libertine text is able to repeat itself with enormous facility. And just as it uses horizontal characterization to integrate paradox, the foundation of a relativistic philosophy, so it puts repetition to work for libertine ends. These novelists follow Peiresc's advice to Gassendi and attempt to find "terms si reservez et si ajustez, qu'il y ayt moyen d'entendre une bonne partie de voz intentions sans que le sens littéral y soit si preciz."[17] They discover that, with this goal in mind, they can successfully employ a form of what might be termed "metaphorical" narration, basically a reiteration of a key passage or situation, slightly altered in each recounting. This is apparently the closest thing possible to an age-old libertine technique, one already practiced by such an illustrious predecessor as Artephius, the "inspiration" for Tristan's Artefius. In the preface to his translation of the *Philosophie naturelle*, Pierre Arnauld explains the manner in which Artephius could be considered a practitioner of narrative artifice:

> Toutes fois que les impies, ignorans, et meschans ne peussent aisément trouver le moyen de nuire aux bons apprenant cette science, il a un peu voilé le principal de l'art, par une artificieuse methode, faisant comme s'il repetoit plusieurs fois une chose, car dans icelles repetitions il change toujours quelques mots semblant souvent dire le contraire de ce qu'il a dit auparavant, voulant laisser au jugement du lecteur le bon chemin.[18]

It is easy to imagine the advantages to be drawn from such a system by an author with a dangerous message. By means of simple changes in his repetitions, he may hint at a great deal while actually saying very little explicitly. As they imply with their use of the first person, all the individual libertine stories vary only slightly from the libertine Ur-text. It is therefore an easy matter to transfer elements from one biography to another, to draw parallelisms between two or more situations, to use a less controversial freethinker to draw attention away from a more or less unmentionable figure. What I have called here the libertine nod of recognition is obviously an important tool used by these novelists to shape their texts along these lines.

Since *L'Autre Monde* contains a greater number of these nods of recognition than any other text in the tradition, one would expect it to make the most complex use of metaphorical narration. Once the web formed by Cyrano's interchangeable situations is even partially unraveled, the reader begins to suspect that a proper evaluation of all the risky implications adumbrated by this lunar voyage would require an almost impossibly close reading. The principal metaphorical chain in *L'Autre Monde* is generated by the figure of a defender of intellectual freedom obliged to spend his days as a wanderer because his ideas are too daring for the society in and for which he developed them. The central figure in this chain is the work's narrator, who, in its opening paragraphs, is the first subject of a repeated vignette portraying the ostracizing of a freethinker.

It is because his imagination is not free in the intellectual circle he frequents that the narrator sets out on his journey to the moon. *L'Autre Monde* begins as he and four of his friends are returning home from a place near Paris. "La lune était dans son plein," the opening phrase, sets the stage for the prefatory conversation, reported by the narrator in indirect speech, in which three of the friends give their definitions of the moon: "une lucarne du ciel par où l'on entrevoyait la gloire des bienheureux"; "la platine où Diane dresse les rabats d'Apollon"; "le soleil lui-même, qui s'étant au soir dépouillé de ses rayons regardait par un trou ce qu'on faisait au monde quand il n'y était plus" (p. 31).[19] The company finds this burlesquing of various systems of belief[20] quite entertaining. When in the first direct speech of the text the narrator offers his own definition, he is greeted by the loudest outburst of laughter thus far: "Et moi, dis-je, qui souhaite mêler mes enthousiasmes aux vôtres, je crois sans m'amuser aux imaginations pointues dont vous chatouillez le temps pour le faire marcher plus vite, que la lune est un monde comme celui-ci, à qui le nôtre sert de lune" (p. 31).

The reasons for finding this formulation so humorous are not immediately evident. The narrator's definition is certainly no more ludicrous than those of his companions. It even fits perfectly into the overall order of presentation: the moon is first compared to two more or less rectangular, flat surfaces, then to two spheres.[21] Moreover, this theory, unlike the others, is presented for serious consideration—"sans m'amuser"—yet, even though the narrator goes on to explain the theories of Copernicus, Kepler, and others, his audience only continues to "s'égosiller de plus belle." The reader is left to wonder if the fact that the narrator chooses to display his ideas in the same informal manner as that used by his friends does not close their minds to any serious consideration of his theory. How can something heard in a comic context be taken seriously? Thus, Cyrano inscribes a familiar problem of the *histoire comique* in the opening of his work. The narrator's companions turn for their jokes to tired mythological systems and to the neutralization of the burlesque. They lack the imagination necessary to integrate his translation into a relativistic system. If the moon is an earth and the earth is a moon, then their moonlight stroll is perhaps not a unique phenomenon. The narrator, like all men with the ability to conceive of alternate systems encountered in *L'Autre Monde*, is mocked because of his intellectual daring.

From time to time in the course of *L'Autre Monde*, certain individuals such as Achab and Campanella are praised because they, too, were at least ridiculed, if not condemned to a harsher fate, when they tried to present new and often seemingly absurd theories. One of the few moments when the novel's narrative tone becomes serious and elevated is reserved for Tristan L'Hermite, who is described by the demon of Socrates in a eulogy that ends: "C'est le seul poète, le seul philosophe et le seul homme libre que vous ayez" (p. 57). There is even a remarkable episode that constitutes a careful parody of both *L'Autre Monde*'s opening scene and, more daringly, of Galileo's trial and subsequent renunciation of his theory. The narrator is accused of heresy by the priests on the moon because "j'avais osé dire que la lune était un monde dont je venais, et que leur monde n'était qu'une lune" (p. 79). The demon of Socrates comes to his defense by explaining that "s'il est homme, quand même il ne serait pas venu de la lune, puisque tout homme est libre, ne lui est-il pas libre de s'imaginer ce qu'il voudra? Quoi! pouvez-vous le contraindre à n'avoir que vos visions? Vous le forcerez bien à dire qu'il croit que la lune n'est pas un monde, mais il ne le croira pas pourtant" (p. 80). The demon is able through his oration to persuade them to do away with the death penalty, but that is replaced by another punishment. Despite the demon's warnings against dogmatism, the narrator is obliged to cry at every crossroads of the city: "Peuple, je vous déclare que cette lune ici n'est pas une lune, mais un monde; et que ce monde de là-bas n'est pas un monde, mais une lune. Tel est ce que les Prêtres trouvent bon que vous croyiez" (p. 81).

The narrator's fellow prisoner on the moon, the Spaniard, explains how he traveled around the world and finally left it for the moon because "il n'avait pu trouver un seul pays où l'imagination même fut en liberté" (p. 66). The demon meets Tristan L'Hermite in England. He, too, is condemned to wander because of the boldness of his thinking: "Je rencontrai un homme, la honte de son pays" (p. 57). And the demon himself is the archetypal traveler/seeker for freedom. He is still referred to by the name of his first "master," Socrates: "Il ajouta . . . qu'on l'appelait le démon de Socrate" (p. 55). His title provides a link with Cyrano and Dyrcona's most famous predecessor in the art of dialogic reasoning—and in the unhappy fates to which it leads. The demon describes his past in some detail: he has spent the centuries since the death of Socrates traveling from country to country advising imaginative thinkers.

The narrator has in common with the various seasoned rebels he either encounters or has described for him the fact that he undertakes his voyages (more or less of his own free will) to escape persecution. The implications of these comparisons between the narrator and historical individuals are crucial. Indeed, if paradox may be called the "negative" structuring principle on which *L'Au-tre Monde* is based, comparisons such as these constitute its "pos-itive" unifying device. *L'Autre Monde* lacks the causal develop-ment of the novel. The reader cannot expect to be led by means of traditional logic to a clearly interpretable conclusion. Cyrano's text is saved from being merely a hopeless muddle of disparate fragments by the presence in it of chains of metaphorical situa-tions: the narrator's position is like Galileo's, and Galileo's is like Tristan's, and Tristan's is like the Spaniard's, whose situation is similar to the narrator's, and so on. Meaning in *L'Autre Monde* is not the result of the rationality of a story line. In Cyrano's aesthet-ics of fragmentation, certain situations and images become obses-sional. In order to comprehend the work's significance, it is neces-sary to replace the links omitted by ellipsis and to connect the obsessive repetitions.

It is already daring for the narrator to be compared to historical individuals persecuted for their ideas, since some of these men, such as Galileo, were considered dangerous thinkers in Cyrano's day. In addition, these parallelisms enter the realm of blasphemy when, during the course of his conversation with Elie in the Garden of Paradise, the narrator establishes by means of explicit and implicit comparisons illustrious precedents for his flights to and from paradise. In the Garden of Eden, as Elie explains to him, "n'ont jamais entré que six personnes: Adam, Eve, Enoch, moi qui suis le vieil Elie, saint Jean l'Evangéliste, et vous" (p. 44). It is apparent that the narrator's enterprise, and with it those of all his predecessors in intellectual daring, is being compared to certain key moments in biblical history. Enoch reaches paradise through a most original use of "le feu du ciel." As the fire is consuming one of his sacrificial victims, Enoch fills with the vapor rising from the sacrifice two vases that he attaches under his armpits, sure that he will get to paradise because of God's words: "L'odeur des sacrifi-ces du juste est montée jusqu'à moi" (p. 45). The narrator's utiliza-tion of vials of dew in his first attempt at interplanetary travel is reminiscent of Elie's technique: "Je m'étais attaché autour de moi quantité de fioles pleines de rosée, et la chaleur du soleil qui les attirait m'éleva si haut, qu'à la fin je me trouvai au-dessus des plus hautes nuées" (pp. 32–33). Later, the narrator is separated from this paradise reached by various forms of evaporation or sublimation because he lacks the patience to receive information at a rhythm dictated by his more prudent guide. This time, the comparison can be drawn, for example, with Adam and Eve's loss of the same paradise, or with Achab's loss of the Ark's shelter. Just as the narrator flees Elie, Adam escapes the vengeance of God by "le feu de son enthousiasme" (p. 44). And since Adam is known to "les idolâtres" under the name of Prometheus (p. 45), the network opens up to include a prebiblical past as well.

Prometheus, who "fut bien autrefois au ciel dérober du feu" (p. 32), is the central figure in the narrator's genealogy. *L'Autre Monde* sketches various possibilities for literal and figurative interpretations of the Prometheus myth. On the moon, the sexual connotations of primitive fire myths become explicit. Nobles may be recognized because they have the right to wear not a sword but "la figure d'un membre viril." The host's son explains to the scandalized narrator the superiority of this symbol, which, instead of honoring an instrument of destruction, exalts "un membre sans qui nous serions au rang de ce qui n'est pas, le Prométhée de chaque animal" (p. 108). And the two systems are united in the figure of the archangel who guards paradise with his "épée flamboyante" (p. 51). The idea of procreation is converted by other codes into different forms of creation that range from inspiration, to vision, to imaginative thinking, to literary creation. The fire symbolic of Prometheus is mentioned frequently in *L'Autre Monde*: "le feu du ciel," "l'ardeur du feu de la charité," "le feu de l'enthousiasme," the "fièvres chaudes" of the narrator's vision of "l'autre monde"—"notre imagination, plus chaude que les autres facultés de l'âme" (p. 100). All forms of liberating desire are equated, and the quest for fire becomes the unifying bond among those who make real and imaginary voyages in Cyrano's work. Those who give free reign to the powers of the imagination, like Enoch, John the Evangelist, Galileo, and even the still anonymous narrator, travel under the sign of fire.

In fact, the narrator, who seeks to unite the (apparently) contradictory ways of living in the new intellectual world he describes in *L'Autre Monde*, can be seen as the next Prometheus the Spaniard is searching for on the moon: "Il nous manque un Prométhée pour faire cet extrait" (p. 73). He himself immediately invites the comparison when he first envisions his lunar voyage in these terms:

> Mais, ajoutais-je, je ne saurais m'éclaircir de ce doute, si je ne monte jusque-là?
> Et pourquoi non? me répondais-je aussitôt. Prométhée fut bien autrefois au ciel (p. 32).

With his explosive book (whose writing is described at the beginning of the *Estats et empires*), the narrator becomes a worthy inheritor of Galileo and Cardano. In *L'Autre Monde*, he shares Galileo's trial. Cardano's works are inspired by the same men the narrator believes to be responsible for opening his copy of Cardano to the page describing their apparition to his Italian predecessor.[22] The narrator, in the same inspirational situation as Cardano and soon to create a work similar to his, is seen reading the passage in Cardano that describes the guidance he received. The libertine *mise en abyme* illustrates the passing on of the torch, as does each of the other links in *L'Autre Monde*'s most essential metaphorical chain.

It is certainly in *L'Autre Monde* that this structuring principle finds its most striking elaboration, hence my decision to use this text as my main example here. No other libertine text matches its structural density, but repetition replaces development in all of them. The use of repetition varies according to each text's particular thematic obsessions. *L'Autre Monde*'s own obsession is centered on the libertine presence, the naming of libertine ancestors. The most frequently repeated themes in the other texts, such as gambling and magic, will be discussed at length in the next chapter. To mention only one example here: though the hero-victimized-as-a-result-of-his-gambling sequence in the *Avantures* does not possess the complexity that is the source of *L'Autre Monde*'s strength, simply because it substitutes a single protagonist for the multiplicity of figures evoked by Cyrano, the blatant simplicity of its repetition is nevertheless sufficient to erase any cause/effect narration in the text.

Cause/effect narration anchored in the developmental must be erased in order to permit the juxtaposition of the segments of a given theme. The most effective play among the various occurrences of each situation is obtained from a narrative based on constant fragmentation. These texts never necessitate the sort of attention span that caused Rousseau's faithful reader to miss her ball. This is true not only because they are concerned with nothing so little as love, generally assumed to be the only novelistic subject capable of awakening and maintaining such sustained curiosity, but also because they are divided into completely autonomous, short units that make possible, and even encourage, a choppy reading. The building blocks of a libertine narrative are so easily separated from the text in its entirety that each appears to encourage its detachment into the sort of independent existence possessed by an anthology piece.[23] In the only reference to division found in any of these texts, Tristan pledges allegiance to a sort of aesthetics of lazy reading, or an aesthetics of reading for a lazy reader. The page explains to model reader Thirinte that "j'ai divisé toute cette histoire en petits chapitres, de peur de vous être ennuyeux par un trop long discours, et pour vous faciliter le moyen de me laisser en tous les lieux où je pourrai vous être moins agréable" (p. 50).

It is true that Tristan's novel sets a pace so brisk that even the demanding page could be reassured. The use of short chapters in Théophile's *Fragments* provides the only real precedent for Tristan's break with dominant tradition. It might even be argued that Tristan fails to live up to the model provided by the *Fragments*. There, in order to replace gripping subject matter with narrative speed, each chapter is made almost completely independent and detachable. In fact, the only elements Théophile's reader must retain from one chapter to the next are the names and identities of the narrator's companions.

Even without the clearly indicated division into chapters favored by Théophile and Tristan, other libertine texts achieve the same goal of narrative fragmentation. Cyrano's extraterrestrial voyages evidently decompose into brief segments. After his initial nocturnal conversation with his friends, the narrator of *L'Autre Monde* is kept busy through discussions with ten interlocutors, and no attempt is made to hide the fact that each of these dialogues leads an independent existence. The *Estats et empires*, likewise, contains a series of Dyrcona's conversations, and the text is further split by the insertion of four brief interpolated stories, the only occurrence in a libertine text of this "narrative aid" otherwise so frequently encountered in seventeenth-century novels. Three of these tales are presented in the classical manner: Dyrcona notices a mysterious phenomenon, and persuades a knowledgeable bystander to provide him with an explanation for it. Thus, the nightingale's story (pp. 142–46) is supplied by the king of the little people, the "Histoire des Arbres Amans" (pp. 168–76) by the "plus sage de tous les Chesnes du Dodonne," and the fight between the *Salamandre* and the *Remore* (pp. 177–81) is described by Campanella. Finally, the narrator himself provides an additional story, that of his capture and trial by birds (pp. 142–64), which actually belongs to the voyage's primary narrative plane, but is presented as though it were a distinct unit, to the point of being set off with its own subtitle, "L'Histoire des Oiseaux."

The two earthly voyages adopt still another means of cutting, a juxtaposition of prose and verse, with its roots in both Menippean satire and burlesque narrative. Chapelle allows verse to intervene at more regular intervals than does D'Assoucy, with an end result that resembles an operatic alternation between recitative and lyric. In the *Voyage*, poetry is frequently assigned the role of description. If, for example, a proper name is mentioned, then a brief verse interlude will be inserted to describe some of the individual's or place's salient features. The narrative status of these moments as *hors d'oeuvres* is made clear by their distinct formal nature. D'Assoucy provides what is certainly the last word in narrative fragmentation, making the *Avantures* a compilation of the various methods employed in previous libertine texts. He combines short chapters characteristic of the *Page* and the *Fragments*, with occasional subtitles, such as "La Rencontre de l'Illustre Savoyard," to set off privileged moments within chapters, a method used by Cyrano in the *Estats et empires*, with a mixture of verse and prose similar to Chapelle's, as though he were concerned that one of these means alone would not be sufficient to stress his rejection of the developmental. Furthermore, D'Assoucy's juxtaposition of prose and verse is far more paratactical than Chapelle's. Passages of poetry composed specifically for the *Avantures* are generally devoted to burlesque flights of fancy and commentaries on events, and are therefore more removed from their context than Chapelle's concrete descriptions. Moreover,

D'Assoucy indulges in moments of self-citation, inserting some of his previously published poems into the sections of his adventures that describe the events surrounding their composition. Into his text, he splices interludes so autonomous that they already possess a previous literary existence, and are therefore perfectly incompatible with any notion of subordination of the part to the whole. At these moments, the *Avantures* seems no more than a showcase for the recycling of moments of past literary glory, for the insertion of frozen refrains that clearly denounce the lack of progression in the text.

In *The Chapter in Fiction*, Philip Stevick discusses at great length some of the ways in which novelists usually leap over the silence between chapters. They try to facilitate the passage over the blank space that marks the transition through the creation of what Stevick calls "cadences", for example, "anticipatory cadences," or remarks at the end of a chapter that provoke suspense or anticipation for what will be found in the following one.[24] Thus, as Stevick demonstrates, the normal way of dealing with the gap between chapters is simply to bridge it. He fails to leave room in his system for a less typical case, such as that of the libertine text, in which no attempt is made to eliminate the blank spaces not only between chapters or other units whose separate status is clearly indicated typographically but also between narrative entities whose boundaries, even if unmarked, are nonetheless clearly implied. In libertine narrative, parataxis is the basic structuring principle. These texts so foster disjunction that they would run the risk of near disintegration into a mass of unrelated segments, were it not for their use of the basic unifying device in early narrative, the appearance of the hero/narrator in all episodes.[25] Only repetition within parataxis assures a form of unity.

It is largely because the libertine text reverses in these ways the generally accepted standards that govern the territories of ending and non-ending in prose fiction that it was so harshly judged for so long. For theoreticians sharing a common vision of logic and the logical, everything about the libertine text is wrong. In the first place, its chapters and other divisional units are all marked by a sense of closure and maintain their autonomy when this is least expected. Then, to make matters worse, the libertine text does an about-face and abandons its autonomy in situations when other texts defend it, abandons the overall closure provided by an ending, or at least a sense of ending. The majority of these texts are unfinished—the *Fragments* and the *Estats et empires* literally so; the first edition of *Francion*, the *Page*, and *L'Autre Monde* because their heroes do not reach the end of their adventures. And because they are opposed to the notion of conclusiveness, they are all open-ended as well.

"There is no story for which the question as to how it continued would not be legitimate. The novelist, on the other hand, cannot hope to take the smallest step beyond that limit at which he invites the reader to a divinatory realization of the meaning of life by writing 'Finis.' "[26] Walter Benjamin contrasts in these terms the contradictory goals of two types of narrative. It is easy to see why the libertine text cannot share the optimism that enables all narrative forms that can be readily classified as novels to impose limits. A novel without a goal is an impossible thing, and the libertine text has nowhere to go, either in its subject matter, stripped of such novelistic end products as love and initiation, or in its philosophical orientation, deprived of the support of a belief in truth and of the ability to stop questioning. Thus, the libertine writers are obliged not only to maintain the paratactical narrative of the *roman héroïque* but even to call attention to its importance for them.

The combination of this narrative form with dialogic subject matter and a philosophy of paradox is certainly an explosive one. *Clélie* sometimes employs what may be termed "accidental" or "unconscious" fragmentation, but, since it tries on the whole to remain faithful to an easily followed developmental logic, it was never judged either incomprehensible or mad. Unlike, for example, *L'Autre Monde*, where fragmentation is not only continuous but perfectly conscious and motivated as well, and which, as a result, has been disdained as being only "un assemblage d'éléments divers et parfois opposés,"[27] and even reviled as a reflection of Cyrano's "madness." "Quand il fit son *Voyage dans la lune*, il en avait déjà le premier quartier dans la tête," as Ménage put it.

Even this summary comparison serves to demonstrate that the simple presence of fragmentation is not sufficient to have a work classified as problematic. On the other hand, any attempt to put this form in the service of a new type of logic, to develop a logic of fragmentation, a logic that could be considered threatening to standard notions of logic, this can never be tolerated by the dominant tradition. In conclusion, I would like to break away from the developmental movement of academic logic, and to borrow just once the libertine notion of the metaphorical chain. In "Galileo's Language: Mathematics and Poetry in a New Science," Stillman Drake situates the origin of Galileo's persecution in the style and the logic he developed:

> The style used in writing a scientific work in any era requires respect for precision. Galileo's predecessors sought logical precision; his successors sought mathematical precision. Galileo did not turn his back on either of these; instead, he recognized and added other ways of making things precise. . . . Modern science tends to be written in technical terms without the slightest tincture of poetic metaphor. It is of interest that Galileo rejected such a style, though it already prevailed around him. Had he adopted it, it is likely that he would have reached the top of the academic profession, would not have left the university to serve the Grand Duke, and would have died in universal esteem rather than as a condemned heretic.[28]

As *L'Autre Monde* seeks to demonstrate, Galileo is like Dyrcona/Cyrano; Dyrcona/Cyrano is like Tristan; Tristan is like Théophile, and so on.

1. For a description of the formal characteristics of the *maqāmāt* and a discussion of their resemblances with subsequent Western literary traditions, see Ben E. Perry's *The Ancient Romances*, pp. 206–7.

2. *Illuminations*, pp. 98, 99.

3. Ibid., p. 101.

4. *Oeuvres comiques*, 1:130.

5. *Illuminations*, p. 89.

6. "On Some Motifs in Baudelaire," in *Illuminations*, p. 164.

7. *Le Page disgracié*, p. 33.

8. "Il lui manque l'ordre, l'harmonieux accord de toutes les parties, l'arrangement définitif qui fait un tout homogène," says Fournel of Cyrano (p. 52). His criticism of *L'Autre Monde*'s narrative logic is representative of an important tradition of its textual interpretation.

9. This distinction between what I term non-poetic and poetic narration has obvious affinities with Barthes's "texte de plaisir" and "texte de jouissance." There are, for example, resemblances between the "texte de jouissance" and poetic narration. "Ce lecteur, il faut que je le cherche (que je le 'drague'), *sans savoir où il est*. Un espace de la jouissance est alors créé. Ce n'est pas la 'personne' de l'autre qui m'est nécessaire, c'est l'espace: la possibilité d'une dialec-

tique du désir, d'une *imprévision* de la jouissance: que les jeux ne soient pas faits, qu'il y ait un jeu." It must be admitted, however, that the poetic text as I have described it here stops short of continuing the notion of narrative freedom to Barthes's conclusion, a permanent state of *coupure*: "Ce qu'il veut, c'est le lieu d'une perte, c'est la faille, la coupure, la déflation" (*Le Plaisir du texte*, pp. 11, 15).

10. Adam, *Histoire,* 4:159–60.

11. The average length of a chapter in the *Page* is, for example, no more than a little over two and a half pages. In my experience, the only seventeenth-century novel outside the libertine tradition to practice a division into short chapters is the *Roman comique.*

12. *Imitation and Illusion in the French Memoir-Novel (1700–50)*, p. 240.

13. Kristeva discusses at some length the question of the logic of poetic narration in "Le Mot, le dialogue, et le roman." I plan to consider her remarks in my last chapter, along with the question of dialogue and the dialogic.

14. Ibid., p. 171.

15. Sunrise and sunset are undoubtedly the most popular moments at which to open a novel, as an examination of the first sentences of works given in Lever's bibliography reveals. In general, only comic novels are ever precise enough about their opening time to indicate an hour. Even then, both of the best-known examples fail to equal Cyrano's precision, because they continue to give a choice of hours. For Scarron, when *Le Roman comique* begins it is "entre cinq et six" (ed. Adam, p. 532), and the first scene of Claude Le Petit's *L'Heure du Berger* takes place "entre huict et neuf du soir" (ed. Lachèvre, *Les Oeuvres libertines de Claude Le Petit*, p. 57). On the first sentences in seventeenth-century novels, see my "Scarron's *Roman comique*: The Other Side of Parody."

16. *Illuminations*, p. 181.

17. See chapter 1, note 53.

18. (Laurent d'Houry, 1682), p. 4. Arnauld is the probable translator of the text and author of this preface.

19. In the versions of *L'Autre Monde* available in the edition published by Le Bret in 1657 under the title *Histoire comique* and in the Munich manuscript, two of the most puzzling divergences with the text of the Paris manuscript occur in the work's first paragraph. The 1657 edition changes the number of friends returning to Paris (from "quatre de mes amis et moi" to the indeterminate "plusieurs de mes amis et moi"), and the Munich manuscript alters both the number of friends (this time, to the equally vague "quelques-uns") and the total number of definitions given (from four to five, as another of the friends pokes fun for a second time at classical mythology: "tantôt un autre, persuadé des fables anciennes, s'imaginait que possible Bacchus tenait taverne là-hault, au Ciel, et qu'il y avait pendu pour enseigne la pleine lune" (*Histoire comique*, pp. 1–2; and *Oeuvres libertines de Cyrano de Bergerac*, 1:5.

20. Maurice Laugaa describes these systems as "sytèmes 'fixistes': le Dieu chrétien, l'Olympe païen, le Soleil mythique ou rationnel des théories hélicocentriques" ("Lune, ou l'Autre," p. 285).

21. If the roundness suggested by "platine" because of its association with watches is dismissed. The additional definition provided by the Munich manuscript and the shifting order in which these definitions are presented in all editions of *L'Autre Monde* prior to Lachèvre's are responsible for a certain degree of confusion in readings of this passage by critics not completely aware of the discrepancies among editions. Jaqueline Van Baelen, for example, analyzes it

only with the inclusion of the Bacchus comparison, despite its dubious origin and the evident syntactic and semantic asymetry created by its presence ("Reality and Illusion in *L'Autre Monde*: The Narrative Voyage," (pp. 179–80). Laugaa realizes that this definition provokes what he terms "une perturbation du sens" (p. 288), but he incorrectly analyzes it as belonging to Le Bret's text, instead of to that of the Munich manuscript, which has its own particular problems of origin.

22. In *De Vita Propria Liber*, Cardano in fact refers on several occasions to a "guardian spirit" who inspired and guided his work. He devotes a chapter to his own case and to the story of others who, like him, were attended by such beings: "all, to be sure, lived happily save Socrates and me" (p. 240). Thereby he documents one phase of the demon's pre-lunar existence.

23. As Laugaa says of *L'Autre Monde*: "La vogue des morceaux choisis autorise les remanieurs à trancher à nouveau dans un texte supposé docile à toutes les mutilations" (p. 282).

24. Stevick, p. 100.

25. The narrator, of course, is generally not present in interpolated stories.

26. *Illuminations*, p. 100.

27. Pietro Toldo, "Les Voyages merveilleux de Cyrano de Bergerac et de Swift et leurs rapports avec l'oeuvre de Rabelais," p. 320.

28. Drake, p. 23.

CHAPTER FOUR

CAMERA LUCIDA

Tous les savants étaient autrefois accusés de magie. Je n'en suis point étonné. Chacun disait en lui-même: "J'ai porté les talents naturels aussi loin qu'ils peuvent aller; cependant un certain savant a des avantages sur moi: il faut bien qu'il y ait là quelque diablerie."

A présent que ces sortes d'accusations sont tombées dans le décri, on a pris un autre tour; et un savant ne saurait guère éviter le reproche d'irréligion ou d'hérésie.—Montesquieu

Je veux tâcher que pour apprendre à s'apprécier, on puisse avoir du moins une pièce de comparaison; que chacun puisse connoitre soi et un autre, et cet autre ce sera moi. . . . Je vais travailler pour ainsi dire dans la chambre obscure; il n'y faut point d'autre art que de suivre exactement les traits que je vois marqués.— Jean-Jacques Rousseau

I. THE WAY IT WAS, OR, WHAT MIGHT HAVE BEEN

The heroes of the libertine novels are all men of letters. The narrator of the *Fragments* is a famous poet, and poetry is also the avocation of the young Francion. By the 1626 version of his life-novel, the part-time poet has developed full-scale novelistic projects. Raymond asks Francion the classic question: Why does he not write his memoirs? He answers that he has already done so: "Il y en a encore un autre où j'ay plaisament descrit quelques unes de mes advantures, lequel j'appelle la Jeunesse de Francion" (p. 437). However, his claims to authorship are disputed, in the books that describe his youthful adventures, by a frame narrative in which Francion is no more than a character referred to in the

101

third person by an "I" who takes responsibility for the narration and who cannot be confused with Francion. No matter. With his *ex post facto* appropriation of the book, Francion also lays claim to the title reserved by Démoris for the page: "Le *héros écrivant* entre dans la fiction; c'est à un livre que conduisaient ses aventures."[1] True, the page is more noticeably an author than Francion. From the start, he is associated with the production of a book. And once this step has been taken with the page, the libertine hero remains an "écrivant." No subsequent narrator hides the fact that his adventures lead to a book.

The majority of the works composed by these libertine hero/ writers are produced through the mediation of a very particular type of *camera obscura*, the prison cell. The composition of the book is generally preceded by time spent in this dark chamber, and may thus be said to result from the experience of enforced confinement, from the realization that the cell door locks the prisoner into a position of difference. When the mother of the page's mistress decides to put him on trial for plotting to help her niece poison her daughter, she has him isolated, first in a room, then in the prison of any would-be hero's dreams, "une vieille tour qui était séparée de tout le reste du bâtiment" (p. 181). In *L'Autre Monde*, the narrator is taken prisoner by soldiers in Canada, and on the moon is twice trapped in a cage. And to prevent his reader from thinking that life is any easier in the land of light and truth, he is captured once again on the sun, this time by birds who hold him prisoner in a tree trunk. As for D'Assoucy, Colombey is forced to admit right at the start of his preface that "chacune des grandes étapes de sa vie est marquée par un cachot" (p. v).

D'Assoucy allegedly lets these captivity sequences build up until their number is quite impressive before he launches into the series of texts he hopes will turn the tables against his various captors. It is significant that for the publication, if not the composition, of these segments, D'Assoucy reverses chronological order, so that he could first unburden himself of the two prison narratives, *La Prison de Monsieur Dassoucy* and the *Pensées de Monsieur Dassoucy, dans le Saint-Office de Rome*.[2] The *Avantures* contains a final (initial?) captivity scene, the description of D'Assoucy's imprisonment as a result of the Montpellier scandal, which is far removed from the romanticism of the page's con-

finement in the tower, or the burlesque vision of Dyrcona restricted to a hollow tree trunk by the swarms of jailor-birds
perched on its branches. In his treatment of the passage, D'Assoucy provides so many graphic details that for once the reader
almost forgets to laugh at his plight: "Je ne reposay point; mon
matelas, qui, dans la septentiéme année de son service, pouvoit
encore disputer de la blancheur avec mes draps, et qui, avec la
couverture, ne faisoient pas tout ensemble l'épaisseur de la
langue d'un chat, ne me donna pas beaucoup d'envie de me
dépoüiller" (p. 142).

In all these instances, the *camera obscura* is also a *camera lucida*, an instrument that enables its inhabitants to project their experiences of confinement onto an exterior surface. There is nothing paradoxical about this transformation, which is simply an
early variant of the standard literary function of the hero's imprisonment. From his period of enforced separation from life, the
page, à la Monte Cristo, draws the courage necessary for the adventures that will eventually form the great book of his life. Since
the actual book of his adventures appears only much later (assuming a "realistic" chronology, in which the hero lives out his story,
then writes his memoirs), and since its existence is at the time of its
composition directly attributed to a friend's prodding, the prison
episode is a source of indirect inspiration at best. In the *Avantures*, on the other hand, the relationship between the cell and the
text is organic. Only D'Assoucy's text lives up to the model set up
by the prologue to *Don Quixote*, in which Cervantes suggests that
he began his novel while in a prison cell. At the end of his description of his imprisonment in Montpellier, D'Assoucy explains that
he composed the account of this episode inside his *cachot*: "Ce
sage Gentilhomme avec plusieurs de mes amis ayant trouvé qu'il
estoit de mon honneur de donner au public la relation de cette
tragicomique avanture, . . . je la fis voir à Monsieur le Juge
Mage, qui en suite me donna la permission de la faire imprimer"
(p. 148). The immense narrative of the *Avantures* and the subsequent volumes may have germinated out of this chapter.[3]

The relatively optimistic pattern of the passage through dark-
ness as a prelude to enlightenment and writing cannot be used,
however, to describe the most developed captivity sequence in a
libertine text, the story in the *Estats et empires* of Dyrcona's en-

forced stays in two prisons, the first in a village near Toulouse, the second in Toulouse itself. *L'Autre Monde* already had portrayed the narrator as a prisoner on several occasions. These imprisonments supposedly precede the composition of the text that describes them, which takes place in the first pages of the *Estats et empires*. Here, Dyrcona, at the urging of his protector, passes from the partial oral accounts of his adventures, of which there are many, both in *L'Autre Monde* and in the beginning of the *Estats et empires*, to a comprehensive written one:

> Je mis donc la plume à la main, et à mesure que j'achevois un cahier, impatient de ma gloire qui luy [i.e., M. de Colignac] démangeoit plus que la sienne, il alloit à Toulouse le proner dans les plus belles assemblées. . . . Mes loüanges dont il sembloit l'infatigable écho, me firent connoistre de tout le monde. Déjà les graveurs, sans m'avoir veu, avoient buriné mon image; et la ville retentissoit, dans chaque carrefour, du gosier enroüe des colporteurs qui crioient à tuë teste: Voilà *le Portrait de l'Autheur* des *Estats et Empires de la Lune* (p. 101).

In this case, the prison pattern becomes double because the account of captivities generates new captivities. The *Estats et empires de la lune* is an immediate and immense *succès de scandale*, a book that polarizes the opinions of all its readers until it becomes no less than the moving force of life in Toulouse:

> Peu après les copies en manuscrit se vendirent sour le manteau; tout le monde et ce qui est hors du monde, c'est-à-dire depuis le gentilhomme jusqu'au moine, acheta cette pièce, et les femmes mesmes prirent party. Chaque famille se divisa, et les intérets de cette querelle allèrent si loin, que la ville fut partagée en deux factions, la *Lunaire* et l'*Antilunaire* (p. 102).

A work that incites even such notorious outsiders as monks and women to take an active part in the functioning of a society, and one that pushes an entire city to the brink of insanity (*lunaire*'s ties to *lunatique* are never denied in Cyrano's works) is clearly a work destined for censorship. All because Dyrcona is self-sacrificing enough to want to make his dear friend happy and unlucky enough to have a controversial best-seller on his hands, the members of the Parlement of Toulouse would reserve a harsh fate for him indeed. They describe this fate to Colignac with the help of a decidedly Tartuffian formula: "Nous engageons nostre hon-

neur de le faire brûler sans scandale" (p. 103). Dyrcona manages
to escape this sentence, only to be hauled off to a country jail by a
band of peasants inspired by the local curé (who in turn is inspired
more by revenge for Colignac's unpaid tithes and a desire for
Dyrcona's fat mule than by consideration for the moral salvation
of his community). He bribes his way out of this first confinement, but not before he has a chance to appreciate the charms of
his surroundings:

> Je demeuray tout seul, et fort mélancolique, le corps arrondi sur
> un boteau de paille en poudre: elle n'estoit pas pourtant si menüe
> que plus de cinquante rats ne la broyassent encor. La voûte, les
> murailles et le plancher, estoient composez de six pierres de tombe,
> afin qu'ayant la mort dessus, dessous, et à l'entour de moy, je ne
> pûsse douter de mon enterrement. La froide bave des limas, et le
> gluant venin des crapauts, me couloient sur le visage; les poux y
> avoient les dents plus longues que le corps (p. 110).

After his escape, Dyrcona is obliged to take up the life of a fugitive. He has a hard time on the run, because "mon estampe m'a-
voit fait connoistre mesme aux harangères" (p. 114).[4] Under the
circumstances, it is not surprising that he is quickly recaptured in
Toulouse and thrown into a dark hole similar to his first "tomb,"
but even more densely populated. In addition to the usual toads
and rats, it contains more exotic lizards and *couleuvres*, even
"une, à la sombre clarté de ses prunelles étincelantes, qui, de sa
gueulle toute noire de venin, dardoit une langue à trois pointes
dont la brusque agitation paroissoit une foudre où ses regards
mettoient le feu" (p. 117).

Of the prison tales that help give birth to a book, only D'Assoucy's goes beyond a romantic or a comic treatment of the experience to suggest the horror of enforced isolation. His evocation
is, however, far surpassed by the details of slimy walls and creatures that make the descriptions of Dyrcona's prisons stand out
among contemporary treatments, despite the presence in them of
a comic element. Cyrano never abandons his burlesque sense of
distancing. Yet, the accumulation of unpleasant details makes it
impossible to dismiss the earth adventures that open the *Estats et
empires* as lightly as Fournel does: "Je laisse de côté le pittoresque
récit du début, où Cyrano . . . après avoir écrit l'histoire de son
premier voyage, raconte comment il est exorcisé, appréhendé au

corps, et jeté dans un cachot."[5] The story of a writer who is imprisoned under harsh conditions because he is the author of a book judged to be heretical and mad—surely this cannot be belittled as merely "pittoresque." This is especially true when the book that opens the prison gates for the fictive author Dyrcona is one that was actually composed by the not-so-fictive man of letters whose name appears on the cover of the *Estats et empires du soleil*, one that was known to Cyrano's contemporaries under the same title used for the fictive work, the *Estats et empires de la lune*, and one that, at the time of the composition of the *Estats et empires du soleil*, was being passed around in manuscript form in certain Parisian circles every bit as avidly as the fictional manuscript in Toulouse.

Actually, the circulation of the "real" manuscript of *L'Autre Monde/Les Estats et empires de la lune* was so carefully controlled that Cyrano never risked the fate he reserves for his fictional substitute. The fame and the infamy so gleefully heaped on the double of his creation may certainly be traced to very evident mythologizing tendencies on Cyrano's part, but even the exaggeration of the self-made scapegoat's fate cannot completely deflect attention from the vignette's serious side. Cyrano chose not to publish *L'Autre Monde*,[6] and simply to inscribe in its sequel a (somewhat inflated) version of the fate he and it certainly would have known, had he allowed it to circulate more widely. Cyrano is not the only author to describe a reversal of the precedence of prison over book established by *Don Quixote*. But whereas many authors are imprisoned because of their books (and Cyrano undoubtedly had examples in mind), it is more unusual to foresee this fate, to avoid it in actuality, and to live it out in fiction.

The role of the outsider assumed by Dyrcona because of the type of novel he chooses to write is a complex one. When he is threatened by the "Barbes à longue robe" of Toulouse (p. 102), he is attacked because he is one of the men of letters of a new school who have no place in the world of the "Barbes." These murderous scholars stand for old systems and old ways of expressing ideas, for the baggage of the pedant so frequently satirized by the libertines: Théophile's Sidias, Cyrano's "nouvel Sidias," Sorel's Hortensius. To the pedant, the libertine is particularly threatening because he is at the same time comprehensible and incomprehensible. Like the pedant, the libertine is primarily concerned with the exploration of philosophy and science, but, unlike him, he chooses to present his reflections on these matters in highly frivolous garb. His rejection of the seriousness and purity of accepted and acceptable philosophical discourse in favor of the tainted lightness of the novel alienates the libertine from the pedant—without even the advantage of gaining for him the support of other novelists as substitute allies. The libertine stresses the distance that separates him from contemporary novelists by refusing to water down his subject matter in order to rejoin the characteristic thematics of the novel. He also attacks the novel's style and its conventions—both Théophile and Sorel choose to open their novels with parodies of the heroic tradition. Too frivolous for some, too serious for others, and eager to thwart any hopes for peaceful coexistence by poking fun at all attempts at intellectual or stylistic codification, the libertine text seems driven by a desire for isolation and by a quest for incomprehension. The libertine broadens his conception of the pedant to include all those who readily and totally adhere to a system of belief that pretends to be airtight. He then logically accompanies his rejection of the pedantic with an attempt to avoid all its pitfalls—in other words, to remain constantly open, constantly doubting, and in constant suspension of belief. This desire to remain marginal translates into a particular vision of the man of letters, one that corresponds historically to the fate reserved for many contemporary libertine authors.

The heroes find themselves in prison on numerous occasions in the course of these novels. Only in the case of Dyrcona at the beginning of the *Estats et empires* does confinement result from the composition of memoirs. Otherwise, the prison doors open for these writers for a variety of reasons that on the surface may seem to have little in common, but that may in fact all be assigned to the same category of offenses against the seventeenth-century's code of sameness. In his *Histoire de la folie à l'âge classique*, Michel Foucault describes the replacement of the single global explanation for the exclusion and confinement of difference in the Middle Ages, leprosy, by a collection of troubles bearing names as different as madness, poverty, and old age. The classical period multiplied the names of otherness, and refined the process of its containment. It did not always bother to distinguish clearly between the crimes of, say, the alchemist and the atheist, but it knew that neither of these figures conformed to its image of sameness. In choosing a mask of alienation for its hero to wear, the libertine text has therefore a wide selection of more or less interchangeable grimaces from which to pick. It may speak of the alchemist, the atheist, the sorcerer, or the possessed. All are destined for similar fates, since all forms of otherness are reunited in prison.

The libertine writers therefore evoke regularly a certain number of subjects about which contemporary literature otherwise adopts one of two attitudes: prudent avoidance (the stance usually chosen by the more respectable literary traditions),[7] or eventual "taming" as a result of a purely stereotypical and comic treatment (as is the case with all baroque portrayals of madness, that of the *Gascon extravagant*, for example).[8] They choose to speak rather than to remain silent, and they refuse to render these forbidden themes palatable by depicting them only in a comic light. This exceptional decision brings the reader to the heart of their conception of the libertine experience.

It can be argued that atheism is the most dangerous image of otherness that could be associated with the hero of a novel in the seventeenth century. For a number of reasons, this issue is particularly difficult for the libertine authors to evoke: it strikes too close to home for a partially comic description; it is perhaps simply too "hot" to handle in a complex way without compromising their always delicate enterprise. Whatever the combination of explanations, the libertine novel rarely develops the character of the religious freethinker. Its heroes are regularly accused of atheism, as is the narrator in *L'Autre Monde* by Elie. D'Assoucy is called an atheist by the Catholics in Montpellier and by many of those he meets on his travels. But such confrontations are handled as quietly as possible. The accusation is either shrugged off as a joke or simply not answered at all. Even more significant is the fact that, of a number of dangerous charges, those of atheism are the only ones not actually provoked by the heroes themselves. They provide few descriptions that might encourage the reader to doubt their religious respectability. Notable exceptions are moments of precocious freethinking on the part of both Francion and the page, such as, for example, the page's evocation of his encounter with a formidable representative of Catholicism when he was only three or four: "Un prince de l'Eglise de mes proches parents . . . fut surpris, lorsque, me caressant un jour et me raillant sur des demandes que j'avais faites de la forme des enfers, je lui témoignai en ma manière de m'exprimer que je doutais qu'il y eut des tenebres où il y avait de si grands feux allumés" (p. 54).

The example is small, and I would not draw from it any theory of hidden clues to an atheistic reading planted in the *Page*. Through an examination of a series of "forbidden" or daring themes that recur with unusual frequency in the libertine text, I hope to establish certain peculiarities about their treatment of these issues. The evocation of atheism or freethinking begins to make a certain pattern clear. In the libertine novels, the hero acts out again and again the drama of his alienation. He must learn repeatedly the hard lesson that there is no place for him in the societies he hopes to frequent. Once it has been established beyond a doubt that he is "other," he is driven out or isolated in some form of prison, or both. However, if we superimpose these scenes of forced separation, a surprising fact stands out. The libertine hero is rarely exiled as a result of accusations that his enemies invent spontaneously. There is almost always complicity between libertine and accuser. It is the libertine who plants the seeds of his own downfall, the libertine who suggests the motivations for his own expulsion. Thus, in this characteristically libertine insistence on alienation, the pattern uncovered in the discussion of autobiography recurs. The libertine writer/hero fosters certain readings. He serves as a ready accomplice in his own (possibly misleading) unmasking.

To return briefly to the accusations of atheism, when these occur, they seem almost thrown in as an afterthought, simply one more in an already impressive list of charges. The Catholics of Montpellier, for example, may scream that D'Assoucy is an atheist, but they are only indulging in a bit of one-upmanship. It does not really matter whether he is an atheist or not, since he is being run out of town on a charge that appears in their eyes to be more than sufficient for his condemnation: homosexuality. Elsewhere, D'Assoucy sheds light on this apparent eclipse of the danger of freethinking. In the scene devoted to his persecution at the hands of his own incarnation of the archetypal libertine foe, the pedant

Triboulet, he describes the moment when Triboulet passes from indirect tormenting and inferences to verbal abuse: "Il m'appela impie, sorcier, athée, hérétique et imposteur, *homo sceleratus atque nefandus*" (p. 75). To be sure, the charge of atheism is present here—with a proliferation of no fewer than three of its synonyms—but Triboulet's outburst is more interesting because of the ways in which it extends the limits of that dangerous word. His accusations are presented in the form of a catalogue, a stylistic choice that performs a leveling process among the terms it juxtaposes. This leveling push is encouraged by the fact that three of the nouns presented are synonyms. In this context, "sorcier," which would normally evoke a quite independent set of meanings, is restricted, through a first movement of assimilation and reduction, to synonymy with "impie, athée, hérétique." The last member of the catalogue sets in motion a second and more significant reduction of meaning. For the summation of his charges, Triboulet, like any pedant worthy of the name, turns to Latin, and in doing so, tips his hand. It seems that, for him, atheists and sorcerers are only "wicked men." With the example of the pedant's curses, D'Assoucy exposes a confusion in terms that springs from the generalized fear of otherness. The accuser driven by this fear does not linger over precision in terms, but simply throws in as many as seem necessary to make clear the distance separating him from his target. In this sense, a writer who wishes to inscribe the persecution of freethinkers in his text need not necessarily depict a freethinker in order to do so—any figure of deviation will carry the necessary implications.

Other figures of difference also provide a certain exoticism that makes a wider range of literary treatments possible. The sorcerer is surely one of these. He is related to the magician and the alchemist, since all three share the power to transform and ultimately control objects and even human beings, a power capable of such diverse manifestations as the sublimation of baser elements to obtain gold and the possession of "diaboliques." These figures—the sorcerer, the magician, and the alchemist—are clearly problematic for anyone aspiring to the title of freethinker in the mid-seventeenth century; hence their Janus-like status in the libertine text. On the one hand, their power is spent, and the only role left for them to play is that of actor in a mythological, epistemological, and intellectual past. Despite the fact that he is living in what appears to be a period rich in witchcraft trials, poisonings, and general belief in the powers of the sorcerer, the libertine, from Gabriel Naudé to Cyrano, laughs in the face of these "diableries," and supports the rising tide of the new science, the only force capable of breaking superstition's back. This is the aspect of libertine thought responsible for such texts as Naudé's *Apologie pour tous les grands personnages qui ont esté faussement soupçonnez de Magie* and Cyrano's letters "Pour les sorciers" and "Contre les sorciers." This attitude also affects their novels, and takes the form of what Démoris calls "une vision critique": "Chez tous . . . une conscience aiguë de leur fascination débouche sur une vision critique: le Page poursuit son alchimiste, Cyrano est pris pour sorcier, Théophile démasque les possédées."[9]

It is true that the libertine hero does not always display a great deal of sympathy for the charms of the occult. In almost all cases, accusations of sorcery, rather than causing alarm, are simply shown to be completely ridiculous. Dyrcona, for example, is never bothered by the fact that, as soon as he sets foot in a new land, its ruling bodies are ready to condemn him as a magician. Thus, upon his arrival in Canada, M. de Montmagny explains that the Jesuits "veulent absolument que vous soyez magicien, et la plus grande grâce que vous puissiez obtenir d'eux, c'est de ne passer que pour imposteur" (p. 35). Back in France, one of the members of the Parlement of Toulouse assures Colignac that he can take his word that the man he is sheltering is a dangerous sorcerer, because "y a-t-il aucun Parlement qui se connoisse en sorciers comme le nostre?" (p. 102).

In neither of these instances is the libertine hero obliged to participate actively in the unmasking of superstition. Ironically, he has only to sit back and let those whose power depends on its existence do his work for him. Other libertine heroes may take a more forceful role. In the *Fragments*, the narrator unmasks the "démoniaque" and her accomplices. Francion mocks the superstitions that give him total power over Valentin. If the reader considers only these uncomplicated passages in the libertine texts, he will readily accept the possibility of extending Madeleine Alcover's description of Cyrano to all their authors: she sees him as a rather cold man of science who does nothing but laugh at anyone or anything concerned with the occult.[10]

It is less easy to defend this opinion in the face of a second image of the sorcerer also prevalent in these novels. As the *barbe* from Toulouse reminds Colignac, any thinker who oversteps the tight limits of acceptable thought quickly finds himself put in his place by those who know a sorcerer when they see one. Many of those accused are charlatans in possession of no secrets more important than their own falseness, but some of them are true men of magic in another sense of the term. As Naudé explains in the preface to *Apologie pour tous les grands personnages qui ont esté faussement soupçonnez de Magie*, almost any thinker ahead of his time is sure to be "written off" by means of such a charge: "D'où venant . . . à me resouvenir que non seulement Virgile, mais presque tous les grands personnages estoient pareillement soupçonnez de magie, je commençay aussi tost de me douter que c'estoit à tort et sans raison."[11] Naudé's choice of Virgil as his first example of a "personnage faussement soupçonnez de Magie" is a characteristic one. In the course of the *Apologie*, he often comes to the defense of writers, a decision that can be explained by his own literary preoccupations, but one that in addition is closely affiliated with the connotations of magic in the libertine text.

The central encounter made by the *page disgracié* is with the alchemist he will afterward refer to by many different names, but most often simply as "le philosophe." This meeting, unlike others involving men of magic in the libertine novel, is not marked by a denunciation scene. Denunciation is an attempt to unmask, and these novels contain only would-be unmaskings in which the accuser never wins. Time after time, he thinks he has found his victim out, lifts the veil—and finds someone completely different from his expectation. From such a perspective of the *trompeur trompé*, the page's alchemist, like the atheist, is of little interest. If his mask is lifted, he does have something to hide. Shortly after their initial encounter, the philosopher explains to the page who has been pursuing him why he flees all human contact. The page has been pursuing him not because of a desire to unmask him, as Démoris implies, but simply because he is driven by an irresistible fascination. In the page's words: "Il me représenta comme en tremblant le danger que couraient ceux qui avaient un secret pareil, quand ils étaient découverts par quelque prince; que le moindre malheur qu'ils en pouvaient attendre était l'entière perte de leur liberté" (p. 100). This is the man the page dreams of serving as an apprentice, in the hope of becoming, like him, a man with a secret. The page believes that coming to maturity should involve the initiation into a certain number of secrets, that there should be a Pandora's box somewhere along the way. No matter that the only man he meets with access to secret knowledge is obliged to remain a fugitive out of constant fear of persecution—the page's desire to share that knowledge is stronger than his fear.

The young page is not yet a writer. He has not yet discovered the comparison implicit behind Naudé's unmasking of an alleged unmasking and behind the repeated denunciations/unmaskings of Dyrcona as a sorcerer. None of these denunciations/unmaskings can be described as completely successful, in that none of them produces the desired effect of uncovering a sorcerer pretending to be like everyone else, pretending to be the same rather than other, that is, a man without secrets. Yet, in a way, all of them are successful because they accidentally expose writers, individuals seeking to be, like sorcerers, men with secrets and men with the power to transform. Instead of sorcerers, they uncover (only) would-be sorcerers, men pretending to be sorcerers, imposters— the Canadian Jesuits' "next-best" dream: "Ils veulent absolument que vous soyez magicien; et la plus grande grâce que vous puissiez obtenir d'eux, c'est de ne passer que pour imposteur" (*L'Autre Monde*, p. 35).[12] These denunciations miss, but just barely, which goes to show that their ability to detect otherness is not entirely off. After all, no Parlement knows its way around sorcerers like the Parlement of Toulouse, so the denouncers cannot be totally wrong, which perhaps explains why alchemy ultimately leads to prison, just like the book.

It certainly explains why the libertine heroes themselves invite all the most interesting accusations of sorcery in these novels. The element of complicity in their own condemnation is especially strong in these cases, probably because all of the libertine heroes share the page's pursuit of Artefius: alchemy and artifice. They, too, are men who seek initiation, who strive to gain possession of a secret. Either to facilitate their quest or to make their audience believe they are already initiates into mysterious knowledge, these heroes play at an unusual game, at which they enjoy immense success: they pretend to be sorcerers. The first example of such a travesty is the opening scene of *Francion* where the hero's claims to magical powers play havoc with everyone's projects, even his own.

Francion succeeds admirably in convincing everyone that he is what he pretends to be: "Monsieur, reprit le Chirurgien en se sousriant, vous me pardonnerez si je vous dy que vous m'obligez à croire que l'opinion que l'on a de vous en ce village cy est veritable, qui est que vous estes tres sçavant en Magie" (p. 89). Although this may be the most obvious instance of the libertine-hero-playing-at-sorcerer, and thus impossible to overlook in this context, it contains nothing of the more problematic complicity elsewhere discernible. Francion plays on the villagers' superstitions, not in an effort to view his power over them in a broader context, but simply to demonstrate a cliché straight out of the more obvious libertine philosophy of magic: that magic has become an empty signifier, just like the formulas Valentin so blindly memorizes and repeats in the hope of regaining his own lost power: "Il se figuroit qu'il y avoit là dessous quelque sens magnifique caché" (p. 68). The adult Francion's portrayal of a sorcerer deliberately never gets beyond the non-depth of a stereotype. It remains a class-conscious joke. Valentin and a few peasants may fall for this cardboard figure, but the *chirurgien*, who describes their credulity "en se sousriant" and, of course, the reader, who shares his intellectual superiority, could never be taken in for a minute by this reminder of a barbaric past.

The mature Francion may wholeheartedly mock the power of magic, but an incident he recounts from his past reveals a certain complicity in its unmasking. When Francion begins to paint his self-portrait, he turns to his own childhood, from which he selects two anecdotes to represent his preschool years. The first of these vignettes, the first image that Francion chooses to give of himself, describes a curious encounter between the child and "un maistre Singe." This canny animal slips into Francion's room when the baby is alone and disguises him by reversing his garments: "faisant entrer mes pieds dans les manches de ma cotte, et mes bras dedans mes chausses" (p. 165). When he is asked who did this to him, Francion replies after an interesting and apparently innocent bit of reasoning: "Parce que j'avois desja ouy appeller du nom de Diable quelque chose laide, je dy que c'estoit un petit garçon laid comme un Diable." The child's remark unleashes the predictable uproar in the household. The servants are convinced "que ce fust un Diable qui estoit venu dedans ma chambre." After the monkey makes several other visits without being seen by anyone else, even Francion's parents come round and "furent contraints de s'imaginer qu'il revenoit un Lutin en nostre maison" (p. 166). Of course, the very natural cause is quickly discovered to eliminate this temporary intrusion of a diabolical form of supernatural magic. No explanation, however, can camouflage the pattern that enters the domain of the libertine novel from Francion's encounter with the devilish monkey. Two subsequent libertine heroes reveal scenes from their young lives dealing with magic and sorcery that are both uncanny and uncannily similar.

One of the page's early disgraces is caused by his fascination with the occult, an obsession that will eventually lead to the mad and ill-fated pursuit of his Artefius. A reading of Jean-Baptiste Porta's *Magie naturelle*[13] inspires him to begin a series of experiments in illusion that eventually backfire and oblige him to run away for the first time. Like baby Francion, it is the young page himself who provides the evidence for a suggestion of diabolical intervention in his life. In the midst of his most "successful" experiment, "il y eut quelqu'un des domestiques qui se ressouvint qu'il avait vu par hasard un de mes livres sur le dos duquel il y avait écrit *Magie*, et qui dit que j'avais fais en ce lieu quelque conjuration diabolique" (p. 86). The page ridicules those who could concoct a diabolical reading of his "malice innocente," yet his own future behavior will belie these protestations of innocence. Almost as if by accident, or unconsciously, he repeats through his experience a classic schema of libertine alienation: the book leads to denunciation, which leads to exile (prison).

The third such scene of youthful self-implication, actually a double one, has D'Assoucy setting himself up as a scapegoat. In general, the *Avantures* finds so much evidence of persecution in the recent past that it is unnecessary to look very far back for inspiration. D'Assoucy brings forth memories from his distant past only once, as a prelude to his account of the events in Montpellier that lead to the imprisonment that nurtures the book. To round out his self-portrait as the eternal victim, he supplies two scenes from his childhood. The first incident, involving D'Assoucy when not quite six, is only narrated once. In this case, it is easy for the reader to see where the blame should be placed: "Je n'avois pas encore six ans que les sots enfans de mon quartier, issus du sang le plus abject de la lie du peuple, me poursuivoient à grands coups de pierres, parce qu'estant dejà plus raisonnable qu'eux, ils connoissoient en moy quelque chose digne de leur aversion" (p. 104). Through the effects of persecution, "I" is shifted from its initial status as subject to a closing one as object. D'Assoucy's persuasiveness is marred only by a certain hesitancy in the sentence's construction. The passage from "I" as subject to "ils" as subject seems bungled because of the presence of a syntactical gap between "estant dejà plus raisonnable qu'eux," and "ils connoissoient en moy" that calls unnecessary attention to the contrived nature of the attribution of blame.

This question recurs in far more blatant fashion with regard to the second incident. In his desperation to establish his innocence by proving once and for all that persecution constantly follows him, and that he does nothing to provoke it, D'Assoucy insists on recounting this second event on two separate occasions. In the continuation of the same sentence, the scene of the six-year-old stoned because his superior intelligence aroused suspicions is linked with a similar event that took place three years later. This incident makes even more explicit the desired identification with the classic vision of the wise men "faussement soupçonnez de Magie": "A neuf ans, estant hors de la maison de mon père, je passay pour magicien parmy le sot peuple de Calais, parce qu'estant doüé d'un esprit vif, et parlant grec et latin, ces gens matériels ne pouvoient pas s'imaginer que sans l'aide d'un esprit malin, je pusse en un âge si tendre estre devenu si sçavant" (p. 104). The Calais incident can obviously serve as a perfect prefiguration of the Montpellier disaster. Either because he is concerned that his reader will miss this point, or because in his intense preoccupation with the theme of his persecution he forgets the first evocation of Calais, D'Assoucy returns to this incident less than twenty pages later to give it a much fuller description. He makes no allusion to the first account, and, supplying more details all along the way, begins again from the beginning: "quoy que je n'eusse encore que neuf ans" (p. 121).

In the retelling, however, the question of blame, more or less neatly established a short time before, becomes problematic. According to the second version, the nine-year-old D'Assoucy enters the service of a widow to act as a companion for her son. Both widow and son are fairly naïve, and the young D'Assoucy, "dejà assez malin pour remarquer en eux cette simplicité" (p. 122), is quick to take advantage of his situation to fabricate a character of mythical proportions for himself: "Comme je parlois dejà Grec, je leur disois que je parlois encore Siriaque, Hébreu et Caldéen; que j'estois Astrologue: et afin qu'ils n'en doutassent nullement, je leur faisois croire que j'estois le fils de ce grand et fameux faiseur d'horoscope nommé César" (p. 122). In the course of the ensuing period of influence, D'Assoucy performs exploits like forecasting the weather and reading palms. He eventually acquires such a reputation that he manages to chase off a hostile crowd of little boys with no more than a simple gesture: "ayant tiré de ma poche un certain livre dont je les menaçois" (p. 123).[14] He even wins credit for the cure of a sick little boy.[15] This last feat serves to confirm his fame and to bring him to the point described in his previous evocation of the event: "Toute la ville fut en rumeur. . . . Ils me prirent à neuf ans pour un celebre magicien. . . . Le sot peuple me vouloit jetter dans la Mer" (pp. 126–27).

By returning at such length to an accusation from which he feels certain to be able to prove his innocence, D'Assoucy manages on the contrary, to provide the only explicit illustration of the complicity of the young libertines in their own condemnation. It is clear from his more detailed analysis of the magician incident that D'Assoucy, far from being solely the object of the hatred and persecution of a series of impersonal subjects—"ils," "la ville," "le sot peuple"—is at the source of his own troubles. This incident, like all the misadventures of young libertines, is presented as an illustration of the stupidity of others, but it backfires by revealing far more about the nascent libertine desire to be other. In fact, these portraits of young sorcerers prefigure the treatment of the adult libertine heroes. They are ominous first signs of the libertine mark.

For example, the link with sorcery follows D'Assoucy through all his persecutions. It is only natural, therefore, that it reappear in Montpellier during what he imagines to be the ultimate moment of his victimization. By the time he reaches the depth/heights of misery for which he schooled himself from age six,

D'Assoucy no longer needs to goad the crowd to come after him by forging an image for denunciation, as he did in Calais. Now, his very own (false) name is sufficient to denounce him, to expose the form of otherness to which he has so long aspired: "Mon destin parmi ce sot et méchant peuple n'auroit pas esté plus doux; je ne pûs pourtant pas éviter qu'ils ne fissent allusion à mon nom, et qu'au lieu de Soucy Musicien, ils ne m'appellassent Sorcier et Magicien" (p. 132). D'Assoucy returns here to his original explanation for the genealogy of incrimination, implying that he did his best to remain part of the faceless "sot peuple," to trick them into believing he was now one of them and no longer an outsider. As always, however, he heard his difference proclaimed all around him: "je ne pus pourtant pas éviter qu'ils." For a moment, he seems an utterly helpless victim: his name, like Akakii Akakievich's overcoat or Kovalijov's nose, apparently has a life of its own. He would have us believe that he was marked at birth by the sign of his ultimate downfall. But, as always, the finger pointing to the guilty party also seems to have a life of its own. It swings round to denounce D'Assoucy himself. It was, after all, he who invented and took on the name D'Assoucy; he who chose as an adult to be reborn under the sign of sorcery, just as he did as a nine-year-old when he decided to become a member of the Nostradamus family. If the people of Montpellier see "Sorcier" in "Soucy" and "Magicien" in "Musicien," D'Assoucy has no one to blame but himself.

His complicity in his own victimization must also be evoked in conjunction with this use of comic etymologies. It is somehow less likely that the people of Montpellier spontaneously invented this splendidly appropriate rallying cry than that, inspired by his own particular mythologizing instincts, D'Assoucy set it up for them to discover. Comic etymologies are certainly compatible with the burlesque spirit that sparkles so often in his prose style, and elsewhere D'Assoucy demonstrates his delight in their whimsical charms. In the *Combat de Cirano de Bergerac, avec le singe de Brioché au bout du Pont-neuf*, he gives free reign to his etymological creativity. His explanation of the origin of "Cirano" (which he claims to have received from Cyrano himself), provides one of the most outrageous examples of the genre: "Bergerac soutenoit en plaisantant, que Mage et Roy étoient *unum et idem*, qu'on appelloit un Roy Cir, en François Sire, et comme ce Mage, ce Roy, ce Cir, pour faire ces enchantemens, se campoit au milieu d'un cercle; c'est-à-dire d'un O, on le nommoit Cir an O."[16] This etymology goes even farther than that of D'Assoucy's sobriquet in stressing numerous ties. D'Assoucy/Cyrano calls attention to the sorcerer's sovereignty, to the magic in names, to the magic in the men who are marked by them. In their striving to be considered as repositories of secret powers, these men would have their public believe that the sorcerer is in "D'Assoucy" and that "Cyrano" leads to the circle of his spells.

As though the difference acquired as a result of his secrets were not enough to complete his separation from the faceless crowd, the sorcerer is often marked with still another stigma of otherness. Time and again, these texts show that great men are accused of magic, and the *Estats et empires* goes one step further to demonstrate that the jump from magic to madness is quickly made. Appropriately, it is a sorcery expert from the Parlement of Toulouse who, in the course of his critique of Dyrcona's book, explains why this is so: "Tant de Lunes, tant de cheminées, tant de voyages par l'air, ne valent rien, je dis rien du tout; et entre vous et moy . . . je n'ay jamais veu de sorcier qui n'eust commerce avec la Lune" (p. 102). For those who, like the venerable parliamentarian, seek to deflate the magic of knowledge and transformation, this is most easily done by dismissing it as lunatic ravings. The circle within which the sorcerer's enchantments take place is the moon's sphere, and the language he speaks is incomprehensible to those unmarked by difference because it is a foreign tongue, the product, not simply of another country, but of another world.

The peculiarities of this foreign tongue make it possible to distinguish the true libertine lunatics from the stereotypical figures of madness so popular in contemporary literature. The baroque madman speaks a language that may range from the slightly incomprehensible to something near gibberish, but is always so bizarre that it is generally thought to be meaningless. Indeed, if there is any sense at all to be made from what he is saying, it is usually overlooked. This madman, far from being an individual with a secret, as is the case with the libertine figures of otherness, is simply a buffoon, whose speeches are no more than comic interludes. The baroque madman does exist in the libertine text in roles that range from the cameo appearance by the "extravagant" Pole the page encounters late in his travels to the fairly developed characters of Hortensius and Collinet in *Francion*. In these cases, the madman is a clown, and his wild language is destined for the amusement of his audience rather than for the eventual decipherment of truths too dangerous to be placed in the mouths of the sane. Of these characters, only Collinet is given a daring role to play out. He has the ability to make those around him see their follies, and is thus a reincarnation of the wise-fool, never so lucid as when he is mad. He represents an important current of baroque madness, one whose philosophy is well defined in the preface to the *Gascon extravagant*: "A penetrer dans ses intentions, on trouve qu'il est Philosophe moral, que les gascons extravagans de cette sorte, sont raisonnables et sçavans, et que si tous les foux leur ressembloient, il n'y auroit pas de difference entre la folie et la sagesse."[17] This is the essence of the baroque madman: different only to be wiser than those who pass judgment on him, different only to annihilate difference, to eliminate the very possibility of otherness: "Si tous les foux leur ressembloient, il n'y auroit pas de difference entre folie et sagesse."

This is certainly the least troubling vision of madness imaginable. As a result, the baroque madman is usually taken in and protected, as is Collinet. And never are his pronouncements startling enough to link him to the more severely punished variants of otherness, such as sorcery. The libertine lunatic, on the other hand, deserves to be compared to the magician because he, too, has a vision, another type of secret. The lunatic is, most literally, an inhabitant of the moon, like Hortensius's mother, according to *L'Autre Monde*.[18] More generally, he is anyone in direct contact with the other world in the moon. Once again according to *L'Autre Monde*, when Noah's Ark, riding the crest of the flood, approaches the moon, no one on board can understand what this land is, so no one wants to undertake the risk of exploring it. No one, that is, but Noah's daughter, Achab, who swims to it: "On eut beau crier après elle, l'appeler cent fois lunatique, protester qu'elle serait cause qu'un jour on reprocherait à toutes les femmes d'avoir dans la tête un quartier de la lune, elle se moqua d'eux" (p. 46).

This lunatic is not the anguished figure described in modern literature's vision of madness, because he/she does not experience otherness within himself[19] but purely in relation to outsiders. The secret that sets him apart from his race is not a power but a voyage. The lunatic has been somewhere almost no one else has been, like the narrator in *L'Autre Monde*, like the occupants of the "Stultifera Navis" described by Foucault: "C'est vers l'autre monde que part le fou sur sa folle nacelle; c'est de l'autre monde qu'il vient quand il débarque."[20] The traveler who returns from such a voyage can never again hope to slip by unnoticed. He remains marked by the other world he has seen. When the narrator drops back to earth and lands in Italy, he is obliged to take refuge behind barred doors, to make himself a prisoner, because he is pursued by a pack of dogs who recognize the moon's odor and are "archarnés contre moi à cause du monde d'où je venais" (p. 117).

The freethinker, the sorcerer, the lunatic—these are the categories of difference so often described in the libertine texts that it is sometimes hard to establish boundaries among them. The obsessiveness with which these visions are repeated can be explained historically. The seventeenth-century man of letters who attempted to explore uncharted territory ran a very real risk of having these labels applied to him. When they describe the persecution of their heroes, the libertines may well be either describing their own present or foretelling their own future. Occasionally, they step outside this personal vision to evoke additional categories of otherness beyond their experience, but ones that provoked the same treatment given the madman and the sorcerer.

Two of these vignettes are especially unusual. Once, D'Assoucy, at a loss to find a comparison striking enough to suggest the extent of his persecution, draws a parallel between his fate and that of the "Enfans d'Israël dans le Desert" (p. 110). The second occurs in the opening sequence of the *Estats et empires*, that catalogue of forms of persecution. Dyrcona not only receives all the accusations already mentioned but even acts out a scene during which he adopts various masks of difference. After escaping from his first prison, he tries to disguise himself from his persecutors and at the same time to pass unnoticed through the crowds of Toulouse. Ironically enough, in his attempt he simply exchanges the mask of otherness forced on him (the sorcerer, the lunatic) for another one, albeit one freely chosen. The peasant who helps him escape provides him with clothes in which Dyrcona hopes to blend in with the masses. He misses this opportunity to lose his difference because "j'avois arrangé sur moy mes haillons si bizarrement qu'avec une démarche qui ni convenoit point à l'habit, je paraissoit moins un pauvre qu'un mascarade" (p. 112). After this initial betrayal, Dyrcona realizes that he is not meant to become just another face in the crowd, and in order to improve his act, he continues to transform himself, becoming, instead of the intellectual outcast that he was, a physical one: "De peur qu'on ne me reconnut à la voix, j'adjoustay à l'exercise de quaisman, l'addresse de contrefaire le muet. Je m'avance donc vers ceux que j'apperçoy qui me regardent; je pointe un doigt dessous le menton, puis dessus la bouche, et je l'ouvre en bâillant, avec un cri non articulé, pour faire entendre par ma grimace qu'un pauvre muet demande l'aumosne." Dyrcona concludes this pantomine worthy of a subsequent "other," Rameau's nephew, by establishing once again the link between otherness and the book: "Enfin, j'appris que la gueuserie est un grand Livre" (p. 114). He then takes on one final mask of the physical outcast, that of a "malade de la contagion," by dirtying his face, putting disorder in his clothing, and even adopting the sign forced on victims of the plague, like a brand, to warn others of their condition: "Ayant étendu mon mouchoir dessus le pavé et disposé aux coins quatre petits cailloux . . . je me couchay vis à vis . . . et me mis à geindre fort langoureusement." This time, his act is successful, and the crowd begins to run by him "en se bouchant le nez" (p. 115). His identification with this form of otherness does not save Dyrcona from his persecutors for long. The scene following his masquerade as a carrier of the plague finds him back in a cell, having demonstrated that the libertine hero is so accustomed to ostracism that, even outside prison, he is forever a victim.

2. ONE-UPMANSHIP

I have insistently maintained that these libertine novels are unusual cases within the novelistic production of their day. On the issue of alienation, however, I am prepared to claim for them an almost unique position in literary history. Rare indeed, in my experience, are the texts that can rival these in their obsessive portrayal of the situation of alienation—certainly they seem to have no predecessors, and no successors before Rousseau. Once it has been established that the subject is omnipresent in them, it seems only natural to ask why. One could possibly begin with a historical explanation. Seventeenth-century freethinkers find themselves in a situation of helplessness before a society that actively seeks to alienate them, and this helplessness is translated in their texts into a recurrent vision both of the accusations they may face and of those actually leveled at other marginal figures with whom they identify. But as they broaden the horizon of otherness they create a vision that defies historical explanation. A close examination of the passages concerned with this issue shows that the historically motivated identification yields to a totally personal vision of alienation, not only without precedent for the libertines, but in most cases with no historical precedent whatsoever.

These completely personal themes of difference represent a related, yet separate, problem from the notion of complicity. Complicity is a basic libertine instinct, but complicity in one's own undoing, to the point of actually giving grounds on which one might be condemned, suggests a diagnosis that grows more inevitable as the cycle of the libertine novels develops: paranoia. The presence of these intensely private themes of alienation serves to complete the impression of claustrophobia that becomes increasingly oppressive in the later libertine texts. It is as if the libertine hero were unable to live without persecution. When not describing himself as a victim on a literal (historical) level, he proceeds with a study of victimization on a metaphorical (personal) level. In the long run, persecution is found everywhere, and the most solitary libertine heroes, Dyrcona and D'Assoucy, are tracked relentlessly by their adversaries. The culminating point of this vision is undoubtedly D'Assoucy's "Epistre à Messieurs les Sots," in which he develops at great length, and with all his fervor, his story as "le plus illustre persecuté de l'univers," from its origin to the then present day in Rome. The extent of D'Assoucy's paranoia becomes apparent at certain moments of this text, which takes the form of an actual litany of persecution (a series of attacks, each answered by a defense: "faire passer pour un Ecrivain ennemy des choses sacrées . . . celuy qui a deffendu"), culminating in a vision of the size of the armies massed against him: "comment cette premiere matiere qui servit à ce premier homme ait pû s'estre assez alterée . . . pour produire des hommes assez méchans et des *peuples entiers* asez sots, pour faire passer un enfant à neuf ans pour magicien" (p. 108; italics mine).

The libertine paranoia is observable first of all in scattered images, such as that of the hero tracked like a beast by bands of men or monsters, which occurs in both Francion's dream (pp. 145, 147) and in the dream narratives of Dyrcona and Colignac (in Colignac's dream, Dyrcona is chased by a "grand monstre noir," and Dyrcona himself dreams that he is pursued by "une troupe d'assassins" [p. 106]). In what is certainly the most unusual of these visions, D'Assoucy describes his arrival in Turin after Loret has announced his death as though he were a ghost returning to life: "peu s'en falut qu'il ne tombast de son haut à la renverse, croyant sans doute que je fusse quelque fantosme, ou l'ame vengeresse des mauvaises offices qu'il m'avoit autrefois rendus" (p. 236). In D'Assoucy's case, not a prison cell but his enemies' success in robbing him of his very existence is at the origin of the book. The *Avantures* is composed to establish the continued existence of the man behind the ghost.

Curiously enough, it is through the passion for gambling shared by D'Assoucy and the page that these heroes develop most insistently their paranoid sense of isolation. Gambling is never described in these texts as either a casual pastime or one that favors a spirit of companionship. It is, on the contrary, a disastrous, uncontrollable force, a "pleasure" certain to culminate in a sense of alienation, yet one to which the libertines feel compelled to return. As such, it has nothing in common with the aristocratic amusement to which Démoris, speaking of the *Avantures*, compares it:

> Comme dans le *Page*, le rappel obsédant du thème du jeu, divertissement aristocratique (et mentionné comme tel dans bien des mémoires), vient indiquer que le poète est tout aussi capable qu'un vrai noble de se donner tout entier à l'instant, dans un total mépris pour des calculs bourgeois. Mais à la différence de Tristan, son vice ne fait éprouver à d'Assoucy aucun remords. Il lui est occasion de se confirmer que la vocation littéraire est une manière de se rendre l'équivalent des gens de qualité.[21]

Granted, the libertine can scorn "calculs bourgeois" as well as any noble. He cannot, however, share the lack of involvement, the depersonalization of the game that keeps the aristocratic amusement a relatively innocent one. An aristocrat does not have a passion for gambling; there is allegedly too little of him present in the game for that to be the case. As a result, he comes out of any contact with games of chance with clean hands. Indeed, gambling in an aristocratic context is not tainted with the bad reputation it acquires in another, one might say bourgeois, environment.

"The disrepute of games of chance is actually based on the fact that the player himself has a hand in it. (An incorrigible patron of a lottery will not be proscribed in the same way as the gambler in a stricter sense.)"[22] Benjamin's comparison may be extended to pinpoint the difference between aristocratic and libertine gambling. The aristocrat gambles like the "patron of a lottery"—his hands are not really "in it."[23] As a result, he simply either wins or loses, with none of the complications that arise from a more passionate approach to the game and its stakes, such as cheating and fleecing. Swindling has no place at an aristocratic table. No aristocrat could descend to the level of the cardsharp: to do so would be to involve himself in a system of values his own milieu could not comprehend. The aristocratic table is, furthermore, closed to all nonaristocrats, so the infiltration of swindlers can be ruled out.

This is unfortunately not the case with libertine games of chance. The description of their unhappy brushes with gambling provided by the page and D'Assoucy evoke, rather than an aristocratic spirit of fairplay and equality within the rules of the game, an ominous atmosphere of paranoid uncertainty, reminiscent of the image of gambling conveyed by Georges de la Tour's painting, *Le Tricheur*. At the center of this powerful canvas is a beautiful prostitute, who, with the help of two of her servants, is quietly fleecing a young nobleman. The painting is a study in silent communication, and the play on eyes and glances shooting from the prostitute, the maid serving her, and the man switching cards behind his back provides a dramatic focus. All those in on the secret (although with less of a "hand in" the game than the man they are duping) use their eyes and have the power to see. The only individual in the painting who remains blind is the young man being swindled. Were he to use his *regard* even briefly, he would instantly unmask the swindle posited on the absence of the fourth pair of eyes. We cannot see the victim's eyes, since he is portrayed as simply and naïvely looking down at his cards, closed into a solitary universe that is invaded by the united forces of his adversaries.

La Tour's four characters give visual form to what could be described as the archetypal swindle of the libertine hero. Whenever the page and D'Assoucy gamble, the swindler and his helpers always watch their victim carefully, but the victim never sees what is happening to him until it is just a little too late. No code of honor whatsoever in their games—the only rule ever respected is that there be a cardsharp present at every hand. What he so mildly refers to as "mon natural enclin au jeu" (p. 228) draws the page into a number of unhappy situations, usually referred to in the chapter titles simply as "nouvelles disgraces." What is certainly the most unsettling of these encounters marks his return to France after the English sojourn. On the road from Dieppe to Paris, the page falls into the trap laid for him by a trio of swindlers. He is traveling in the company of the two helpers, who have gained his confidence, when they are joined by the chief crook. It never occurs to the page that his two very ordinary and very French traveling companions might have anything to do with the incredible stranger who overtakes them and who is variously described as: "ce personnage vêtu de drap gris, couvert d'agrafes d'argent, ayant sur la tête un bonnet de fourrures fort fantasque," "l'espèce de Polonais," "cet homme qui faisait l'enragé," "cet extravagant affligé." The Pole has a tale of woe: he has been robbed by his valet. In order to console him, they all retire to a nearby inn for a quiet evening of wine and cards. There, the page learns all the latest games from Moscow—and loses everything he owns in the process.

The page realizes only much later that he has been duped by a reenactment of the drama depicted in *Le Tricheur*: "Aussi c'était un effet dont je ne connaissais pas la cause; et j'ai fort bien reconnu depuis, à force de ratiociner, qu'il y avait entre ceux qui feignaient être avec moi, des jeux de cartes tout ajustés, qu'ils mettaient entre les mains du faux Polonais, escamotant adroitement les autres, lorsqu'ils faisaient semblant de les mêler" (p. 219). Perhaps the page is unable to break through the web of glances of exchanged complicity in which he is entrapped, unable to unmask the "étranger prétendu," precisely because the "faux Polonais" dupes him by means of an old libertine trick. The cardsharp clearly belongs to the world of difference, but he disguises his primary form of otherness by adopting still another mask of alienation. In this case, the mask is a double one: he pretends to be both a foreigner and a madman (the page calls him "enragé," "extravagant," and says that he "vint faire le démoniaque"). He acts as though the multiplication of false forms of otherness, forms of otherness alien even to him, could keep his victims off the trail of the more dangerous form of difference they protect.

The young nobleman in La Tour's painting falls for the swindler hidden inside the prostitute, and the page for the card-sharp masked by foreign madness. In D'Assoucy's case, he en-counters only crooks wearing every possible disguise and falls for every one of them. The *Avantures* is just beginning, and its hero has hardly gotten out of Paris when he meets his first cardsharp. On this occasion, the wolf does not even bother to dress up elabo-rately as another kind of wolf, but simply slips into the oldest disguise known to his kind, that of the wolf in sheep's clothing. The resulting "homme en qui il sembloit que la nature eust ra-massé ce que le monde a de plus simple, et de plus innocent" (p. 15) pretends to understand nothing of the language of cards: "Il prenoit les Roys pour les Dames, et les Dames pour les Valets." D'Assoucy, ever willing to help a stranger in need and appro-priately incredulous at the good fortune he is encountering, val-iantly tries to explain the basics to him: "Je commençay de luy donner une carte et d'en prendre une carte pour moy, mais je fus plus d'un gros quart d'heure avant que de luy pouvoir faire com-prendre." Of course, the naïveté wears away bit by bit, and the teacher has soon been taken for everything he is worth by his gifted pupil.

D'Assoucy's initial brush with a swindler does nothing to de-ter him from his passion for cards. He gambles his way through city after city, rushing immediately upon his arrival to find the "Académie de jeu," even though he fully realizes that his conduct is obsessive: "Je sçay qu'on dira que j'estois un fou de joüer davan-tage" (p. 320). Each new loss confirms him in his paranoid cer-tainty that all his opponents are united in a giant plot to fleece D'Assoucy. He comes to see himself as completely alone of his kind, faced with the growing ranks of his enemies, all of the same race. Witness his description of the Avignon "Academy": "Comme dans ce lieu il n'y avoit autre Chrétien que moy, et que, jusqu'au maistre qui donnoit les dez et les cartes, tout y estoit juif, il me fallut passer par les rigeurs de la Synagogue. Un grand Juif nommé Melchisedech, qui avoit le nez long et le visage pasle, me gagna mon argent" (p. 101).[24]

This impression that his enemies are identical, that they all wear the same face, finds its ultimate confirmation for D'Assoucy at the time of his last victimization in the *Avantures*. On the way to Avignon just after his escape from Montpellier, D'Assoucy encounters a fellow voyager, a priest with a plaster on one eye. They have hardly begun to share their route when D'Assoucy "discovers" that the priest is also his long-lost "cousin de Carpentras." Both the reunion and the voyage are joyous, and only once is D'Assoucy's gaiety troubled by suspicions that his cousin is not entirely on the level: "Plus je le regardois, plus il me sembloit, à l'emplâtre près, avoir veu cet homme en quelque autre endroit du monde" (p. 157). It is certainly no surprise to the reader that all these diverse trappings—the priest's robes, the plaster, the title of cousin—turn out to be components of the most elaborate disguise put together by any of D'Assoucy's swindlers. What is surprising is that the priest/cousin/thief turns out to be none other than D'Assoucy's former student, the first cardsharp to have the honor of taking his money in the course of the *Avantures*. As if that were not enough, he is also none other than the German who fleeced him in Lyon, and who was described by D'Assoucy at the time as "un très-habile et très-expeditif Allemand qui, par miracle, avoit tout l'air et le visage de mon tueur de temps" (i.e., his "student" [p. 97]). Once he has been swindled no fewer than three times by the same man, D'Assoucy of course finds himself with all the proof he needs to be certain that he is always the victim of the same man, that his persecutors, whether they wear the same face or a series of different masks, all share a single identity.

On this point, the question of complicity, so often evoked in these pages, cannot be avoided. D'Assoucy's desire to be "robbed," as he calls it, is so strong that he almost manages to reverse the situation and give his money away. He cannot help but know what will happen if he gambles. His archetypal cardsharp, just after his first victory, gives him a detailed list of instructions telling him how to avoid a repetition of the event, a warning of which he reminds D'Assoucy in a letter left for him after his third successful swindle: "Ressouvenez-vous . . . de la grace que je vous fais, et n'accusez que vous de vostre desastre, puisqu'après les protestations que vous aviez faites de profiter de mes conseils, vous avez esté assez fol pour perdre cinquante pistolles à Lyon contre moy qui estoit cet Allemand qui vous les gagna chez la Lere; et icy contre un Prieur Provençal que vous ne connoissiez pas" (p. 160). D'Assoucy, like the page, loses because he chooses to do so.

Thus far, the libertine hero in his role as cardsharp's victim would not seem terribly different from the libertine hero accused of sorcery or any other mode of otherness. This similarity, in fact, almost succeeds in masking the fundamental incomparability of these types of victimization. The unlucky gambler does not belong to the historically definable victims of this period, and is quite possibly outside any schema of difference but the libertine's. The libertine is always a victim, but there is a vast difference in the stakes—next to losing one's freedom and one's life, losing one's money hardly seems important enough to merit the same trappings of victimization. Furthermore, for the great majority of the libertine novel's readers, the hero's association with the historically defined other can only have positive connotations—the hero emerges a more sympathetic character from his brushes with the prison cell. To be trapped by a wearer of masks, however, can hardly be expected to add to his favorable image.

And yet, bizarrely enough, the libertine hero does not see things this way, as a passage from the *Avantures* demonstrates. Just after winning his money for the first time, D'Assoucy's ubiquitous swindler attempts to justify his profession in a speech full of burlesque flair:

> Quoy, le Capitaine plumera le soldat, le soldat plumera le paysan, et le goujat plumera la poule, et vous, Monsieur le Poëte, pour vous parer du bien d'autruy vous plumerez impunément tous les autheurs, et moy, à qui mieux qu'à vous appartient le droit de plumage, je n'oseray seulement arracher une de vos plumes? . . . O gens barbares et dénaturez, cruels Anthropophages, qui, ne vivans que de la substance d'autruy, ne pouvez souffrir qu'on touche à la vostre, que trouvez-vous en moy qui ne soit point en vous? . . . Autant d'hommes, autant de larrons; et, autant de

larcins differens, autant de titres particuliers: comme *rançonner, faire venir l'eau au moulin, faire un trou à la nuit, tirer d'un sac deux moutons, joüer de la harpe, griveler, grapiller, plumer la poule sans crier, sophistiquer, frelatter, faire du bien d'autruy large courroye, donner à manger à la pie, mettre de la paille en ses souliers, plier la toilette, alliage, corvée, monopole* (pp. 26, 29).

It is evident that, for D'Assoucy, his lack of luck with cards represents some sort of a "qui perd, gagne" situation, and the cardsharp's remarks provide a clue to understanding just what he feels he gains. By losing when he gambles, D'Assoucy proves that he is not like the rest of men, who, as the swindler teaches him, are all thieves, from the cradle to the grave. With this shift in roles, from wearer of masks to victim of masks, he is, paradoxically, able to maintain his status as an outsider and to make that category even more exclusive.

The total isolation reached by the compulsive gambler is a situation not found outside the *Page* and the *Avantures*. The only other comparable vision of solitude is found in Cyrano's two voyages. Here the reduction of human faculties and rights inherent in the notion of victimization is pushed to its limit to create what might be termed a burlesque variant on the images of otherness—Dyrcona confined not to a prison cell but to a cage, as when he is taken to be either a monkey or a bird. He has barely arrived on the moon when the narrator is classified as "la femelle du petit animal de la reine" and is imprisoned in the same cage as his male, so they can reproduce (p. 55). His male turns out to be a freethinking Spaniard who left the earth for the moon because "il n'avait pu trouver un seul pays où l'imagination même fut en liberté" (p. 66). He is able to explain to the narrator why he has been confined to a cage. When the Spaniard arrived on the moon, he was immediately taken for a monkey, since on the moon monkeys are dressed "à l'espagnole." The lunar judges maintain this opinion, so the next creature they see who looks like the Spaniard is simply placed in the same category, even though he is not dressed like their monkeys. (Why they are so certain the narrator is a female rather than a second male is never explained.) In another phase of his new life as a monkey, the narrator temporarily becomes the property of a "bateleur" charged with his training: "Il m'instruisait à faire le godenot, à passer des culbutes, à figurer des grimaces" (p. 55). Once his act has been perfected, he is taken out to entertain the crowds, and, like a true organ grinder's monkey, is obliged to keep performing, or be punished if he is not active enough to keep his audience amused: "Il se remit de plus belle à tirer ma corde pour me faire sauter, jusqu'à ce que les spectateurs étant souls de rire et d'assurer que j'avais presque autant d'esprit que les bêtes de leur pays" (p. 59).

When the narrator fails to become pregnant, and when, contrary to all their experience with monkeys, he is able to master their "human" language, the lunar experts revise their initial opinion and reclassify him as a "perroquet plumé." This decision at least allows them to keep him in a cage, but does necessitate new training, in the hope of making a proper bird out of the unsuccessful monkey: "Là tous les jours l'oiseleur de la Reine prenait le soin de me venir siffler la langue comme on fait ici aux sansonnets" (p. 74). When this method also fails, the narrator is given a final examination, which determines that he is "possible quelque espèce d'autruche" (p. 75).

These problems of taxonomy continue to plague Dyrcona on the sun, and even reach new heights of complexity there. He may have looked like a bird to his lunar evaluators, but on the sun, when such a resemblance could save his life, he does not stand a chance of passing for one. There, Dyrcona is put on trial by angry birds who accuse him of being a human and therefore a representative of their most hated race. In an effort to establish his (false) innocence, Dyrcona replies to their accusation by trying to play on the identity found for him on the moon: "Quant à ce qui concernoit mon espèce, que je n'estois point Homme comme ils se le figuroient mais Singe; que des hommes m'avoient enlevé au berceau fort jeune et nourry parmi eux" (p. 151).[25] Dyrcona's solar accusers have more evolved methods than their lunar counterparts, so they are able to unmask him very quickly. In the course of his trial, they explain:

> Nous avons beau sauter, marcher, piroüter et inventer en sa présence cent tours de passe par lesquels nous pretendions l'émouvoir à faire de mesme, selon la coutume des Singes. Or quoy qu'il euste esté nourry parmi les Hommes, comme le Singe est toujours Singe, nous soutenons qu'il n'eût pas esté en sa puissance de s'abstenir de contrefaire nos singeries (p. 152).

The birds' account of their unmasking of Dyrcona reveals a possible explanation of his desire to adopt this role. The monkey could be described as the very principle of otherness masked as sameness. For the spectators who observe him, a monkey exists as a monkey only insofar as he is able to eliminate any personal element in his behavior, in order to imitate, "singer," his audience. Furthermore, this imitation cannot stop: "Un Singe est toujours Singe." It can be said that a monkey, like a mirror, has no function, no life, without an audience before it. I imitate, therefore I am (not). The monkey is successful in amusing his audience because he can make himself look like them, while at the same time retaining the difference that leaves them free to indulge in "safe" laughter at this resemblance. The monkey may look like a "little man,"[26] but the spectators remain calm, safe with the security of their superiority to this creature whose similarity might seem frightening were it not defused by his ridiculousness.

Describing a libertine hero as a monkey or a bird (who can imitate man's voice and language) might seem a sad commentary on the reduction of his individuality to the series of masks imposed on him both by his enemies and by himself. He is denounced (unmasked) so often that in the long run there is nothing left behind the masks. But, like D'Assoucy's notion of the "supreme victim," the image of the monkey may also be viewed in a more positive light—at least, that is, from the libertine's particular vantage point. To be a monkey is also to be safe from denunciation. A monkey is only a reflection of what he sees, and that reflection is constantly changing and therefore impossible to pin down. The demon of Socrates explains why this is an image of power for the libertine when he lets the narrator in on Campanella's secret weapon:[27] "Ce fut moi qui l'avisai, pendant qu'il était à l'Inquisition à Rome, de styler son visage et son corps aux grimaces et aux postures ordinaires de ceux dont il avait besoin de connaître l'intérieur afin d'exciter chez soi par une même assiette les pensées que cette même situation avait appelées dans ses adversaires, parce qu'ainsi il ménagerait mieux leur âme quand il la connaîtrait" (p. 56).

The man/monkey can control his alienation—by maintaining it at all times. Furthermore, the man may play monkey, but he remains man. His resemblance to his public is, therefore, more frightening, and their laughter less safe. D'Assoucy, in the *Combat de Cirano de Bergerac avec le singe de Brioché*, describes the consequences of a performance by a marionnette troupe in a Swiss village that had never before witnessed this type of imitation: "Le peuple brule-sorcier . . . dénonça Brioché aux Magistrats. Des témoins attestoient avoir oüy jargonner, parlementer, et deviser de petites figures qui ne pouvoient être que des diables."[28] It is the diabolical power sensed in both the marionnettes and in Francion's monkey that transcends the absurdity of this vision of the libertine hero to link it to the more public masks of otherness.

The libertine hero as monkey is also the ultimate in otherness because he, like the loser, seeks uniqueness in difference. No one can be more other than the perfect monkey, who changes faces every second. I do not use the adjective "perfect" lightly here, because it is precisely the notion of perfection that presents the only obstacle to the positive valorization of these two images of otherness. Both of them are based on the premise that the hero as loser or monkey is not like the rest of men. Even in these apparently ridiculous situations, he is worthy of sympathy because he alone is pure, he alone is always a victim, never a victimizer. As soon, however, as anyone else portrays himself in these roles, the spell is broken. The hero can no longer be different from the rest of men, only different from most men. He is no longer the victim of all other men so united in their persecution of him that they share the same face, but simply the victim of almost all men— with the few exceptions of those who are neither like the rest of men nor really exactly like him. In short, such heroes are like the phoenix described in the *Estats et empires*—there is room on any given planet for only one of them at any given time.

D'Assoucy illustrates perfectly both the functioning of this principle and its application to the libertines' transformation of autobiography. Curiously enough, he chooses as his model not himself but Cyrano. In the *Combat de Cirano de Bergerac avec le singe de Brioché*, he imagines Cyrano's "murder" of a monkey he describes as the "presqu'homme des marionnettes." In order to remain unique, Cyrano is obliged to kill the other who is like him, the other who, in clothes similar to his, entertains the crowd with swashbuckling sword thrusts performed with a miniature sword in a display reminiscent of Cyrano's own simian antics. Brioché's monkey threatens the very foundations of Cyrano's act. If he allows himself to be out-monkeyed by a monkey, he will afterward be classified, no longer as fabulous, fantastic, or mad, but simply as a common buffoon. He must use his life-size weapon to impale this miniature version of himself brandishing an equally miniature sword, in order to avoid becoming one of a series—a Quaker Oats' man looking at himself looking at himself, and so on.

Another incident from Cyrano's apocryphal biography illustrates this desire for uniqueness in his particular brand of flamboyant behavior. It is widely chronicled that Cyrano, after a quarrel with the actor Montfleury, forbid him to act for a month. When, arriving at the theater a few days later, he caught him in the act, Cyrano threatened the frightened actor with his ever-present sword, until he ran trembling from the stage. In his public letter "Contre le gras Montfleury, mauvais auteur et comédien," Cyrano pretends that his persecution was motivated only by Montfleury's obesity and the poor quality of his acting. These reasons are certainly valid, but they must not be allowed to distract attention from the fact that chasing his rivals in the act of imitating others from the stage where they perform is an active fantasy for Cyrano. He defends the image of the libertine as permanent actor, as one who literally takes his theater to the streets. This eternal other with his personal vision of living theater rejects not only the potential rival he sees in the actor but also the integrated otherness that is the theater.

3. SOLITARY CONFINEMENT

Obviously, this obsessive desire for uniqueness in their victimization, this quest for perfect difference, would make peaceful coexistence within any type of society a highly problematic venture for the libertines. The ostracizing that was the lot of all freethinkers of their day initially fostered their withdrawal into circles whose access was limited to those who shared certain beliefs. In the end, however, the libertine cooperation of the Gassendi years was broken down by paranoia and a desire for self-punishment. Solidarity disintegrated into slander, as each member of the group wanted to be unique in his alienation. Already alienated from society, the last survivors of the group originally united under Gassendi borrowed tactics learned from official repression and used them until they succeeded in alienating themselves from each other. Their refusal to live with the concept of sameness even on so small a scale led them to a new form of prison, the *chambre obscure* in the sense in which Rousseau employs the term, that is, a state of isolation so advanced that "I" is the only figure of sameness[29] admitted: "que chacun puisse connoitre soi et un autre, et cet autre ce sera moi. . . . Je vais travailler pour ainsi dire dans la chambre obscure."[30]

"Deffiez-vous generallement de tout le monde, et surtout de vos plus grands amis; car, quoyque tous les amis ne soient pas perfides, les grands coups ne se font jamais que par les grands amis" (p. 38). The cardsharp with a thousand faces shares these words of personal wisdom with D'Assoucy, and thereby provides him with what is ultimately the best piece of advice in any libertine text. A comparison developed by Claude Lévi-Strauss in *Tristes tropiques* provides a means of distinguishing this persecution from within the ranks of the initiate from its external counterpart. Our societies practice the isolation of those they call possessed, their expulsion, or what Lévi-Strauss calls "anthropémie." To these he opposes the so-called "sociétés anthropophages" who "voient dans l'absorption de certains individus, détenteurs de forces redoutables, le seul moyen de neutraliser celles-ci et même de les mettre à profit."[31] External persecution attempts to deal with the libertines by means of expulsion, but the persecution that comes from within uses tactics that could better be qualified as "anthropophages." In a so-called "société anthropophage," the dead possessor of secrets is consumed, so that his secrets can be understood. On the moon, as the narrator of *L'Autre Monde* learns, a philosopher passes on his secrets to his disciples by calling them to his deathbed, in order to have them eat his flesh and drink his blood just after his death, and then immediately make love[32] so that in the babies produced while they are nourished with his body, "ils soient comme assurés que c'est leur ami qui revit" (p. 107).[33]

The positive connotations of this form of cannibalism stressed by both Lévi-Strauss and Cyrano disappear, however, in its "practical" libertine application. When, in an effort to preserve the purity of their sense of victimization, the libertines begin to attack each other, they engage in a form of verbal cannibalism. Once they become aware of the importance of uniqueness for all the images they seek to present, they begin to perceive each other as rivals. They attempt to "neutralize" their rivals by devouring their reputations, and eventually their identities, in the hope of gaining unique access to the secrets they possess. In his description of Chapelle and Bachaumont's attacks, D'Assoucy prefigures Lévi-Strauss's terminology: "Ils ont enrichi leurs écrits de l'honneur d'autruy, plus cruels que . . . les Antropophages" (p. 147).

The principal means they employ to neutralize each other is an accusation as explosive as any of those already discussed here, that of homosexuality. Chapelle first throws it out against D'Assoucy, who returns the favor by increasing the number of those implicated. Both the meaning and the intentions of the relevant passages are absolutely clear, making the silence of the majority of critics on this subject difficult to interpret as anything but an attempt to suppress the undesirable. Even those who dare mention the unmentionable usually do so in such a veiled manner that the effects of its intrusion are muted. Colombey, for example, defends D'Assoucy so completely that he does not feel it necessary to pronounce the name of the accusation: "Le pauvre musicien/poète avait le tort de marcher flanqué de deux jeunes garçons d'allure équivoque, et qui, en réalité, n'étaient que des pages de musique chargés de prêter la fraîcheur de leur voix aux airs que leur maître composait" (p. v). Would that it were so easy to dismiss the pages, especially Pierrotin, and the episodes in which they are evoked! Or that it were possible to agree with Neubert's allegation that D'Assoucy tries to cover up the whole unpleasant situation as quickly as possible[34]—or even that the question of libertine homosexuality could be suspended with a question mark: "Tous ces hommes avaient-ils donc cela de commun d'être peu capable d'amour?"[35]

Only Démoris faces up to the weight of the issue, at least as far as D'Assoucy is concerned. He categorically denies the existence of an attempted cover-up, and stresses the invitation to scandal presented by the text: "Le récit . . . n'ébauche pas l'ombre d'une justification. . . . D'Assoucy . . . consacre la plus grande partie de son récit à décrire avec application les rapports de nature

assez évidemment passionnelle, qui le lient au page."[36] Even Démoris does not go beyond this first step to examine the wider
implications of this question, both for the *Avantures* and for other libertine texts as well.

It cannot be denied that the libertine text presents a sexuality
that can only be termed unusual from a novelistic point of view, if
not frankly marginal. There is no need to turn to Freudian interpretations, such as gambling as masturbation, in order to document this point. One may simply remark, along with Adam, that
there are indeed few women in these texts, and further show that,
when they portray a figure of desire, it is rarely a woman and more
often a "bel adolescent."[37] This is most evident in *L'Autre Monde*,
where, in the list of figures who serve as guides for the narrator,
maleness is privileged over femaleness, youth over age, and daring over traditional wisdom: the archangel guarding paradise
with his "épée flamboyante," "le fils de l'hôte," and even the demon of Socrates, who first appears to the narrator as an old man,
but soon afterward slips into the body of an adolescent. In the
majority of libertine texts, woman is not only removed from her
pedestal but also on many occasions demoted to a negative role.
D'Assoucy is driven out of Montpellier by hordes of outraged
women. The page is put on trial by his mistress's mother, and
when Dyrcona goes on trial on the sun, the birds who attack him
most violently are all female ("Je repondis à mon accusatrice" [p.
151]).

This paranoid vision of women may be linked to the sexual
implications of the libertine fascination with alchemy. As Bachelard explains in *La Psychanalyse du feu*, "toute l'Alchimie était
traversée par une immense rêverie sexuelle, par une rêverie de
richesse et de rajeunissement, par une rêverie de puissance." The
alchemist's "rêverie de puissance" is exceptional not only for its
intensity but even more so, as Bachelard goes on to explain, for its
self-reflexiveness. Alchemy upholds an absolute distinction between a principle of male fire and that of a female one. It maintains a "valorisation nettement prédominante du feu masculin,"
which has definite consequences for the composition of its universe: "Il ne faut pas oublier que l'alchimie est uniquement une
science d'hommes, de célibataires, d'hommes sans femme, d'in-
itiés retranchés de la communauté humaine au profit d'une so-

ciété masculine. Elle ne reçoit pas directement les influences de la rêverie féminine. Sa doctrine du feu est donc fortement polarisée par des désirs inassouvis."[38]

If I make these observations about the sexuality portrayed in the libertine texts, it is certainly not because I want to draw conclusions about the sexual preferences of either their heroes or their authors. This question seems no more relevant to me than to decide whether or not they were sorcerers—another specter of otherness that ultimately has its origin within the group itself. The texts themselves add homosexuality to their list of deviations. I would like to confront this accusation in order to evaluate its importance in the schema of difference they trace and, at the same time, to see if it can be used to establish a broader definition of otherness.

The homosexual rejects the other in the form of the female, and thereby chooses for himself a marginal status. If he continues his rejection of others to include all those not part of a very exclusive group, then the element of narcissism in this sexual inversion becomes flagrant. A pronounced incestuous quality greatly limits the scope of the prefix "homo-" in the homo-sexual/intellectual bonds that originally unite these libertines. This notion of incest could provide an explanation for the eventual dissolution of these seemingly stable bonds. When D'Assoucy begins what is quite evidently, in Démoris's terms, some sort of "passionate relationship" with an outsider, he breaks out of this established pattern. In so doing, he destroys its circle of power, which must remain airtight in order to function properly. For this infringement of the rules governing their isolation, for this attempt to let an outsider in on their secrets, D'Assoucy, like any member of a secret society in similar circumstances, must be punished. Chapelle's attack is an example of brutal slander, but it also an attempt to ostracize a partner who merits punishment.

The element of complicity involved in these denunciations cannot be properly situated without running the risk of appearing to indulge in what Démoris refers to as "quelque secrète jubilation dans cette représentation du scandale,"[39] that is, without quoting at some length from the passages involved. Chapelle describes with an exceptional dose of glee the high/low point of D'Assoucy's *Avantures*, his sudden departure from Montpellier. In his account of the incident, D'Assoucy admits only to his persecution at

the hands of certain "femmes galantes" who "m'appelloient hérétique, non en fait de religion, mais en fait d'amour" (p. 133), and
who succeed in having him briefly imprisoned. He describes no
mob scenes, and claims to have left the city, though sooner than
planned, nevertheless of his own free will.

Chapelle's version, the first to appear in print, concentrates on
precisely those "colorful" moments omitted by D'Assoucy. He
especially relishes the description of the women's riot:

> Là d'hommes on voyoit fort peu;
> Cent mille femmes animées,
> Toutes de colère enflammées,
> Accouroient en foule en ce lieu
> Avec des torches allumées.

> Elles écumoient toutes de rage, et jamais on n'a rien vu de si
> terrible. Les unes disoient que c'était trop peu de le bruler; et les
> autres, qu'il falloit l'écorcher vif auparavant, et toutes, que, si la
> justice le leur vouloit livrer, elles inventeroit de nouveaux suppli-
> ces pour le tourmenter (p. 84).

In Chapelle's description, D'Assoucy's punishment is rig-
orously parallel to that reserved for atheists. But, whereas that
punishment was essentially a case of men being punished by men,
the former concentrates on a much rarer type of revolt, of women
against men, or rather, against a man. Given the nature of the
allegations, this seems more appropriate, but it is also more ter-
rifying because so unusual. One thinks of Dumas's *Ange Pitou*,
in which Gilbert repeatedly warns the king and queen that the
day the women join the Revolution is the day it will become
serious.

Chapelle closes his description of the Montpellier expulsion by
evoking D'Assoucy slinking out of town, a broken man (p. 85).
This image of D'Assoucy recurs to dominate the *Voyage*'s final
scene. Chapelle recognizes his former friend, despite the fact that
he is trying to hide behind his cloak, which he has pulled up over
his face. Rather than respecting his embarrassment, Chapelle refuses to let D'Assoucy off the hook, and chooses just this moment
to press him for more information on his relationship with
Pierrotin:

> "Ce petit garçon qui vous suit
> Et qui derrière vous se glisse,

> Que sait-il? En quel exercise,
> En quel art l'avez-vous instruit?"
> "Il sait tout, dit-il. S'il vous duit,
> Il est bien à votre service."

(Pp. 97–98)

Although he simply thanks D'Assoucy for his offer, declines it, and takes his leave of him, the very fact that Chapelle chooses to mention this proposal provides a basis for the accusation of complicity D'Assoucy will level at him. In connection with this issue, a rather curious passage from the *Voyage* comes to mind. Before the Montpellier incident, Chapelle evokes in some detail his pleasant memories of Agen and his stay there. Agen is described as a city of enchanting women who have already succeeded in holding prisoner ("arrêter") for long periods of time a number of their (Chapelle and Bachaumont's) friends, among them a certain d'Ortis, who arranges a dinner to introduce them to these dangerous beauties. They realize that no one has escaped these women before, without at least leaving his heart "pour ôtage d'un prompt retour."

> Ainsi donc qu'avoient fait les autres,
> Il fallut y laisser les nôtres.
> Là tous deux ils furent pris;
> Mais, n'en déplaise à tant de belles,
> Ce fut par l'aimable d'Ortis
> . . . .

Elles ne lui envièrent point cette conquête, et, nous jugeant apparemment très infirmes, elles ne daignèrent point employer le moindre de leurs charmes pour nous retenir (pp. 62–63).

The passage can of course be read simply as a declaration of friendship and loyalty, but its use of a love vocabulary makes this unclear and draws attention to this friendship in a rather suspicious manner. Without trying to continue D'Assoucy's habit of throwing out accusations, I would simply like to point out that it seems imprudent for anyone trying to denounce a friend's homosexuality to dwell on an incident that leaves him open to the same suspicion.

Prudence does not dominate D'Assoucy's response to Chapelle's slander either, but by this stage the stakes are slightly al-

tered. D'Assoucy so relishes an accusation that he is constitution-
ally incapable of categorical denials. The question is no longer
whether or not the accusation is a just one but whether or not it
can be given a broader application. As a result, he throws Chapelle's words right back in his face, explaining that firsthand
knowledge leaves Chapelle well placed to judge D'Assoucy's preferences.[40] In another of his so-called defenses against Chapelle's
attacks, he implicates Cyrano in the affair, even though his name
is never mentioned by Chapelle. When D'Assoucy explains that
the women of Montpellier are attacking him because of the
"longues habitudes que j'avois eues avec C., feu D.B." (p. 133), he
does nothing to clear his own name, and merely succeeds in gra-
tuitously complicating the matter.

It seems quite evident from D'Assoucy's handling of this issue,
and reasonably evident from Chapelle's, that homosexuality is
the most dangerous accusation of otherness for the libertines, the
one they were least willing simply to laugh off. They can talk as
much as they please about being sorcerers, or madmen, or monkeys, but they run no risk of being taken seriously. At most, the
metaphorical implications of these figures will be considered.
But, when from within the circle of initiates the figure of the homosexual is added to the family of exiles, the opposite is true. In
this case, it is highly probable that the question will be given a
completely literal interpretation—hence the silence of subsequent
commentators afraid to take sides in what they feel to be the only
issue: whether or not the libertines really were homosexuals.

Since the question of homosexuality is generally avoided because of this dominance of the literal, the possibility of its figurative manifestations is, of course, never even evoked. Yet, if homosexuality, the category of difference adopted by the libertines for
themselves and never chosen for them by anyone from outside, is
viewed in broader terms, it can deepen our understanding of the
libertine compulsion to be other. In a study entitled "The Differ-
ing Seed: Dante's Brunetto Latini," Eugene Vance develops just
such a wider definition of homosexuality. In an attempt to understand the place Dante assigns Brunetto in hell with the sodomists,
Vance concludes:

> If sodomy was considered to be a sin against nature, the concept of
> "nature" over and against which sodomy was believed to consti-

tute a class of corruptive behaviour had become such a broad
ideological construct by Dante's time that sodomy could now
easily be seen as but one member of a whole family of more subtle
—and for poets, perhaps, more interesting—perversions. . . .
In this case, the relationship is embodied above all in the order
and the process of language.[41]

With the libertines, as with Brunetto Latini, the question of
homosexuality ultimately leads back once again not only to prison but also to the book. This time, however, I am not referring to
the "concrete" object from which the text originates, or in which
the attacks culminate, but, more basically, to the tool manipulated by the *héros écrivant*, language. Vance discusses the reasons
why, for Dante, Brunetto's language could be described as artificial, unnatural, perverted. Homosexuality can be read as a metaphor for linguistic "perversion," and certainly no other writers in
seventeenth-century France produced more unnatural language
than the libertines. They stripped their language as much as possible of names and other "natural" signs of origin, signs that attempt to perpetuate (the myth of) the transparency of language.
For the genealogical transparency that is the hallmark of so-
called natural language, they substitute a dialect largely of their
own creation, the burlesque. The burlesque is perhaps the most
extreme manifestation of linguistic self-consciousness. Constantly calling attention to its verbal functioning, it tries to make linguistic play more important than referential content. Their linguistic creativity earns the libertine writers an additional ostracizing. Their books are not only referred to as poorly constructed
treatments of unworthy themes, but they also gain the literary
establishment's scorn because of their medium of expression.

The libertines choose to reject the codes of literary sameness
advanced in their day, and to create instead their own language of
otherness, based on a reevaluation of an important term in the
contemporary critical vocabulary, the sublime. In this new definition, "sublime" means simply what is most imaginative rather
than what is most elevated or lofty or what inspires veneration or
awe—what is able to elevate the mind from the base to the noble,
as it was interpreted in dominant theories. Not that the idea of
elevation is absent from the libertine definition of the sublime.

Cyrano describes the imagination as "notre imagination, plus chaude que les autres facultés de l'âme" (*L'Autre Monde*, p. 100), and attributes to it the ability to liberate the lightest particles from the weight of matter, to vaporize, to produce "fièvres chaudes" (p. 32). The difference between their goals denounces the distance between the two conceptions: the proponent of Classicism seeks to extract the beautiful while leaving the vile behind, and to lift the mind from the disorder of base ideas to the calm of noble aspirations. The libertine makes no such distinctions between beautiful and nonbeautiful, and even scorns harmony in favor of the fiery disorder of thought exploding simultaneously in multiple directions.

It is obvious that the libertines are, for once, simply being faithful to origin. They are concerned not with the vile but the vial, since they do not forget that "sublime" is tied to the alchemists' *sublimatio*, sublimation, defined by Furetière as "action par laquelle on fait élever dans un vaisseau par le moyen du feu, les plus seches, les plus subtiles parties d'un corps." Just as the page watches his alchemist extract liquid gold from a solid,[42] so the libertines hope to replace the alchemist's fire with that of the imagination, and thereby to explore "l'alchimie du verbe." Paradoxically, a system like the burlesque, which at the time of its creation was harshly criticized for its vulgarity, for its Rabelaisian insistence on bodily functions, proves with its use of sublimation that the opposite is true. Boileau and its other detractors were perhaps so violent in their attacks on the burlesque because they somehow sensed, and were threatened by, the sameness beneath the difference. The burlesque is not, as everyone said, a product of a too close contact with nature but a pure product of sublimation in the sense of a deflection of vital, sexual energy.[43] "Sublimation is the use made of bodily energy by a soul which sets itself apart from the body," in Norman O. Brown's definition.[44] After all, Cyrano exchanged the sword for the pen[45]—he never did succeed in combining their use as he does in Rostand's fairy tale. There is no naming in these texts, since there can be no procreation.

The libertine heroes are alienated from their bodies. Repeatedly, they view them as objects with an independent existence, as though projected outside of them by the action of a *camera luci-*

da. As he approaches the sun, Dyrcona's body becomes transparent, until he is able to perceive his so-called vital organs as foreign to him:

> J'estois devenu diaphane . . . aucun endroit, ny de ma chair, ny de mes os, ny de mes entrailles, quoy que transparents n'avoit perdu sa couleur naturelle; au contraire, mes poulmons conservoient encor sous un rouge incarnat leur mole délicatesse; mon coeur toujours vermeil balançoit aisément entre le sistolle et le diastole; mon foye sembloit brûler dans un pourpre de feu, et cuisant l'air que je respirois continuoit la circulation du sang; enfin je me voyois, me touchois, me sentois le mesme, et si pourtant je ne l'estois plus (pp. 134–35).

A similar image of alienation from the life-sustaining parts of his body occurs in Francion's dream, when Valentin rips a hole in Francion's stomach with his cuckold's horns: "Je me mis à contempler mes boyaux et tout ce qui estoit aupres d'eux de plus secret. Je les tiray hors de leur place et eus la curiosité de les mesurer avecque mes mains" (p. 152).

The source of this alienation, of this impotence, is explained in the scene of Dyrcona's seizure outside Toulouse by a man who might be described as a living book: "Une longue robe tissue de feuillets d'un livre de plain-chant le couvroit jusqu'aux ongles et son visage estoit caché d'une carte où l'on avoit écrit: l'*In principio*" (p. 107). As a result of this capture, Dyrcona is forced to become mute.[46] When the words missing from his captor's name tag are supplied, however, the result is the genealogy not only of the world but also of his impotence. *In principio erat verbum*: the libertine hero is castrated by the text, by the text that is the story of his alienation (castration, unnaming) by society. He is not only outside his body but outside language as well.

The libertine hero must endure this state of self-alienation in order to produce/find the language to describe the story of his otherness. The texts suggest different metaphors to characterize the process by which sublimation results in the (re)production of the book. The *Estats et empires* evokes on two occasions the libertine dream of a self-enclosed procreation "machine," in describing the birth of the first hermaphrodite (pp. 172–73), and in defining a mysterious bird with whom the narrator converses: "Le Phénix est hermaphrodite." When the Phoenix describes the conditions for his existence, it becomes clear why he is a key figure in libertine mythology. There is only one Phoenix at a time in a given world. Each lives for a hundred years longing for the sun, at the end of which he lays a single egg, before setting the fire in which his body is consumed (p. 149). This scenario is evidently a libertine utopia. It offers a guarantee of uniqueness, with no one else of your race to fear, and no need for anyone else at any point in the life cycle. The Phoenix can perform all functions and still reach the sun, the ultimate alchemist's fire and the center of intellectual freedom.

In this context, the identification of the narrator in *L'Autre Monde* as the "femelle du petit animal de la reine" seems less startling. After all, the narrator himself says in the work's opening sentences that he is "gros de mille définitions de lune, dont je ne pouvois accoucher" (p. 31). He is pregnant with definitions, with words, with the knowledge that will enable him to create the book that seeks to define the moon's plurality ("mille définitions de lune"), that seeks to re-create/procreate plurality. The narrator is also pregnant with identities, as the other occurrence of the adjective "gros" in Cyrano's novels makes clear. This time, his pregnancy is visible to an outsider. The Phoenix remarks to Dyrcona: "Je voy bien que vous estes gros d'apprendre qui je suis" (p. 148).[47] The narrator is pregnant with definitions and with an identity. The answer to the Phoenix's question, "Who am I?", is obviously "mille définitions de lune." His identity, and Dyrcona's, are in the book.

This identification of the libertine with his book provides the key to D'Assoucy's use of *anthropophage*. He explains that Chapelle and his book exist only because he stole D'Assoucy's life and reputation: "vous qui n'avez presque de nom que ce que vostre médisance et mes disgraces vous ont acquis" (p. 183), and, furthermore, that he stole them only to be able to hand D'Assoucy over to the rabble to be eaten alive: "Il ne faut pas s'étonner si la canaille, qui est toujours affamée de poison, a dévoré ce libelle et s'en lèche encore les doigts avec d'autant plus d'avidité, qu'elle trouve dans ces sortes d'ouvrages des alimens plus conformes à sa nature" (p. 202). This is the essential difference between the way the libertines persecute each other and the way they are persecuted from the outside. They are unable to hide from each other what is perhaps the ultimate libertine secret: even though they remain outside the language that castrates them, it remains, nevertheless, the only source of identity they can accept.

To steal their language is, therefore, to steal the only thing they accept as belonging to them, to steal what they are protecting behind all the masks. Since, as D'Assoucy's cardsharp says, all men are thieves, even poets, and especially your best friend, the situation is particularly critical if your best friend happens to be a poet. For the poet alone can steal from the libertine that last bit of otherness accepted as sameness and, in so doing, make it overtly other, thereby leaving the circle of alienation absolutely airtight. Thus, the libertines' accusations of plagiarism are a sort of desperate fight for life. Because of the particular nature of the libertine writer's relationship to his text, it is not surprising that he almost never goes outside his immediate circle to find suspects. Cyrano turns out public letters with accusations of plagiarism against half of the writers he knows—"Contre La Mothe, brigand de pensées," "Contre Chapelle, brigand de pensées," "Contre Soucidas." D'Assoucy claims that Cyrano and Chapelle owe their success to plagiarism, and they all agree that it would be better to be threatened by "le singe de Brioché" than to have no more originality than D'Assoucy, commonly known as "le singe de Scarron."[48] When the libertine's language is copied, his mask of protective bravado has outlived its usefulness.

The libertine texts are centered around a conflict between the liveliness, the verve, and the vitality usually associated with the so-called "élément gaulois" in the French literary tradition, and the sense of physical and verbal alienation I have been describing here—in other words, a conflict between the mask and what lies behind it. Nowhere is this conflict so clear as in what is probably the best known "morceau choisi" from any libertine text, Francion's controversial dream. Francion's account of his imaginary exploits is so baroquely rich in an apparently joyful celebration of the body and its functions (with a heavy emphasis on the sexual and the excremental) that it is usually treated as an especially glorious "réminscence rabelaisienne," to borrow an expression from Wolfgang Leiner.[49] This explosive text makes an extreme use of paratactical narration, which is, after all, as the marquis de Cussan explains in the *Estats et empires*'s own oneiric section, the logic of dreams: "un pot pourri de toutes les choses à quoy nous avons pensé en veillant . . . un assemblage d'espèces confuses, que la fantaisie qui dans le sommeil n'est plus guidée par la Raison nous présente sans ordre" (p. 107). Francion justifies the wildness of his narrative at the outset by explaining to his listener, the "Gentil-homme Bourguignon," that "tous les songes ne se font ainsy qu'à bastons rompus" (p. 141). He then proceeds, under the cover of these rapid dislocations, to indulge in an astounding physical explicitness.

It is indeed tempting to be carried away by this bravado performance, to allow oneself to be dazzled to the point of never peeking behind the heavy curtain of wild playfulness. Leiner is among the few critics to penetrate to the level of the dream's less positive implications:

> Le rêve de Francion est inquiétant. Il n'y est question que d'amour non récompensé, de projets et de plans traversés, de rencontres avec des monstres et avec des êtres bizarres, souvent méchants et grossiers. Cet univers où les dieux et les êtres sont hostiles au rêveur nous révèle l'inquiétude et l'angoisse du héros. Il est seul dans sa nacelle, entouré d'éléments ennemis, ne disposant que de son ingéniosité pour se maintenir dans un monde dangereux.

Leiner unmasks the dissimulation of the dream's baroque cover-up, but in his discussion of its disquieting aspects, he remains too close to the surface. Not only does "le rêve exprime parfaitement bien l'insatisfaction et la frustration que Francion expérimente dans la vie 'réelle,' " especially with regard to "les rapports de Francion avec la femme,"[50] but it goes far beyond the hero's personal dissatisfactions to broach wider-reaching and more unsettling problems. Leiner stresses, quite convincingly, both the internal coherence of the dream sequence and its links with the novel as a whole, thus joining forces with such critics as Serroy and Garavini in their attempt to trace the patterns of unity in *Francion*'s wild profusion.[51] Although I agree that Francion's dream is no *hors d'oeuvre*, and that many of its themes find echoes elsewhere in the novel, I nevertheless contend that it is wrong not to insist on the exceptional status that it enjoys. Even in a novelistic space as free as that of the first edition of *Francion*, it is impossible not to feel that the dream possesses a narrative and thematic uniqueness. Of all the libertine novels, *Francion* is generally the most hopeful regarding the success and the power of the libertine experience, and its hero rarely finds himself a victim of persecution. The dream sequence belies such optimism, and, in its powerful expression of the most frightening manifestations of alienation already discussed here, can be said to prefigure the eventual dissolution of the libertine movement.

I have already quoted the passage in which Francion, his stomach ripped open, is able to contemplate his organs, a moment of alienation from his body that is far from unique in the course of the dream. In fact, one of its most obsessive recurrent themes is the dismemberment of bodies. Dismemberment is, furthermore, usually linked to an almost infinite multiplication of one bodily part, which results in its total objectification, in an unsettling mechanization of the body. Penises are used as corks (p. 148); an entire temple is filled with vials of a liquor that Francion learns is "les pucellages des femmes" (p. 151); its counterpart is lined with cuckholds' horns (p. 151); Francion even finds himself in a room wallpapered "de jeunes tetons collez ensemble deux à deux, qui estoient comme des balons, balons sur lesquels je me plus longtemps a me rouler" (p. 149). When treated in this Busby Berkeley fashion, breasts become balloons, and all members, completely cut off from their original function, are no more than toys. The most severe of these instances of dismemberment carries this tendency to a frightening extreme. A woman has forced Francion to drink urine, so he slaps her:

> Son corps tomba par pieces. D'un costé estoit la teste, d'un autre les bras, un peu plus loing estoient les cuisses: bref tout estoit divisé: et ce qui me sembla esmerveillable, c'est que la pluspart de tous ces membres ne laisserent pas peu apres de faire leurs offices. Les jambes se promenoient par la caverne, les bras me venoient frapper, la teste me faisoit des grimasses, et la langue me chantoit injures (p. 149).

He tries to put her back together, "mais sa langue s'escria que je n'avois pas pris ses tetons mesmes et que ceux que j'avois mis en son corps estoient d'autres que j'avois ramassés emmy la caverne" (pp. 149–50). Here, the alienation is so complete that the parts/toys are no longer in the control of either their rightful owner or of Francion, but have a sort of mechanized life of their own.

The most notorious form of dismemberment, castration, is also present in the dream, and becomes more threatening as the sequence progresses. The opening scene takes place on a lake when it is raining sausages and cucumbers. A nude Francion uses his penis as a cork to stop up a hole in the *cuve* in which he is floating, and is thus able to grab at this phallic manna. His invention is not as successful for his companions on the lake: "Leur pauvre piece estoit si menuë qu'au lieu de bondon, elle n'eust pu servir que de fausser: De sorte qu'ils furent pitoyablement noyez." The specter of impotence is evoked here, although it apparently presents no immediate threat to Francion himself, who reacts with character-istic bravado: "Moy qui ne craignois pas que ce malheur m'avint, parce que j'estoy fourny, autant que pas un, de ce qui m'estoit necessaire" (p. 141).

His second encounter with the phenomenon is much more im-mediate. Francion is ordered by a group of monsters to pay hom-age to their king by performing a bizarre ritual. He is given scis-sors with which to cut off a hair growing on the king's stomach, but instead, "je couppay un morceau du membre qui eust servy a la generation d'une infinité de petits diablotins comme leur pere" (p. 146). The progression continues to bring the fear closer and closer to home until, in the last scene of his dream, we pass from the castration of others to the long-expected scene of Francion's own castration. The woman who brings him to see Laurette

> me fit accoire que j'estois aussi impuissans que luy (Valentin) aux combas de l'amour, mais qu'elle avoit des remedes pour me donner de la vigueur. M'ayant donc fait coucher tout de mon long, elle me fourra une baguette dedans le fondement, dont elle fit sortir un bout par la verge. . . . Je vy que la baguette poussa de petites branches chargées de fueilles et peu apres poussa un bouton de fleur incogneue. . . . J'eusse bien voulu sçavoir s'il avoit une odeur qui peust aussi bien contenter le nez, et ne l'en pouvant pas approcher, je couppay sa queue avec mes ongles pour la séparer de la tige. Mais je fus bien estonné de voir que le sang sortit aussi tost par l'endroit où j'avois rompu la plante, et peu apres je commençay de souffrir un peu de mal (p. 153).

Here, in the dream's final image of impotence, the tables have turned. The self-assurance of the *cuve* sequence, when Francion seems convinced that he has no rival in virility, has disappeared. Instead, he finds himself in exactly the same situation as the much ridiculed Valentin (with whom his impotence is compared) in the novel's opening scene—obliged to submit passively to quack treatments. Not only is he demoted from the role of doctor to that of patient, but when he carries out the prescribed treatment, he suffers a fate far worse than Valentin's. Francion, the joyful prankster and great unmasker, supplies the only scene of auto-castration in a libertine text.

The dream reaffirms the link between physical and verbal impotence. Francion begs forgiveness from the monsters for having castrated their king, but they are unable to pardon him because "ils n'avoient point de voix humaine" (p. 146). He himself shares their fate after drinking water from a magic fountain: "Je me retournay vers la Dame pour l'appeller traitresse, mais au lieu d'une voix articulée, il ne sortit de ma bouche qu'un hurlement" (p. 145). He thus announces the situation of Dyrcona, the mute beggar (pretending to be) unable to produce anything more than "un cri non articulé" (*Estats et empires*, p. 114).

Perhaps the most extraordinary scene of this extraordinary narrative evokes simultaneously the form of castration reserved for Vanini and other libertines, the alienating power of the text, and the notion of the libertine hero as a figure outside language:

> Je trouvay un vieillard qui avoit de grandes oreilles et la bouche fermée d'un cadenas qui ne se pouvoit ouvrir que quand l'on faisoit rencontrer en certains endroits quelques lettres qui faisoient ces mots, *il est temps*, lorsqu'on les assembloit. Voyant que l'usage de la parole luy estoit interdit, je luy demanday pourquoy, croyant qu'il me respondroit par signes. Apres qu'il eust mis de certains cornets a ses oreilles pour mieux recevoir ma voix, il me monstra de la main un petit boccage, comme s'il m'eust voulu dire que c'estoit là que je pourrois avoir response de ce que je luy demandois. Quand j'en fus proche, j'ouys un caquet continuel sans voir aucunement ceux qui le faisoient et m'imaginay alors que l'on parloit là pour le vieillard. Il y avoit six arbres au milieu des autres qui au lieu de fueilles avoient des langues menuës attachées aux branches avec des fils de fer fort desliez, si bien qu'un vent impetueux qui souffloit contre les faisoit tousjours jargonner. . . . Un grant geant qui estoit caché à leur ombre, oyant qu'elles me descouvroient ce qu'il avoit de plus secret, tira un grand cimeterre, et ne donna point de repos à son bras qu'il ne les eust toutes abbatuës et tranchées en pieces; encore estoient elles si vives qu'elles se remuoient à terre et taschoient de parler comme auparavant. Mais sa rage eut bien apres plus d'occasion de s'accroistre, parce que passant plus loing il me vit contre un rocher où il cogneut que je lisois un ample recit de tous les mauvais deportemens de sa vie. Il s'ap-

procha pour hacher aussi en pieces ce tesmoin de ses crimes, et fut
bien courroucé de ce que sa lame rejaillissoit contre luy sans avoir
seulement escaillé la pierre (p. 148).

I quote this scene in its entirety, because it provides the most
complete illustration of the fear lodged at the center of the libertine message. In this passage, language is totally alienated from
man, exists only outside him, is a perpetual "other" for him. The
old man is a Tantalus-figure, with his big ears that enable him to
take in all the language of others, while he is unable to produce
any of his own. On his mouth can be formed the words *il est
temps*, which, like the *in principio* sign of Dyrcona's living book,
may be described as a hollow presence, a presence that exists only
to call attention to an absence—in the example from Cyrano, the
suppression of the key words, in the dream, a double suppression.
Like *in principio*, *il est temps* is an incomplete expression. What is
it time for? The logical answer is "to speak," but the man cannot
speak, so *il est temps* is an empty signifier, has no meaning other
than the impossibility or the inadequacy of language.

The old man's language, and the language of all the original
owners of the disembodied tongues, has been reduced to an end-
less, uncontrolled, and uncontrollable babble. Even though it is
impersonal and incomprehensible, this language still remains
dangerous because it retains its secret. More disquieting than ev-
en the images of the body in pieces and out of control presented by
the dream is this vision of language in the form of a frozen
signifier—a tongue—beaten, hacked, and sliced at, yet still continuing to exist as sound without meaning. Language with no function, language that exists only to threaten man and to alienate
him, and that cannot be destroyed by him. Even when driven by
all the strength of his abnormal size, and by all the energy of his
paranoia, the giant cannot destroy written language in the form of
a text with an all-powerful secret, the "ample recit de tous les
mauvais deportemens de sa vie" (p. 148). Clearly, in Francion's
dream, man is no longer either the master or the possessor of
language.

It is this vision that is the unsettling conclusion to the libertine
exploration of alienation. If one accepts the picture painted by the
libertine texts at face value, then they can be read as a cry against
the oppression of a system that admits no difference. Although

such a reading is certainly not false, neither is it complete. When these "originaux" choose to liberate themselves from the limitations of their past by altering their names, and from those of the present by inventing personal histories, they do so in an attempt to transform themselves into human monkeys, who exist only to take on the bodies of the other. They are not strangers to the sensation Starobinski attributes to Stendhal, "l'impatience d'avoir à supporter un corps."[52] They are uncomfortable in their own bodies, so they seek to escape them by creating a public mask so shifting that it can never be pinpointed. Hence the dreams of invisible bodies in *Francion* and the *Estats et empires* and the desire to be able to transport oneself elsewhere simply through the force of imagination, a desire announced in *L'Autre Monde* and made explicit in a passage of the *Estats et empires* that betrays the limits of Cyrano's confidence. Not only can men use their imaginations to move themselves but, like spirits, they can alter their bodies, take on any form they wish: "Cippus, roy d'Italie, qui pour avoir assisté à un combat de taureaux et avoir eu toute la nuit son imagination occupée à des cornes, trouva son front cornu le lendemain; Gallus Vitius qui banda son âme et l'excita si vigoureusement à concevoir l'essence de la folie, qu'ayant donné à sa matière par un effort d'imagination les mesmes mouvemens que cette matière doit avoir pour constituer la folie, devient fol" (p. 146). This force culminates on the transparent side of the sun in the race of miniature people Dyrcona meets whose bodies do not resist their imagination's desires, so that they have the power to gather themselves into any shape. When Dyrcona sees them in the form of a nightingale, he exclaims, "ce Rossignol, créateur de soy-mesme" (p. 146).

Once outside the *camera obscura* of their bodies, the libertines are projected through the light chamber into the universe of words where they can indulge in wild, uncontrolled free falls through language. This is the last stage of their dream of total freedom, and it is here that the question of its viability intervenes to break the fall. Can this much freedom really be handled? Can isolation be airtight? Can the body be maintained in pieces? In the case of the libertine, the master of linguistic creativity always realizes, like Francion's giant, that he cannot control either the babbling tongues or the text of his life. He cannot destroy them because, like the alchemist, he is ultimately controlled by his secret.

1. Démoris, p. 43.

2. The *Prison* was published in 1674, the *Pensées* in 1676, whereas their logical place in the narrative is after the tales told by the *Avantures* and the *Avantures d'Italie*, which did not appear until 1677. D'Assoucy explains in the preface to the *Pensées* that "cette pièce est un fragment que j'ai arraché de mes Avantures d'Italie pour ce qu'il interrompit le cours de mon histoire" (p. 343). His statement indicates that only the order of publication was reversed, making this decision all the more exceptional. It is obvious to anyone familiar with the organization of the *Avantures* that digressiveness is generally not considered a negative quality.

3. "Je me desistay de cette entreprise, pour continuer celle que tant de fâcheux obstacles et accidens avoient interrompuë" (p. 148). Since D'Assoucy explains that he chose to abandon the printed text for the book of his life, it cannot be established that the first version of his captivity corresponds to the final text. The fact remains, however, that, by his own account, the *Avantures* originates in the story of his first experience in the *chambre obscure*.

4. Since, as he admits earlier, his portrait was drawn by artists who had never seen him, the fact that he can be so easily recognized from it is unfortunate indeed!

5. Fournel, pp. 106–7.

6. Prévot defends the opposite opinion: "Cyrano étant mort avant d'avoir fait publier son roman." "En ce qui concerne *Les Estats et Empires de la Lune*, on ne saura jamais quel texte l'auteur aurait livré à l'impression" (pp. 7, 9). There is, however, no evidence to justify this point of view. On other occasions, with the *Mazarinades*, for example, Cyrano proved himself an author capable of getting a text to press very rapidly. By 1650, Cyrano was known as the author of *L'Autre Monde* (whose completion is dated even earlier by some critics). If he did in fact intend to publish his novel, it is strange indeed that he did not include it in the 1654 collection of his *Oeuvres diverses*, which does contain works whose composition in all probability followed that of *L'Autre Monde*, such as *La Mort d'Agrippine* (1653).

7. As Maurice Lever stresses in "Sorcellerie et littérature au dix-septième siècle," the difformities of otherness are absent to a remarkable extent in classical literature: "Décidément, l'Enfer n'est pas classique. Nos auteurs du 'grand siècle' n'osent encore s'y aventurer, fût-ce pour une saison, et les champs du mal ne produisent pas de fleurs: les cendres fumantes des bûchers demeurent désespérément steriles. Vous ne trouverez dans la littérature de cette époque ni l'écho des sabbats, ni les cris des sorcières, ni la pestilence des charniers rituels. Rien ne vient troubler la sereine transparence de l'onde dans le bassin d'Apollon. . . . La sorcellerie, empire du désordre, de la laideur, et du mal, échappe aux rigeurs de l'ordonnance classique, qui est aussi un ordre de classe" (p. 14). I question only Lever's omission of the decidedly different treatment of these questions in less "orderly" seventeenth-century literature.

8. Jean Rousset describes the blandness of what he calls the "folie baroque": "Combien cette folie est différente de la folie romantique! A cette folie-jeu qui plaque sur l'être un personnage factice et provisoire endossé comme un vêtement, s'oppose la déchirante folie d'*Aurélia* . . . où il faut voir, au contraire, un arrachement de tous les voiles et une marche vers le secret de l'être" (*La Littérature de l'âge baroque en France*, p. 57).

9. Démoris, p. 54.

10. *La Pensée philosophique et scientifique de Cyrano*, pp. 50–51. This opinion is echoed by other commentators, Georges Mongrédien, for example, in *Madame de Montespan et l'affaire des poisons*, p. 13.

11. Preface, n.p.

12. "Imposter" is in this sense the one term in Triboulet's list that escapes the reduction of meaning: "Il m'appela impie, sorcier, athée, héretique et imposteur, *homo sceleratus atque nefandus*" (p. 75).

13. Porta's work happens to contain an early description of the optical effects of the *camera obscura* (*Magiae naturalis* [Naples, 1558], pp. 135–36).

14. Although D'Assoucy does not identify the book, it is obvious that the little boys believe it to be some mysterious treatise of magic. A link is thereby established with the role of the book of magic for the young page, and with the role of the book in all these self-incriminations.

15. It is interesting to note that all D'Assoucy's adventures as a young magician take place on a boy-size scale. When he is threatened by a crowd—and the parallel with the mob that will later drive him from Montpellier is clear—his attackers, even if numerous, are at least of his own size. And when he manages to effect a cure, it is on someone of his age that he concentrates his powers.

16. *Combat*, pp. 5–6. For a discussion of the relationship between these burlesque etymologies and the *nom d'auteur*, see chapter 2.

17. Preface, n.p.

18. When the narrator of *L'Autre Monde* learns that poetry is accepted as money on the moon, he remembers having encountered this idea before: "Voilà justement la monnaie dont Sorel fait servir Hortensius dans *Francion*, je m'en souviens. C'est là sans doute, qu'il l'a dérobé; mais de qui diable peut-il l'avoir appris? Il faut que ce soit de sa mère, car j'ai ouï dire qu'elle était lunatique" (p. 64). From this genealogy, it might be deduced that (mad) pedants are the descendants of lunatics.

19. In Barthes's description: "Depuis cent ans, la folie (littéraire) est réputée consister en ceci: 'Je est un autre': la folie est une expérience de dépersonnalisation" (*Fragments d'un discours amoureux*, p. 142).

20. *Histoire de la folie à l'âge classique*, p. 22.

21. Démoris, p. 123.

22. Benjamin, *Illuminations*, p. 181.

23. The Freudian interpretation of gambling as masturbation developed in "Dostoevsky and Parricide" would seem to be invalidated by this aloofness: "The 'vice' of masturbation is replaced by the mania for gambling; and the emphasis laid upon the passionate activity of the hands betrays this derivation" (*Character and Culture*, p. 292).

24. One must never expect consistency in his paranoia. Only ten pages later, in a passage I have already cited, D'Assoucy will unite himself as a companion in misery to the "Enfans d'Israël dans le Désert."

25. With this story, Dyrcona adds to the libertine collection of attempts to eliminate parental authority the myth of the child raised by false parents. His particular variant of the dream also allows him to exclude France as his native country:

> Messieurs, s'ecria une Arondelle . . . vous n'avez pas oublié qu'il vient de

dire que le païs qui l'avoit veu naistre estoit la France; mais vous sçavez qu'en France les Singes n'engendrent point: apres cela jugez s'il est ce qu'il se vante d'estre.

Je repondis à mon accusatrice que j'avois esté enlevé si jeune du sein de mes parens et transporté en France, qu'à bon droict je pouvois appeler mon païs natal celuy duquel je me souvenois le plus loin" (p. 151).

26. So much so that on one occasion in *Francion* the baby hero believes the "diabolical" monkey to be a little boy. In this scene, Francion is dressed up by the monkey, (who reverses his clothes), thereby becoming a monkey's monkey and providing a reversal of roles that could be linked with that found on the moon, where men are (lunar) men's monkeys.

27. When they eventually meet in the *Estats et empires*, Campanella himself will explain the source of his power in a more detailed manner.

28. D'Assoucy, *Combat*, p. 9.

29. And eventually of otherness, in a progression that will be examined in the next pages.

30. Introduction of the Neuchâtel manuscript of the *Confessions, Oeuvres complètes*, 1:1149, 1154.

31. *Tristes tropiques*, p. 418.

32. In order to avoid a neat parody of the mass, Cyrano adds a libertine twist to the eating of the flesh and the drinking of the blood.

33. The link between the demon's theory that one may understand the secret workings of someone's thought by imitating his facial expression and gestures and this belief in the transmission of secrets by eating the body is obvious.

34. Neubert, p. 45.

35. Adam, *Théophile de Viau*, p. 242.

36. Démoris, pp. 124–25.

37. This is not the case with *Francion* and the *Page*, where women remain in this traditional role. In general, the question of marginal sexuality is not evoked by these texts, except, in a sense, by Francion's dream.

38. Bachelard, pp. 106, 109.

39. Démoris, p. 125.

40. "Comme en ce temps-là il estoit fort genereux, quand il m'avoit retenu à souper chez lui, et que, pour me retirer chez moi l'heure estoit induë, il me cedoit fort librement la moitié de son lit. C'est pourquoy, après avoir eu de si longues preuves de la qualité de mes desirs, et m'avoir bien daigné honorer plusieurs fois de sa couche, il me semble que c'estoit plutost à luy à me justifier qu'à Messieurs du Presidial de Montpellier, avec lesquels je n'ay jamais couché" (pp. 200–201). I am not proposing a deliberate misreading of this passage. D'Assoucy claims to be giving irrefutable proof of his innocence here, and I only find it strange that he manages to do so in a manner that, for all its apparent inocence, creates more doubts than it erases by bringing up additional controversial incidents.

41. I quote from the unpublished English version of this article, which has appeared in French under the title "Désir, rhétorique, et texte."

42. The link between alchemy and writing is made clear during this scene. When he hears his orders to the servant, the page believes the philosopher is preparing to write: "et surtout il demanda beaucoup de bois, comme s'il eût

voulu veiller à écrire quelques mémoires d'importance" (p. 95), but instead he is about to use the fire and his art to produce gold.

43. On this point, I rejoin the basic thesis of Ferdinand Brunetière's "La Maladie du burlesque."

44. *Life against Death* (Middletown, Conn.: Wesleyan University Press, 1959), p. 157.

45. As if there could be any doubts, he makes the sexual connotation of his favorite weapon clear in *L'Autre Monde*. Nobles on the moon do not wear swords, but "la figure d'un membre viril" (p. 108). Besides, in this antiprocreative land, the image may be all there is. The "membre viril" is defined as "le Prométhée de chaque animal," and the Spaniard explains to the narrator that "il nous manque un Prométhée" (p. 73).

46. Dyrcona therefore loses his tongue in Toulouse, where Vanini's was torn out in 1619.

47. Lachèvre attempts to defuse the adjective by adding in a footnote that it means simply "impatient, avide," but its occurrence in the passage that defines the Phoenix's sexuality belies the straightforwardness of his explanation.

48. Scarron is also accused of plagiarism by Cyrano in "Contre Ronscar," so at least the source of all their ideas is clear.

49. "Le Rêve de Francion: considérations sur la cohésion intérieure de l'*Histoire comique* de Sorel," p. 166.

50. Ibid., pp. 167, 171.

51. Jean Serroy, "D'un roman à métamorphoses: la composition du *Francion* de Charles Sorel"; Fausta Garavini, "*Francion* rivisitato: Diacronia di una struttura."

52. Starobinski, *L'Oeil vivant*, pp. 199–200.

CHAPTER FIVE

THE OTHER IN THE *GRAND SIECLE*

Il faut escrire à la moderne.—Théophile (de Viau)

On sera bien surpris de retrouver dans Théophile des idées qui paraissaient, il y a dix ou douze ans, de la plus audacieuse nouveauté. — Car c'est lui, il faut le dire, qui a commencé le mouvement romantique.—Théophile (Gautier)

1. A NEW ORDER OF THINGS

Certes, les fils chicanent volontiers les pères, s'imaginant qu'ils vont refaire un monde qui n'attendait qu'eux pour devenir meilleur: mais les remous qui agitent les générations successives ne suffisent pas à expliquer un changement si rapide et si décisif. La majorité des Français pensait comme Bossuet; tout d'un coup, les Français pensent comme Voltaire: c'est une révolution.[1]

Today many literary and intellectual historians would find much to criticize in the description given by Hazard's *La Crise de la conscience européenne* of the transformation in French thought from the seventeenth to the eighteenth centuries. A surprising number of theoreticians have turned their attention to the intellectual upheavals of these centuries. Many agree with Hazard that, in any schema of the period, room must be made for one or more times of crisis marking the transition between different world views, and that somewhere in this slice of time the ultimate crisis that signals the beginnings of our modernity can be situated.[2] This quest for the origins of contemporary problematics leads to a reevaluation of the lines that divide "Renaissance" from "Classicism" and "Classicism" from "Enlightenment." I do not plan to take sides in this variant of the problem of periodization,

157

but rather to superimpose several theories, each of which concludes, for different reasons, that fundamental changes occur
somewhere near 1650.

Intellectual historians like Pintard and Spink present this period as the beginning of the modern age, because it marked the
collapse of all systems of belief that had previously obtained nearly total allegiance. As Spink describes it:

> The collapse of medieval teaching was becoming unmistak-
> able . . . outside the classrooms it was already discredited. To
> fill the gap there was as yet only the revised version of Aristotle
> professed in the University of Padua by Pomponazzi and Cre-
> monini and certain themes of hylozoic or panpsychistic natural-
> ism, also of Italian origin and propagated in the works of Cardano
> and Bruno. Even these were under fire before their position was
> established; Renaissance science, the science of the astrologers
> and alchemists was following Scholasticism in collapse, while
> the new science, the science of modern times, was only at its
> beginnings.[3]

Pintard completes Spink's testimony on the scientific void by
stressing the religious void faced by the period: "Le seizième siècle
avait hérité du Moyen Age et réajusté le compromis de l'aristoté-
lisme et du christianisme; il avait, par ses propres forces, organisé
l'union de la sagesse antique et de la foi. . . . Le dix-septième, au
contraire, les recevait épuisées."[4] For Pintard and Spink, the age
immediately following what Spink terms "the crisis of 1619–25" is
a particularly crucial one intellectually, because it provides the
small number of thinkers aware of the consequences of that crisis
with no system of belief they could use to stabilize their existence.
Confronted with the crumbling of the combined forces of Catholicism and Aristotelianism, the intellectual initiate of the mid-
seventeenth century experiences a second fall from Paradise:
from a theo- and geocentric universe, he is rather unexpectedly
thrust into a largely unexplored anthropo- and heliocentric one.
With no acceptable beliefs to break his fall, he has no choice but
to become a renegade and a freethinker.

Traditional intellectual historians divide the seventeenth century in two in order to account for the presence in the mid-
seventeenth century of a brand of freethinking that seems unmistakably "modern," one that can be held up as an ancestor for the
eighteenth-century movement to which they trace the origins of

contemporary thought. More recently, 1650 reappears as a turning point in several less orthodox structural histories of thought. Having found the period of my research mentioned when I least expected it, I began to pool the descriptions made of it in various theoretical contexts. Each of the schemas I plan to examine here develops a theory that can help situate and account for the exceptional nature of the libertine novel. I do not intend to pass judgment on these various systems. I will discuss them neither as though they reflected historical realities, nor as though they presented a vision of the past filtered through personal mythology and an individual's theoretical obsessions. I will simply juxtapose the two most striking interpretations of the period. By outlining what their authors believe to have been at stake at this turning point, I hope both to provide a framework in which to discuss the status of the libertine text and to answer the question of how a small and, in many ways, minor group of authors could renew and (re)create a novelistic form.

The first unexpected encounter with the mid-seventeenth century occurs in Roland Barthes's *Le Degré zéro de l'écriture*. In the course of his attempt to trace the evolution of *écriture*, Barthes reaffirms the conclusion advanced by Spink and Pintard: through 1650 passes a major line of demarcation in French intellectual history. For Barthes, prior to this period French literature had not yet reached a turning point in the development of modernity: "On peut dire que jusque vers 1650, la Littérature française n'avait pas encore dépassé une problématique de la langue, et que par là même elle ignorait encore l'écriture. En effet, tant que la langue hésite sur sa structure même, une morale du language est impossible."[5] Barthes's sense of the importance of the changes taking place at this period can be related to Foucault's discussion in *Les Mots et les choses* of the shift from a medieval to a classical *episteme*.[6] In the section entitled "Représenter," Foucault documents the change he sees in the role of language, the movement by which, during the reign of classical thought, words were perceived as having lost the direct, mimetic relationship with things posited by the Middle Ages and the Renaissance. Once the old order based on resemblance disappears, "le language n'est plus une des figures du monde."[7] For the view of the linguistic sign as a sort of eternal signature branding its object, the seventeenth century substitutes the notion of its arbitrariness. Questions of resemblance yield to questions of representation. This is amply supported by the texts Foucault terms central to this episteme, the *Logique* and the *Grammaire* of Port-Royal. In Cartesian linguistics, words and things are neatly sealed off into separate realms, and language, liberated from its identification with a system of referents, is free to be studied as the autonomous, synchronic system Saussure describes as *langue*. In Foucault's reconstruction of the classical episteme, the time is ripe, as Barthes remarks, for the emergence of *écriture*.

The year 1650 turns up as a pivotal date in another recent description of linguistic and literary evolution, a theory that refers to the role of several of the libertine novelists, but one that weighs much of Foucault's evidence in a very different manner. This second interpretation, that of Mikhail Bakhtin, constitutes the most important recent attack on the foundations of Cartesian linguistics, especially the notion of the arbitrariness of the linguistic sign. Bakhtin and his followers, unlike Barthes and Foucault, consider the changes taking place in 1650 as essentially negative. Rather than glorifying a break responsible for the growth into Structuralist modernity, Bakhtin describes with nostalgia a spirit and a consciousness that existed before 1650, that lost much of their substance and underwent profound transformations about this time, but that are essential for the creation of what he considers the greatest works in modern literature.[8]

Among the theories discussed here, Bakhtin's will enjoy a privileged status, not only because he actually takes these libertine texts into account, but also because the central concepts defined by his work are those I find most illuminating for them. Bakhtin's principal studies, *Marxism and the Philosophy of Language*, *Dostoevsky's Poetics*, and *Rabelais and His World*,[9] often overlap each other as they develop a semiotic schema that attempts to trace the history and ramifications of three literary (and partially sociological) notions: carnival and carnivalized literature, dialogue and the dialogic, and Menippean satire or the menippea.[10] In Bakhtin's system, the notions are intimately related historically, and 1650 is a critical date in the history they share. I will return to these concepts shortly to define them in more detail, but I would first like to discuss Bakhtin's view of the importance of this periodization.

Bakhtin traces the evolution of an extralinguistic concept that he holds responsible for certain changes in language. In his system, 1650 marks the separation between an age in which carnival and the spirit of carnival flourished and were glorified in literature, and one in which they became extinct, no more than memories, occasionally and fleetingly evoked by literary texts that could do no more than artificially re-create their myth. Bakhtin defines the carnival spirit as the spirit of folk humor, "the sense of the gay relativity of prevailing truth and authorities." It is a force that overthrows all hierarchies and systems of belief since it strives "to consecrate interior freedom . . . to liberate from the prevailing point of view of the world, from conventions and established truths, from clichés. . . . This carnival spirit offers the chance . . . to realize the relative nature of all that exists, and to enter a completely new order of things."[11] When carnival reigned over the universe, fools became kings, and kings became fools, as opposites were reconciled. Anything was possible, in a world constantly à l'envers. Systems of separation were defied. The body, for example, was the grotesque body triumphant in its union with its surroundings: "Contrary to modern canons, the grotesque body is not separated from the rest of the world. It is not a closed, completed unit; it is unfinished, outgrows itself, transgresses its own limits."[12]

Carnival became institutionalized at the time of the development of Foucault's classical episteme. Without natural sources, literature could no longer transmit the true spirit of carnival. During the domination of the classical canon, the grotesque and folk humor were excluded from "great" literature and were confined to the harmless space of low comic genres. The carnival spirit itself became trivialized, until its utopian vision of freedom was reduced to nothing more than a sort of carefree holiday mood. In the end, the essence and imagery of the grotesque were passed on only as a purely literary tradition, one associated with the Renaissance.[13]

Bakhtin discusses the traditions that kept the grotesque alive during the period of the classical canon's domination: the comic novel, the travesty, traditions of particular interest to him because they are borderline cases, almost, but not totally, removed from their roots. Despite his nostalgia for an age in which carnival was still alive, Bakhtin ultimately reaches some of the same interpretations for the transformations of 1650 as Foucault: without the direct influence of carnival, words and things are (irrevocably) separated in this period. Even the texts he describes as struggling against this separation of the word from the context of its utterance are able to reproduce, no longer a reality, but only a reality already fictionalized by other texts. Bakhtin enters at this point in his discussion the realm of what is currently referred to as the meta- and intertextual.[14] The first texts marked by the death of carnival convey an awareness of their being less re-creations of some microcosm than readings of previous creations. Their primary *signifié* is "literature."

For Bakhtin, the texts born of this movement toward pure literariness—the comic and libertine novels, for example—are bastardized products of a fall from past glory. They at least share the merit of struggling to preserve the fading contact with the world of relativism and physical reality. The intellectual tradition covered with glory in the course of its rediscovery by Foucault and other contemporary thinkers does not fare as well in Bakhtin's system. His *Marxism and the Philosophy of Language* attacks the premises on which the logic of Cartesian linguistics and Port-Royal's universal grammar are founded:

> The idea of the conventionality, the arbitrariness, of language is a typical one for rationalism as a whole; and no less typical is the comparison of language to the system of mathematical signs. What interests the mathematically minded rationalists is not the relationship of the sign to the actual reality it reflects or to the individual who is its originator, but the relationship of sign to sign within a closed system already accepted and authorized. In other words, they are interested only in the inner logic of the system of signs itself, taken, as in algebra, completely independently of the meanings that give signs their content.[15]

In *Rabelais and His World*, Bakhtin stresses the destruction of the grotesque body cut off from direct contact with the world. In *Marxism and the Philosophy of Language*, he deplores the belief that language can be removed from the reality in which it is anchored. "A sign is a phenomenon of the external world."[16]

To separate words from things is to deny them the context in which they evolve. For Bakhtin, language should be studied primarily on the level of what Saussure terms *parole*. Signs exist first and foremost in verbal communication, in the process of interaction between two individual consciousnesses. By remaining blind to the dialogic structure of the word, through which one reality reflects and alters another, Cartesian linguistics fosters the creation of literary texts hopelessly anchored in linguistic and philosophical monologism. In Bakhtin's system, the greatest literary texts are, on the contrary, those that manage somehow to overcome the legacy of the split of 1650 and to re-create an anti-system of relativism by maintaining an awareness of their existence in a context of verbal communication, at the point of intersection of various speech acts. Such texts are distinguished by the type of discourse they develop, which Bakhtin calls dialogic or polyphonic, and are placed under a very flexible generic heading, menippea.

Bakhtin traces the development of the menippea, beginning with its origins in antiquity, and devotes a major study to an author representative of the tradition before the disappearance of carnival, Rabelais, and one to a novelist who demonstrates its re-creation, Dostoevsky. In *Dostoevsky's Poetics*, Bakhtin discusses the rejection of linguistic arbitrariness by dialogic discourse that situates itself at the point of collision between voices. A work may be described as dialogic if, first, it is centered on the act of verbal communication, and, second, it takes this polyphony to its logical polysemic conclusion. In the dialogic text, all voices are equal and unmerged, and no one voice controls the others and has power to establish truth. To give expression to its polyphony, the dialogic text functions best within the most flexible type of formal organization. The menippea is just that: a prose (anti-) genre, based on the integration of disparate elements (verse interludes, interpolated stories, letters), on open-endedness, and on parataxis.[17]

I evoke these theories of 1650 at the outset of my concluding remarks on seventeenth-century French libertine fiction in order to illustrate the particular tensions that form a backdrop for its creation. The answer proposed by the libertine authors to the crisis of 1650 is a type of novel that, in its dialogic and carnivalized aspects, corresponds to the model proposed by Bakhtin. Yet the libertine novel is not free of the sense of its own arbitrariness to which Foucault and Barthes accord priority. It is with these apparently conflicting forces in mind that I would like to return to the texts.

2. A POETICS OF MODERNITY

> Un discours qui contient beacoup de passages différents, non seulement pour le style, mais même pour le language ressemble à une robe de diverses couleurs et de plusieurs pièces rapportées qui la rendent ridicule. (La Mothe Le Vayer)

Describing the crisis of 1619–25, Spink stresses its lack of contemporary public impact. Only a handful of specialists could have been fully acquainted with the terms and consequences of the new physics developed by scientists such as Copernicus, Tycho-Brahe, Kepler, and Galileo, and even they prudently refrained from commenting freely on these matters. Despite the limitation of, at best, only a secondhand and limited knowledge of the recent theories, the libertine novelists, never known for their prudence, were quick to realize that they could speak where others were silent. They were conscious of the fact that, in the world of Copernicus, writers could no longer content themselves with the same means of expression developed for that of Aristotle. A literary revolution had to follow the scientific one. The challenge of scientific expansion had to be met with a discourse of freedom. The discourse they chose was dialogic, and their choice cannot be explained solely on the basis of Rudolf Hirzel's conclusion, supported by John Cosentini, that dialogue flourishes in periods of dissolution of old dogmas and in times of political and social upheaval.[18] The libertines turn to various manifestations of the dialogic to express their liberation and their relativism, and are able thereby to renew a narrative tradition with an important heritage. They announce the new by resurrecting the memory of their predecessors who wrote freely. They do so, not only by adopting the narrative form Bakhtin refers to as the menippea, but also by means of a complex network of references to a past in language.

The desire to develop a theory of literary modernity is immediately evident in the earliest libertine novels. *L'Histoire comique de Francion* proves itself to be worthy of its title with its opening sentence:

> Les voiles de la nuict avoient couvert tout l'Orison lorsqu'un vieillard qui s'appelloit Valentin sortit d'un chasteau de Bourgogne avec une robbe de chambre, un bonnet rouge en teste et un gros pacquet sous son bras, encore ne sçay-je pourquoy il n'avoit point ses lunettes, car c'estoit sa coustume de les porter tousjours à son nez ou à sa ceinture (p. 66).

Francion can be called an *histoire comique* because it is a funny novel, but also because, like the other seventeenth-century novels that bear this generic label, it can be seen as an attack on what its author views as outmoded forms of prose fiction. The description of Valentin is made in the narrator's own language, but "les voiles de la nuict avoient couvert tout l'Orison" is clearly a borrowed utterance, foreign words that sound ludicrous in what is for them an unnatural context.[19] The phrase is more than ludicrous, it is empty. By inserting a foreign element at the beginning of his novel, Sorel attempts to demonstrate how meaningless inflated style is, and by contrast, to show how meaningful his own will be. In 1623, the style that will be known as the burlesque is beginning to make its presence felt on the French literary scene, and the first message it transmits is a warning against the prevalence of cliché. Rhetorical repetitiousness is the target most often associated with the burlesque's literary aggressivity. Sorel's opening phrase must have been immediately recognizable to those of his contemporaries who were also readers of more heroic novels. This is, so they had been told, the way a novel should begin. In Sorel's opinion, the novelists who were busy telling them so could have put their energy to more profitable use had they turned to the creation of new forms rather than repeating the faded language of cliché.

That Théophile shares Sorel's concern with a theory of modernity is immediately evident from his decision to begin the *Fragments* with what is arguably the most aggressive moment of literary polemic ever to find its way into the pages of a novel. The novel's first chapter might be considered the founding text of the seventeenth-century parodic tradition. The novelists who come after Théophile will be able to insert a parody of heroic language into the first sentences of their novels and feel certain that their polemical intentions will be understood. Théophile, on the other hand, far surpasses this pale and limited dialogue with unnamed adversaries. The first chapter of the *Fragments* is completely unnovelistic. Here, Théophile does more than insert borrowed clichés: he makes place in the narrative he is about to begin for a representative of a non-narrative, non-fictional genre, the literary manifesto. Chapter one of the *Fragments* is an example of interpolation, like the *Roman comique's nouvelles espagnoles* or the catalogues in the *Roman bourgeois*. The separation between Théophile's prescription for literary modernity and the other chapters of the *Fragments* is "punctuated" by formal differences: the manifesto is written in the present tense, as opposed to the past that dominates the rest of the novel; it is almost entirely narrated in the first person plural ("je" intervenes only twice), and it makes a rather extraordinary use of the imperative mode ("il faut" appears five times, "devoir" twice). In so straightforward a context, the humorous juxtaposition found in *Francion*'s opening sentence would be out of place.

The *Fragments* begins: "L'élégance ordinaire de nos Ecrivains est à peu pres selon ces termes." This opening clause immediately counteracts any potentially comic effects to which the subsequent exceptionally long parodic *incipit* might otherwise give rise:

> L'Aurore, toute d'or et d'azur, brodée de perles et de rubis, paroissoit aux portes de l'Orient; les Estoiles, eblouÿes, d'une plus vive clarté, laissoient effacer leur blancheur et devenoient peu à peu de la couleur du ciel; les bestes de la queste revenoient aux bois et les hommes à leur travail; le silence faisoit place au bruit et les tenebres à la lumiere (p. 1).

After he demonstrates what not to do with this interpolation of empty rhetoric, Théophile is able to offer his theory of a modern style: "Il faut que le discours soit ferme; que le sens y soit naturel et facile; le langage exprès et signifiant" (p. 2). Théophile's manifesto, like a burlesque text, constantly juxtaposes and maintains a distinction between two discourses ("mine" and "other"). Unlike the burlesque, it does so solely for polemical, and never for comic, ends. Théophile chastises writers for what his contemporary Guy de la Brosse calls "le superstitieux respet de l'antiquité" that prevents them "de passer plus outre que l'Alphabet de [leurs] devanciers."[20] By setting up with precision in four pages of examples the two voices in the dialogue (ancient and modern, trite and innovative, foreign and French), Théophile contributes the first clear example of parodic intertextuality in the libertine novels. The *Fragments* and *Francion* are engaged in a dialogue with texts past and present with which they disagree. Like the burlesque tradition, they call attention to the malfunctioning of language that is so codified that it is no longer meaningful. They inaugurate a polemical dialogue with cliché.

The parodic dialogues with alien literary texts opened by the first sentences of the *Fragments* and *Francion* provide an immediate indication of the "literariness" of these novels. From the beginning, Théophile and Sorel take pains to inscribe in their works an atmosphere of self-consciousness. Their narrators/heroes are not only *écrivants* or *écrivains*: they are above all readers of novels.[21] No libertine text illustrates this function more elaborately than the *Page*. Here, reading is more than a pastime or avocation: it is the source of the page's greatest successes. As far back as he can remember, his love of stories and his prodigious memory win him the attention he craves. Already at age four, he is an avid reader of novels. Since he retains every detail of their adventures, "je débitais agréablement à mon aïeule et à mon grand-père" (p. 54). He reads and reads, until he is able to call himself "le vivant répertoire des romans et des contes fabuleux" (p. 59).

When he begins his career as a page, he puts this talent to good use in his duties. He tells his tales to the young princes he serves to help them fall asleep when they are sick. Eventually, like other faithful readers of fiction, he comes to identify himself with its heroes: "Je me figurais . . . que j'étais quelqu'un des héros d'Homère, ou pour le moins quelque paladin, ou chevalier de la Table ronde" (p. 81). His literary storytelling serves him best when he uses it to further his love interests. In the chapter entitled "Les Premières Amours du page disgracié," the adventures of the lovers in the novels he narrates to his young mistress form an intentional *mise en abyme* for the love story he is hoping to begin. Just as he plans, she falls in love with him by projecting herself into the narratives he uses to enchant her, the *Aethiopica* and a strong dose of "ces romans héroïques dont on fait estime" (p. 122). Indeed, his mistress is so pleased with her page's talents that she delights in showing them off. On a family journey, all of the entertainment value of his vast reading is exploited, as "j'entrepris de conter à ma maîtresse tout ce que j'avais lu de l'*Astrée*. . . . J'en entretenais tous les jours cinq ou six heures ma maîtresse sans que ses oreilles en fussent fatiguées . . . et c'était un charme dont j'endormais la mère et une de ses confidentes, afin qu'elles ne pussent prendre garde aux oeillades que nous nous lancions" (pp. 146–47). Like Scheherazade, the page knows how to use story to disarm the watchful dragon.

It seems that in this role he can produce any effect desired. Only once does he fail to control his powerful talent, and his slip has fatal results. His mistress, ever desirous of finding a wider audience for her protégé, invites one of her cousins to hear his stories. "Pour obéir à ce commandement et ne m'engager pas en une matière qui leur pût être ennuyeuse, j'entrepris de leur raconter les aventures de Psyché," the page remarks with perfectly feigned naïveté (p. 124). Like his mistress, the cousin is young and beautiful, and she of course shares her fate. As a result of what the page terms his "jeune et folle éloquence" (p. 125), the cousin is soon hopelessly in love with him. The page is too successful at Scheherazade's game, and the conquests he obtains from his vulgarizations of heroic fiction lead to his banishment from England.[22] Another type of text, however, is healthier for him, and near the end of his adventures we see the page, living proof of the victory of the comic style, happily spinning tales once again, this time to his new master in France: "Bien souvent, je lui contais quelque aventure nouvelle que j'avais apprise; d'autres fois, c'était une vieille histoire renouvelée que j'avais prise ou dans le *Décameron* de Boccace, ou dans Straparole, Pogge Florentin . . . et d'autres auteurs qui se sont voulu charitablement appliquer à guérir la mélancolie" (p. 257). With its web of intertextual references, the *Page* gives ample testimony to the seductiveness of storytelling.

Although its composition is less firmly anchored in a literary atmosphere, the *Voyage* nevertheless lays much stress on the narrator/reader relationship. It contains references to literary works of the period and reports one extensive conversation with a group of *précieuses* from Montpellier about men of letters (Sarrasin, Voiture, Ménage, and so on) and heroic novels. In a manner reminiscent of Molière, the *précieuses* are mocked because they praise the likes of *Cassandre*, *Cyrus*, and *Clélie* "pour la magnificence de l'expression et la grandeur des événements" (p. 82). In the context of as passively chatty a voyage narrative as Chapelle's, the narrator has a special relationship to the reader, as Jean Rousset points out: "On voit que le narrateur est moins acteur que spectateur et auditeur; auditeur de récits offerts par les surprises de la route, selon une ancienne tradition, il est ici une figure du lecteur de romans, oubliant ses 'chagrins' dans les aventures d'autrui."[23] Such a narrator is a perpetual reader of novels, literally and metaphorically.

In Cyrano's two imaginary voyages, the question of intertextuality attains a far greater complexity than in other libertine texts. The key intertextual references in *L'Autre Monde* act first of all as signs of homage. When the narrator returns home from the moonlight stroll narrated in the novel's opening scene, he finds the works of Cardano open on his table:

> Je tombai de vue, comme par force, justement dans une histoire que raconte ce philosophe: il écrit qu'étudiant un soir à la chandelle, il aperçut entrer, à travers les portes fermées de sa chambre, deux grands vieillards, lesquels, après beaucoup d'interrogations qu'il leur fit, répondirent qu'ils étaient habitants de la lune, et cela dit, ils disparurent (p. 32).

The lunar intervention to which Cyrano refers here is actually described by Cardano, who claims to have benefited from such an inspirational visit on more than one occasion in his *De la subtilité et subtiles inventions, ensemble les causes occultes et raisons d'icelles.* By mentioning the visit at the beginning of his novel, Cyrano immediately demonstrates an awareness of literary precedent as keen as the sense of stylistic and metaphoric relativity embodied in *L'Autre Monde*'s first paragraph. Other books have dealt with men from the moon before his, and Cyrano deliberately flaunts his novel's literary origins (unlike Théophile and Sorel, who begin by flaunting their literary adversaries).

His narrator is not only a reader of literature. He is a reader of works that present parallels to his own situation more striking than those found by the page in his heroic love stories, works that can have an active influence on his adventures. The page merely uses novelistic plots to program his fate, but the narrator's story is preordained by literature, is generated by previous literary texts. In the case of Cardano's lunar visitors, for example, they gain a second literary existence in the pages of *L'Autre Monde*, since they can provide an explanation for the coincidence of the open book: "Sans doute . . . les deux vieillards qui apparurent à ce grand homme sont ceux-là mêmes qui ont derangé mon livre, et qui l'ont ouvert sur cette page, pour s'épargner la peine de me faire cette harangue qu'ils ont faite à Cardan" (p. 32). Cyrano begins by citing an incident from Cardano, thereby giving it a second life, the indirect, passive life of quotation. He then goes beyond this first movement to reanimate quotation by giving the incident a new active literary existence. When Cyrano attributes an action in his book to characters cited from Cardano's, he succeeds in blurring the boundaries between quotation and original. In this case, quotation can even replace the primary text. The narrator needs neither to see the lunar visitors nor to hear what they have to say to him. The ideal scene to begin his adventures already exists, so reading can be substituted for action. An extreme use of Cyrano's "blurring" would lead to a type of *livre sur rien* in which the hero would do nothing but read about what happened to previous heroes.

In order to make his point absolutely clear, Cyrano does not abandon the question of the extraterrestial inspiration of Cardano's works after this initial reference. Shortly after they meet, the demon of Socrates describes for the narrator a similar intrusion into Cardano's life for which he was responsible: "Un jour, entre autres, j'apparus à Cardan comme il étudiait; je l'instruisis de quantité de choses, et en récompense il me promit qu'il témoignerait à la posterité de qui il tenait les miracles qu'il s'attendait d'écrire" (p. 56). This passage proves that Cardano keeps his promise, for, once again, Cyrano does not invent the incident described in *L'Autre Monde* but cites it from Cardano's autobiography. Cardano's book precedes Cyrano's and may have inspired it. Cyrano returns the literary favor by giving the passage from his predecessor in freethinking a second life in print, thereby refulfilling Cardano's promise to share credit with a demon.

He does the same thing a few lines later for another of his libertine and literary ancestors. In the course of his genealogy, the demon lists a second fruitful encounter: "Je connus aussi Campanella . . . il commença à ma prière un livre que nous intitulâmes *de Sensu rerum*" (p. 56). In the case of Campanella, the inspirational link (at least with the *Estats et empires*) is certain. Cyrano pays homage to him not only by citing an incident from his work but also by connecting him with Cardano by means of the demon they shared. Furthermore, his use of quotation does not end here. Extraterrestrial inspiration is brought closer to home when the spirit involved is one actually seen by the narrator. Cyrano makes it clear that even the demon of Socrates has a previous literary existence. His name, as the demon himself is the first to point out, already marks him with his borrowed status. He may explain the inspiration of his narrator's book (this is never said, although perhaps implicit in the citation from Cardano), but he was not created by Cyrano. The demon is borrowed from previous accounts, those of Socrates, Cardano, and Campanella. He serves not only as a character but also as an extended citation from the printed pages that first gave him life.

This type of borrowing is most unusual in literature. It is not uncommon to see a historical figure re-created in the pages of a novel; a well-known name is both likely to intrigue the reader and to facilitate his acceptance of the character, to encourage a "suspension of disbelief" at least as far as this element of the novel is concerned.[24] The brand of re-creation practiced by Cyrano, however, works in the opposite direction. The demon of Socrates is not invented by Cyrano, any more than the faces from the then recent past used by Madame de Lafayette; but he, unlike the vidame de Chartres or Diane de Poitiers, can hardly be said to anchor the text in authenticity. The demon is not accepted by history: no documents or events guarantee his physical reality. Only strange accounts, which might be described as metaphorical renditions of personal adventures, attest to his acts. Cyrano repeats without alteration all the proofs available of the demon's existence. Since this existence is literary rather than historical, it contributes to *L'Autre Monde*'s denunciation of its own fictionality. By introducing a "citation character" like the demon of Socrates, Cyrano continues the blurrings between history and fiction practiced by the libertines with regard to their own origins, and he also evokes a problematics of quotation.

Two other characters in *L'Autre Monde* might be termed citations. The Spaniard who plays male to the narrator's female on the moon, like the majority of characters in the novel, has no proper name to identify him. He must be distinguished from the other *porte paroles* the narrator encounters, however, because, like the demon, he has a literary past. In this case, Cyrano simply does not bother to make this fact explicit. A Spaniard on the moon for Cyrano, and for any reader familiar with the texts he evidently considers his literary predecessors, can only be Domingo Gonzales, the hero and alleged author of Francis Godwin's *The Man in the Moon* (1638). Cardano may have mentioned men from the moon, but Godwin came much closer to Cyrano's project when he told the story of a man on the moon. Once this reference is traced, it is clear that the narrator and the Spaniard form a couple more unique than the lunar race, the Selenians, imagined: as Christian Barbe points out, Gonzales is the narrator's "précurseur fictif."[25] The Spaniard is a citation from Godwin. Like the demon of Socrates, he is a character with a literary past. Furthermore, that literary past is parallel to the literary present being acted out by *L'Autre Monde*'s own narrator.

The third instance of the use of character as citation in *L'Autre Monde* is the most complex. This citation is made by the demon of Socrates. Shortly after suggesting his relationship to Cardano's work, the demon tells of meeting Tristan L'Hermite. In a passage (wisely) expurgated by Le Bret, the demon delivers an elaborate eulogy of Cyrano's contemporary and sometime friend, which he concludes with an incident from Tristan's life intended to provide the ultimate confirmation of his status as virtue incarnate ("la vertu dont il est le trône"):

> Quand je vis une vertu si haute, j'appréhendai qu'elle ne fût pas reconnue; c'est pourquoi je tâchai de lui faire accepter trois fioles; la première était pleine d'huile de talc, l'autre de poudre de projection, et la dernière d'or potable, c'est-à-dire de ce sel végétatif dont vos chimistes promettent l'éternité. Mais il les refusa avec un dédain plus généreux que Diogène ne reçut les compliments d'Alexandre quand il le vint visiter à son tonneau (p. 57).

The scene narrated by the demon here is no more of Cyrano's invention than is the demon's appearance to Cardano. To the reader familiar with a certain textual tradition, it becomes clear that the demon's literary past is even more complicated than originally suspected. Not only is he the demon of inspiration who visited Socrates, Cardano, and all the others listed in his impressive genealogy (pp. 55–56),[26] but he lays claim to a recent literary past in which he played a role somewhat different from his earlier ones.

The demon's anecdote of the three vials is an explicit reference to a scene in the *Page* acted out by the novel's hero and his "nouvel Artefius" just before their separation. On their last day together, the philosopher wakes the page with a demonstration of his powers: he shows his pupil three little glass bottles, each containing a beautifully colored substance, and describes their special powers.

The bottles are filled with "huile de talc," "poudre de projection," and "médecine universelle."[27] Until this point, the two versions are identical, as though Cyrano/the demon wished to make certain of his audience's confidence before moving to alter literary history. Far from scornfully refusing these substances, the page is only too eager to accept, and immediately tastes the "médecine universelle." No sooner has he begun to drink, however, when "l'excès de la joie me fit ouvrir la main et le breuvage précieux tomba par terre." At this sight, the alchemist "fut épouvanté de cet accident et l'interpréta possible à mauvais augure" (p. 105). Shortly afterward, he is called away, and they part forever, with the master displeased at his pupil's behavior. The changes in the demon's rendition of this tale completely alter its significance. Whereas in his own version the page bungles his much-desired initiation into alchemy and fails to win even the confidence, much less the admiration, of the alchemist, according to the demon (who should know, since he claims to have been there in the form of the alchemist himself), Tristan uses the encounter to his advantage, and emerges from it "tout esprit . . . tout coeur," the freest man in France, a true libertine hero.

This lesson in contradiction and subjective vision is Cyrano's most interesting use of a particular form of citation. With it, the demon of Socrates establishes a new facet of his literary past: if they have not already read about him, readers who enjoy him can turn for additional adventures to the *Page*, where he has previously played the role of the magician (who was playing the role of Artefius, who was playing the role of Apollonius of Tyana). But when he identifies himself as the magician, he at the same time, and without even calling attention to the substitution, equates Tristan with his page. While it is surprising to find that the fictional demon is partially a quotation of other characters, it is harder to accept either the fictionalization of Tristan by someone else (even though he himself certainly encouraged the tendency) or the assimilation of his novel's hero into his autobiography (we have already seen the dangers that entails). Furthermore, the demon's drive to fictionalize strains the boundaries of citation, thereby putting its functioning into question. How exact does quotation have to be in order to operate as quotation? Is it simple perception as quotation enough? If the reader does not know the text quoted, does a citation still retain its status as citation? These questions are posed in a footnote by the "rédacteur" of one of the greatest monuments to borrowed speech, *Les Liaisons dangereuses*: "On croit que c'est Rousseau dans *Emile*, mais la citation n'est pas exacte, et l'application qu'en fait Valmont est bien fausse; et puis, madame de Touvel avait-elle lu *Emile?*"[28]

Related to these intertextual assimilations in *L'Autre Monde* are certain well-documented references to *Francion*. In the last edition of his novel, Sorel has his pedant Hortensius describe at great length the world on the moon and the lunar novel he plans to compose. At times, Hortensius's account "prefigures" *L'Autre Monde*. For example, he says of the earth: "Il faut croire qu'elle sert de lune à cet autre monde" (p. 427). He makes the same analogy later developed at great length by one of Cyrano's lunar philosophers: for a mite or a louse, a human body is as big as the whole world is for that human being (p. 428). It is clear that Cyrano does not want these parallelisms to be missed. Citation is an act of homage for him, so he is never ashamed to acknowledge his predecessors. After all, *L'Autre Monde* is the lunar novel Hortensius never wrote. Thus, he quotes one of the pedant's visions: on the moon, poets are relieved of financial worries, since their poems are accepted as money.[29] And this time he does not close the episode without inscribing his source's name in his text:

> Ha! vraiment . . . voilà justement la monnaie dont Sorel fait servir Hortensius dans *Francion*, je m'en souviens. C'est là sans doute, qu'il l'a dérobé; mais de qui diable peut-il l'avoir appris? Il faut que ce soit de sa mère, car j'ai ouï dire qu'elle était lunatique (p. 64).

His discovery of Hortensius's genealogy repeats a movement found in all of Cyrano's explicit intertextual references, a movement that sets them apart from simple inscriptions of the names of previous novels in novels. For Cyrano, quotation is practiced in conjunction with an implicit reflection on its limits. Each time he quotes, Cyrano builds into his own text a scene inspired by a previous literary work, a literary work of a tradition with which his own presents affinities, and one that his reader is therefore likely to know. Then he announces his citation, with an initial effect of calling attention to the fictionality of the universe in which his text inscribes itself, of flaunting its self-consciousness. Cyrano's originality comes from the fact that he accompanies self-conscious denunciation, an awareness of citation, with a denial of citation. Hortensius/Sorel did not invent the idea of poems used as money; it already existed on the moon. He is not, therefore, inventing, but copying, just like the narrator/Cyrano. In the same manner, Tristan did not create the alchemist in his novel, since he existed, and Cyrano can prove it because his narrator met the demon, who was the alchemist, who met Tristan (who perhaps called himself the page?). Nothing more than flashy games, it might be argued. Perhaps. But through his manipulation of quotation, Cyrano is able to make a move beyond self-consciousness in the direction of a new representational "fallacy." He reunites books with their referents, at least on the moon.

Can Cyrano's free "tampering" with texts be used to document the libertine obsession with plagiarism? Did he himself lavish accusations of plagiarism on all those writers whose styles had affinities with his own because of an awareness of his own literary crimes? Many critics would agree with this view, Emile Roy, for example, who comments at length on Cyrano's "emprunts" from Sorel and concludes: "Les quelques pages où le pédant Hortensius expose ses projets de voyage fantastique dans la lune . . . ont plus servi à Cyrano de Bergerac, que tous les livres analogues publiés dans les trente années suivantes; il doit la moitié de ses 'burlesques audaces' à *l'Histoire comique de Francion* et au *Berger extravagant*."[30] Alcover speaks of Cyrano's "larcins," and contends that "aucune des coutumes, souvent ingénieuses, rencontrées dans la Lune n'est de Savinien: il a plagié partout."[31] The opinion that everything in Cyrano comes from someone else is responsible for the enormous number of pages devoted to the sources of his novels. The study of influences on him makes up the major part of Cyrano criticism.[32] Such a perspective, faithfully adopted, can lead to a judgment as severe as Jacques Denis's condemnation of the entire contemporary French libertine movement: "En général, leur esprit était tout d'emprunt, et leur science regardait plus vers le passé que vers l'avenir . . . A la différence de Descartes, qui semble jaloux de ne rien avancer que de lui-même, ils mettent leur esprit et leur gloire à citer."[33]

It is impossible to deny the libertine penchant for copying. However, the question of sources has now been sufficiently documented to allow the focus of the discussion to be shifted to the originality of such an enterprise. Maurice Blanchot says of Cyrano and *L'Autre Monde*: "Il n'invente rien . . . Et pourtant, il a une 'imagination de feu,' et *L'Autre Monde* est un livre qui frappe encore par son étrangeté et sa nouveauté."[34] It is the difference between borrowing and an art of quotation that can unravel Blanchot's paradox, that can explain why writers who, for some, are of interest only because of the sources they compile can also be described as "new" by Blanchot's modernity.

The problem of quotation in literary narrative has been treated in two complementary studies, Herman Meyer's *The Poetics of Quotation in the European Novel* and Bakhtin's *Marxism and the Philosophy of Language*. Both of these works articulate definitions of quotation that stress the dual nature of the relationship an incorporating text entertains with the discourse it incorporates. The relationship is based on similarity and difference, on rapprochement and distancing. As Meyer phrases it: "The charm of quotation emanates from a unique tension between assimilation and dissimulation: it links itself closely with its new environment, but at the same time detaches itself from it, thus permitting another world to radiate into the self-contained world of the novel."[35] Quoted discourse maintains a certain independence with regard to its new context. It is recognizable as a foreign element because it retains some or all of the exact words of its original author, and/or because it retains at least part of its first content.[36] Quotation represents the concrete linguistic presence of the other. This other is kept under control by being removed from its original context and inserted into a new, foreign one. Such an uprooting of necessity entails at least a minimal blurring of intentions.

It is this simultaneous otherness and sameness, this hide-and-seek effect, that Meyer uses to distinguish quotation from borrowing and thereby to separate its study from the search for influences or sources. A borrowing does not have a double nature, first, because it is completely severed from the context of its origin, and second, because its author's intentions are never blurred, simply repeated. All that is gained from tracing it to its source is what Meyer terms "a certain philological clarification" or "philological satisfaction."[37] The discovery of a borrowing neither enriches the meaning of the englobing text nor provides any clue to the aesthetic value of that text. Hence the failure of source studies to treat many passages in a text like Cyrano's composed of quoted material that is not severed from its original context, and that does not merely repeat the author's intentions in that context. Tracking down the numerous sources of ideas expressed in *L'Autre Monde* is an enterprise of a concrete value for the history of ideas, but one that does not necessarily contribute to an understanding of the works "nouveauté." To reduce *L'Autre Monde* to a list of authors whose theories it develops is to enrich the *livre à clef* theory with a new facet, to make yet another attempt to discover the mythical "*Grand Cyrus* libertin." Such a treatment is contrary to the spirit of libertine aesthetics as I have attempted to define it here. Ideas in *L'Autre Monde* are ultimately subordinated to a theory of knowledge, and this explains why quotation plays such an important role in the novel. The realization that the demon claims to have been Tristan's alchemist, for example, provides more than a philological satisfaction. It is essential for the comprehension of Cyrano's view of the nature and the status of fiction.

"Reported speech is speech within speech, utterance within utterance, and at the same time also *speech about speech, utterance about utterance*." Bakhtin's broadest definition of quotation[38] explains why the study of this phenomenon occupies such a privileged position in his work. Since there is no change of intention involved, speech that is merely borrowed does not require an act of recognition. But quotation is, in Hjelmslev's terminology, a connotative system because its signifier is already a language, someone else's language. Its signified is a calling into question of the nature and functioning of discourse. It must be seen for what it is, and it must be reunited with its original environment in order for its dialogue with and about language to flourish. For Bakhtin, quotation is one of the means by which texts created after the fall from carnival can recapture its spirit and reenter the kingdom of relativity.[39] It is the type of linguistic and intertextual dialogue generated by quotation that allows texts to escape imprisonment in a world of hierarchies and avoid the monologism that serves their cause.[40]

Dialogue is a model sketched everywhere in the libertine novels. The storytelling positions, first oral, then written, so frequently adopted in early first-person fiction are more than nominally present here. Francion stages a command performance of his life story for his "Gentil-homme Bourguignon." Contrary to standard practice for this particular convention, he does not launch into his tale and immediately forget the presence of the listener who had so eagerly begged for his rendition. By regularly proving that he is tailoring his performance to his audience, Francion maintains contact with the character who gives him a pretext for telling his life story. He foresees his objections ("Vous me direz que"). He demonstrates his faith in the other's ability to fill in the gaps ("Je vous laisse à juger si").

The narrator of the *Fragments* maintains a separate "frame" dialogue in each of the novel's sections: with the implied reader for whom he describes his tastes and habits, and with the readers sufficiently versed in contemporary polemics to be included in the first chapter's clearly literary "nous" ("nos vers d'aujourd'huy"; "Démosthene et Virgile n'ont point escrit en nostre temps, et nous ne saurions escrire en leur siecle"). *L'Autre Monde*'s series of conversations provide a model of dialogic solicitude. The interlocutors often engage in long tirades, but they persistently try to foresee the opinions of their partners in dialogue. While the Spaniard presents his ideas on the existence of a vacuum, for example, he constantly makes place in his discourse for the objections he imagines are being formed in the silent narrator's mind. By leaving room for antagonism, he creates a progressively larger and more hostile audience for his discourse: "Je vois fort bien que *vous* me demandez pourquoi donc. . . . Qu'*il* me réponde donc, je l'en supplie. . . . Mais, sans m'amuser à répondre à toutes *leurs* objections" (p. 69; italics mine).[41]

The mission D'Assoucy assigned to the *Avantures*—to justify his actions and save his reputation—is omnipresent. On the one hand, he takes the offensive and addresses his enemies by name in the hope of engaging them in a dialogue that will ultimately prove his innocence. Hence the diatribes directed at Loret, at Cyrano, at Chapelle ("Ample réponse de Dassoucy au Voyage de m. Chapelle") and at "Messieurs les sots," the legions of readers of Chapelle's *Voyage* who D'Assoucy imagines are convinced of his guilt ("Epistre à messieurs les Sots . . . contenant les actions de grace de l'autheur, des biens et des faveurs infinies que par toute terre il en a reçues"). This dialogue of aggression is complemented by a defensive dialogue with the "tres-sage Lecteur" (significantly in the more intimate singular), whom he constantly calls upon as the last purely innocent presence capable of believing in his virtue. This reader is asked to make judgments, to take sides (D'Assoucy's side) in his dialogue with the texts that have slandered him, with their writers and the readers who have accepted their testimony. To this reader alone, D'Assoucy will bear his soul: "Je te confesse, Lecteur" (p. 125).

In the libertine novels, dialogue is ubiquitous. The presence of levels of dialogue, from the situational (serving to recall the presence of a silent audience, and largely conventional) to the intertextual (with admired and scorned predecessors), is certainly worthy of note because of a degree of complexity and continuity uncommon at the period. However, dialogue does not in itself embody a philosophy of relativity. This is a function of the use of quotation. Citation provides the most convincing means of implying an essential tenet of freethinking, what Jan Miel has called the "discovery that all knowledge is hollow at the center."[42]

This awareness is often expressed in libertine texts by means of a device borrowed from the seminal work of self-conscious fiction, *Don Quixote*. The innkeeper gives the priest a copy of one of Cervantes's own *Exemplary Novels* (actually a double wink at the reader, since these were published after the first part of *Don Quixote*, in which the reference is placed). Early in the second part of the novel, Sancho reveals to the Don that "the story of your Grace has already been put into a book called *The Ingenious Gentleman, Don Quixote de la Mancha*, they mention me in it, under my own name, Sancho Panza . . . along with things that happened to us when we were alone together."[43] At these moments, the reader finds his foothold in fiction shaken.

Sorel, the libertine novelist closest to the self-conscious tradition, repeats this effect in the passage of *Francion* in which its hero discusses his novelistic projects.[44] Sorel uses both types of self-citation found in Cervantes in the same passage: he has Francion claim authorship of a not yet published text (*Le Berger extravagant*) and the text in which he is actually appearing (pp. 436–37). He thereby indulges in a game played out time and again in *Quixote*'s wake: the weakening of the boundaries between fiction and reality, and the destruction of the neatly established chronological territory assigned to a work of fiction. *Le Berger extravagant* is allowed a sort of impossible preview by being cited before its publication, before, therefore, it has a right to literary life. But this bit of anachronistic fireworks is surpassed by Francion's revelation that the book of his youth (*La Jeunesse de Francion*) already exists. Since *Francion* was originally published in serial form, for its contemporary readers the literary game is parallel to that created by Sancho Panza's discovery of the first part of *Don Quixote*. Francion, like Sancho and the Don, acquires a simultaneous and inconceivable double existence. Characters have no right to stick around to comment on the books that contain the story of their adventures. Furthermore, for the twentieth-century reader faced with the complete text of Francion's life, the issue is still more complicated: how can he describe the book of his life as though it were an independent volume, when the narrative in which those adventures are contained is not yet completed?

Cyrano continues such speculations in his pair of voyages. I have already discussed at some length the account of the composition of *Les Estats et empires de la lune* given at the beginning of *Les Estats et empires du soleil*. In this passage, Cyrano does not step outside the realm of the possible. Just as D'Assoucy mentions works he has already published, the *Ovide* and the volumes of his burlesque poetry, Cyrano stays within accepted literary chronology. Cyrano's reference is, nonetheless, more startling than D'Assoucy's self-conscious allusions because of his alterations, of his fictionalizing of fiction. Far from disturbing the reassuring chronology of literature, he creates for it a stability, in this case, one that is too good to be true. Cyrano describes the composition and publication of the first part of a two-volume work in that work's second volume, thereby providing both a transition between the two parts and a literary past for the second half. The transition is quite effective, since it establishes an intertextual identity between the two works: Dyrcona has been to the moon, has met the demon of Socrates; the narrator of the lunar voyage continues to exist, and acquires a name (which in turn involves him with Cyrano in the same way as the demon involved the page with Tristan). The past, however, is largely false. The *Estats et em-*

pires de la lune certainly had an existence at the time of the composition of the *Estats et empires du soleil*, but not a public one.
The action of choosing a place for it on the shelves of the library is
premature. But then, the only public existence to which a truly
libertine text can aspire is fictional.

This idea receives a more explicit treatment in a passage from
L'Autre Monde in which the demon makes the narrator a present
of two books he has selected to entertain the narrator while he
waits for the vehicle the demon is building for his voyage back to
earth. The first, brought to the moon from the demon's "pays
natal," the sun, is called *Les Etats et empires du soleil.* Cyrano's
anachronism, while following the model proposed by Cervantes
and already repeated by Sorel, adds a new twist to its speculations. The *Exemplary Novels* and *Le Berger extravagant* were
published only after they had acquired a fictional existence as
completed books, but their narratives in no way depend on those
of the works in which they are inscribed. The relationship between Cyrano's two voyages, however, is symbiotic. Can a sequel
exist as a completed, published volume before the narration of its
first half has been completed? Can, furthermore, this volume be
handed over to the individual who is identified in its opening
pages as its author? He is thus able to read it and his own story. He
can discover not only that he has written this book but that he will
write (therefore, has already written, if its composition and publication can be described in the book he is given) the story of the
voyage he is still living out on the moon.

The demon gives the narrator ("afin de vous divertir") not only
the story of his past life to read but also the story of his present life,
and even the story of the end of this phase of his life and much of
his future life as well. Sancho Panza is frightened when he thinks
of someone knowing about the past he had believed he alone possessed: "I had to cross myself, for I could not help wondering how
the one who wrote all those things down could have come to know
about them." Imagine his reaction if he had been asked, like the
narrator, to make a leap through several modernities, to be transformed into a character out of Borges. The narrator, fortunately,
is far less emotional than his Spanish predecessor, and he does not
even bat an eye. Perhaps he is able to preserve his *sang-froid* because he is in on the secret of the birth of all libertine texts. The

demon from the sun, who inspired Cardano and Campanella directly and Tristan (the page) indirectly, goes even further in the narrator's case, and hands him the book to be written, the *Estats et empires du soleil* (which also tells him how to write/how he wrote *L'Autre Monde*). This Socratic (dialogic) demon offered Tristan in "real" life magic potions. Disguised as Artefius, he gave Tristan's double, the page, both elixirs and impetus. He inspired Cardano's books, and was responsible for Campanella's subject and even his title ("un livre que nous intitulâmes *de Sensu rerum*," he says [p. 56], graciously sharing the credit with him). He reduces the narrator (Cyrano's double) to the level of a scribe as unoriginal as Flaubert's copy-clerks. Origin has been thwarted once again.

The demon does even more than that. Along with the narrator/ Dyrcona/Cyrano's book-to-be-that-already-is, he presents him with a second volume, about which he is more explicit:

> Je vous donne encore celui-ci que j'estime beaucoup davantage; c'est le *Grand Oeuvre des philosophes*, qu'un des plus forts esprits du soleil a composé. Il prouve là-dedans que toutes choses sont vraies, et déclare la façon d'unir physiquement les vérités de chaque contradictoire, comme par exemple que le blanc est noir et que le noir est blanc; qu'on peut être et n'être pas en même temps; qu'il peut y avoir une montagne sans vallée; que le néant est quelque chose, et que toutes les choses qui sont ne sont point. Mais remarquez qu'il prouve ces inouïs paradoxes, sans aucune raison captieuse, ni sophistique (pp. 103-4).

Within the context of libertine intertextuality, the reference to the *Grand Oeuvre des philosophes* enjoys an exceptional status. This is the only instance in which the work cited does not exist. Furthermore, from the demon's description, it is clear that this text would have a particular appeal for a libertine reader. The *Grand Oeuvre* is the ultimate work of freethinking, a book that stretches the dialogic reasoning of the demon's first master/pupil and of the freethinkers' first example/warning to its extreme (anti)conclusion: the destruction of the notion of opposites. No trace of hierarchy or the monologic in its universe. All systems of thought can peacefully coexist when "toutes choses sont vraies."

L'Autre Monde is Cyrano's web of other voices and other discourses, all pushed through a sieve until they lose their individual textures, and then glazed with a comic style and the rhetoric of dialogue, so that all its characters ultimately speak with the same voice. These different homogenized discourses are then juxtaposed, without the judgmental markers that would enable a reader to decide which one is "right." *L'Autre Monde*, in other words, aspires to be *Le Grand Oeuvre des philosophes*, the book of every libertine author's dreams. Next to his citation of his own, perhaps as yet only dreamed of, book, Cyrano inscribes the most curious of his libertine *mises en abyme*. The demon's second gift to the narrator provides a clue to the importance of all these citations, and, after his presentation, he makes his message clear in his salutation and last words to the narrator: "Songez à librement vivre" (p. 104).

By means of these citations, the dialogue is kept open, and the voices of the past continue to be heard. *L'Autre Monde* even contains a vision of a dialogic utopia: the books the demon gives the narrator are "oral." They are boxes carved from precious stones that contain metal disks with ridges. Each box is wound up with a key, and its needle is placed on the ridge of the desired chapter. The lunar books have the advantage of reproducing an author's voice as his text: "Ainsi vous avez éternellement autour de vous tous les grands hommes et morts et vivants qui vous entretiennent de vive voix" (p. 105). They can thus defy what Bakhtin perceived to be the ultimate barrier to the realization of the dialogic in a literary text: the inability of the work held prisoner within the pages of a book to do more than faintly suggest (through *skaz*) the voice of its author and thereby the oral language to which his system accords primacy.

Regarded in this light, citation's role in a libertine system seems positive, blending the past, the present, and the possible in a discourse of progressive liberation. However, this overlooks one implication of the structure of the demon's presentation. When Cyrano juxtaposes his own would-be book with another book also, in a sense, of his own invention but impossible on earth, a dream book, he puts into question the importance of his own intellectual enterprise. Can his own book ever have any real value, or might it just as well be only imaginary? The narrator's lunar visitors do not bother to speak to him because they have already told Cardano what they want to say to him, and Cardano has transcribed their message for all to read. If the *Grand Oeuvre des philosophes* already exists in some other world(s), is it necessary to repeat its message in an imperfect, earthly book? Quotation may be a valuable tool for the expression of freethinking, but it is impossible to maintain a sense of self-importance in its presence. After all, as Edward Said points out: "Quotation is a constant reminder that writing is a form of displacement. For although quotation can take many forms, in every one the quoted passage symbolizes other writing as encroachment, as a disturbing force moving potentially to take over what is presently being written. . . . It is a reminder that other writing serves to displace present writing . . . from its absolutely central, proper place."[45] Thus, the libertine penchant for quotation is born of the same sense of alienation that spreads their fear of plagiarism. Writers constantly aware of the slippage between discourses, of the impossibility of staking a claim and policing it in the territory of language, know that they can have no voice of their own. They must adopt the voice of the other, annihilate the self to facilitate its blending into the other.

There are striking illustrations of this in the libertine novels. The "singe de Scarron" who writes about the "singe de Brioché" makes an extravagant use of his own previous works. He frequently refers to the number and importance of the "gros volumes" he has already published. More surprisingly, he even inserts (quotes) entire poems of his composition. These texts have been in print previously in one or another of the fat volumes, but D'Assoucy feels compelled to give them a second literary existence, in a last-ditch attempt to defend himself against slander and to guarantee that at least his poetic voice will be heard. In the event that his latest literary creation, the *Avantures* (an additional "cinq gros volumes," as he tells the king in his dedication), is not sufficient to speak for him, he juxtaposes his old literary voice and his new one. But just as he realizes that the juxtaposition of his version of his life with Chapelle's contradictory one will ultimately annihilate both of them ("Mais pour dire la vérité, / L'un et l'autre de son costé / N'a rien écrit de véritable." [p. 188]), so he must sense that his poems will suffer a loss of importance from their reduction to the status of quotation. Because of their interpolation, his own poems become foreign. The territory of D'Assoucy's "new" literary voice in the *Avantures* is so overrun by other voices, both friendly and enemy, that its force, and that of the present it represents, are weakened. Once again, D'Assoucy manages to help his enemies in their task of destroying him.

Repetition also undermines the auctorial or narrative voice in Cyrano's voyages. In the course of an interior monologue during his solar sojourn, Dyrcona considers four examples that illustrate the imagination's power over the body. His reflections are immediately followed by a conversation with a bird who explains to him that "la Nature a imprimé aux oiseaux une secrette envie de voler jusqu'icy, et peut-estre que cette emotion de nostre volonté est ce qui nous a fait croistre des ailes." The bird goes on to give four examples of similar occurrences involving humans, in which it is disconcerting to recognize two of the four incidents cited by the narrator only two pages earlier: that of the pregnant women whose babies take on the shape of their desires and that of Cippus, who, dreaming of bulls, made horns grow from his forehead. These vignettes are in no way disguised to keep the reader from recognizing them as those just used, and the only change is in their order (Dyrcona's first example becomes the bird's last, and his last is the first used by the bird). This is a strange case of repetition afraid to go unnoticed. Although the *Estats et empires* is perhaps not the most polished of texts, this figure is certainly intentional, for surely any author could remember a passage for two pages. Such a blatant repetition raises questions about the possession and the uniqueness of discourse. If the same thing can be said by two speakers, then the speaker's identity is no longer important.

L'Autre Monde poses this question of narrative identity more forcefully still. When the narrator lands on the moon, he finds himself in the *Paradis terrestre* whose beauties he proceeds to describe at some length (pp. 41–43). This passage is clearly parenthetical, different in tone and form from the rest of the text. In a work as bare of obvious rhetoric as *L'Autre Monde*, this elaborate figure seems out of place. It is reminiscent of Cyrano's public letters, such as those about the four seasons, whose carefully codified elegance is a far cry from the seventeenth-century comic tradition. Moreover, the passage seems contrary in intention to Cyrano's small *Oeuvre des philosophes*: it is the only segment in *L'Autre Monde* in which the monologic manages to drown out the dialogic. In a work devoted, if not to causal development, at least to unfolding narrative elements through repetition and addition, it represents a moment of stasis that challenges the text's momentum, all the more remarkable because it stands alone in a work hostile to description and does not form one link in a chain of ornaments. This carefully sculptured digression seems a more likely candidate for Scudery's *Ibrahim* than for Cyrano's manifesto against closure.

Such clues, for once, are not meant to lead the reader astray. The unmistakeable sensation of difference generated by the narrator's description of the Earthly Paradise on the moon stems from its very real literary independence. It is not without reason that Cyrano's descriptive parenthesis recalls the style of his public letters: it is (or was) part of one of them. The charms of Paradise were first enumerated as part of a (fictional) seduction plot with a scenario reminiscent of that which allegedly motivated the writing of *La Religieuse*. In a letter usually referred to as "D'une maison de campagne," but also as "Le Campagnard," the narrator tries to convince an unidentified friend to leave Paris and return to his country home. To prepare the text for insertion in *L'Autre Monde*, Cyrano simply eliminated the frame seduction motif and made minor alterations and cuts in the descriptive body of the text.[46] He thereby removes the text from its original *raison d'être*, leaving it free to be manipulated as a prefabricated literary building block. Cyrano then performs a maneuver rare in literary history: he indulges in a lengthy self-citation. This citation must be distinguished from any other enclave of foreign influence in *L'Autre Monde*. It is completely unrelated to the borrowings from the systems of Gassendi, Copernicus, and others that frequently subtend its discussions. It is also different from its fellow citations because its source is not mentioned and it bears no other habitual signal of its status, and because there is nothing in it of Cyrano's playful sleight of hand. No real changes are made in the passage. No fun can be had and no insight gained from returning it to the context of its creation. This is the only section of *L'Autre Monde* that refuses to dialogue, either internally or externally. Due to its array of superlatives and the preciosity of its images, the description can function equally well and equally blandly in any situation calling for a beautiful spot, an estate thought to be heaven on earth, or the "real" earthly heaven in the other world.

This much links the passage to the question of narrative identity. The speaker loses importance when what he has to say can be shifted verbatim from mouth to mouth. But that point alone is not sufficient to explain why Cyrano chooses to double his narrative voice, without either calling attention to his trick or covering it up by pushing this discourse, like all the other ones, through his stylistic sieve to make it blend in. Perhaps the doubling goes undenounced because, for once, quotation is totally dissociated from self-conscious games and the comic tradition. Its implications here are far more serious. If Cyrano does not use original words to describe utopia, it is not because he is unable to find them but because he chooses not to. This self-avowed amateur of citation and obsessive borrower who does nothing to hide either his borrowing or its obsessiveness, this writer so afraid that his words will be pillaged that he accuses even his closest friends of plagiarism, gives utopia the form of self-citation. If ideas can come from other books and inspiration can be attributed to other books, why not a vision of paradise as well? In this case, Cyrano, instead of having his text violated by foreigners, as he feared would happen, is able to indulge in a moment of auto-mutilation (castration). Instead of having his voice displaced only by the foreign voices whose presence he constantly senses around him, he is displaced by one of his own other voices. This is without question the most dangerous invasion in *L'Autre Monde*. Cyrano's self-citation casts doubts on the originality of both utopia and his own voice.

This evocation of the pitfalls of cliché and copying can be linked to the parody of an inflated "heroic" style discussed early in this chapter in relation to Théophile and Sorel. The sin of merely repeating what has already been said by others must be avoided at any price. The crucial point of the literary manifesto that opens the *Fragments* is a simple one: a writer must find his own language, not the language of others: "Il faut comme Homere faire bien une description; mais non point par ses termes, ny par ses Epithetes: il faut escrire comme il a escrit, mais non pas ce qu'il a escrit" (p. 3). After his initial declarations in favor of originality, Théophile proceeds to fill his text with examples of language that fails to communicate. There is Ronsard's pedantic and cumbersome return to Greek and Latin roots ("Il semble qu'il se veuille rendre incogneu pour paroitre Docte. . . . Dans ces termes estrangers il n'est point intelligible pour François" [pp. 2–3]). There

are those who hide behind Latin and assume, like Ronsard for his
"mots forgés," that it is intelligible to all: Sidias peppers his sentences with Latin phrases that he does not bother to translate into
French and that remain empty signifiers. There are the nonsense
sounds of the "fille obsédée" who has learned what her teachers
consider a convincing language of possession: "Elle . . . court
en gromelant quelques mots de Latin mal prononcé: je luy parlay
Latin le plus distinctement qu'il m'estoit possible, mais je ne vis
jamais aucune apparence qu'elle l'entendit" (p. 16). These incorrectly assimilated foreign tongues illustrate language's communicative breakdown when it is blindly repeated and distanced from
its original function. The enclaves of empty signifiers the narrator
cites, like Cyrano's self-quotation, are hopelessly monologic
when they are cut off from their roots in conversation and seduction and cannot find the dialogue that would give them meaning.

The libertine meditations on cliché, quotation, and other
phenomena of linguistic uprootedness are rarely counteracted by
moments of linguistic creativity capable of indicating routes out
of the quagmire of the already said or ways of returning the
speaker's sense of identity and property to him. If one overlooks
the progressiveness and vitality of the *Fragments'* manifesto,
there is not much evidence elsewhere to indicate that the modernity forecast by these texts is really that of the Romantics, as Gautier would have us believe, and not that of a far more nihilistic
vision, constantly displaced by inter- and meta-textuality. The
libertine awareness, with only rare exceptions, is unable to go
beyond the sense of invasion by other voices in order to reassert
power over the aggressor.

Early in the *Avantures*, D'Assoucy receives a gift more precious than any magic potion: he learns how to break out of the
vicious circle of his repeated misfortunes. The thief-with-a-
thousand-faces teaches him how to avoid being robbed, and this
lesson simultaneously indicates a method for surmounting his literary paranoia. First he explains that everyone is a thief, and then
he exposes the complex linguistic system devised by men to hide
both their activity and their awareness of its status:

> Chaque métier a son nom, chaque permission de dérober a son
> titre.
>   Si le Capitaine vole le soldat, cela s'appelle le *tour du baston*; le

soldat volé par son capitaine vole le paysan, et ce vol s'appelle *vivre sur le bon homme*. Le paysan volé par le soldat prend tout ce qui se rencontre dans son desespoir, et ce vol s'appelle

Butiner,

Fourager,

Aller à la petite guerre,

Aller en course,

Faire contribuer, etc.,

sont les titres honorables dont les nobles enfans de Mars se servent pour s'emparer honnestement du bien d'autruy. . . .

Que diray-je de plus? autant d'hommes, autant de larrons; et, autant de larcins differens, autant de titres particuliers: comme *Rançonner, faire venir l'eau au moulin, faire un trou à la nuit, tirer d'un sac deux moutures, jouer de la harpe, griveler, grapiller, plumer la poule sans crier, sophistiquer, frelatter, faire du bien d'autruy large courroye, donner à manger a la pie, mettre de la paille en ses souliers, plier la toilette, alliage, corvée, monopole*. . . .

Ainsi dans le monde dérobant et dérobé, chacun dérobe sous ses titres spécieux, et les plus puissans comme les plus dignes d'estre respectez erigent leurs larcins en titre d'honneur, ainsi, il faut qu'un honneste larron, s'il veut dérober honnestement et sans reproche, ait ses patentes (pp. 28–29).

An instinctive first response to this passage might link it to the problematic of language's nonfunctioning so often evoked in the libertine texts. After all, the thief describes another instance of subversion of the communicative function. Words are used here in order to camouflage, to remain opaque to all but a small number of initiate who alone are capable of discerning the thief's paradox: though expressions like "faire un trou à la nuit" and "jouer de la harpe" would appear to the outsider to belong to completely different semantic worlds, in fact they are synonyms. The range of expressions he is able to elucidate makes evident why this impressive passage is confided to the thief. Through him, language becomes an active accomplice in an act faithful to its nature of deception and duplicity: the instrument of the libertine's loss of identity helps rob others of their material property.

It cannot be argued, however, that the passage in its entirety remains nihilistic. In fact, the notion of language's ability to conceal and impoverish is almost taken for granted. Far more striking than the idea that everything the thief says can be reduced to a unique *signifié* is the dazzling richness of the *signifiants* that can be used to convey that one meaning. Signifying here is clearly subordinated to connotation. This passage is the antithesis of those moments in the *Avantures* where D'Assoucy, like a caged beast, grovels for scraps of pity. Here the emperor reigns in new clothes, brilliant in their opacity. For a moment, he revels in the secret of his extraction from the alienation of linguistic *singeries*. And the thief's method is as easy as child's play. Instead of trying to get around language's deceptiveness, flaunt it, indulge in it, enjoy it. The catalogue of thievery explodes with the paradoxical riches of language's nonfunctioning, verbal proof that "larcins" can become "titres d'honneur."[47] There is no doubt that the ill-gotten gains D'Assoucy parades before his "cher Lecteur" are fascinating. He taps the deepest source of synonyms and metaphors, the realms of slang and popular language, and uses them to create a brilliant verbal carnival. D'Assoucy demonstrates that linguistic play and the games of language can ward off displacement by quotation and cliché and can return his text to a context of relativism as surely as do the images of the union of opposites and the systems of reversal in *L'Autre Monde* and *Francion*.[48]

"Quotation and proverb have as a common denominator the fact that both are preformed linguistic material. Proverbs in their totality constitute an unwritten literature, as it were, and represent a popular analogue to the quotation for written literature," Meyer affirms.[49] Thus, proverb can be used to "fight" quotation because they are in this sense equal arms. D'Assoucy is not the only libertine novelist to sense the potential of proverbs for making the essence of oral dialogue accessible to written texts. Some of the most Promethean (Prometheus was, after all, a thief) moments in *L'Autre Monde* involve an exploration of proverbs and lexicalized expressions. But whereas D'Assoucy accumulates gleaming heaps of proverbs in order to glorify their variety and suggestiveness, Cyrano scrutinizes them one by one and painstakingly dissects them. For Blanchot, this literal interpretation of metaphor—or, rather, this giving life to situations inscribed in proverbial expressions—is the central creative impetus behind *L'Autre Monde*: "Presque toutes les situations importantes de *L'Autre Monde* sont des métaphores qui se réalisent par de vraies métamorphoses. Le language prend le pas sur le contenu théorique."[50] The carnival D'Assoucy describes is a nocturnal one (thieves prefer the dark; if necessary, they can always "faire un trou à la nuit"), so it is only natural that Cyrano's exploration of its creative consequences take place in the lunar dimness. And the original "trou à la nuit" is, of course, the moon, which may also be the sun, according to *L'Autre Monde*'s opening paragraph: "Ce pourrait bien être . . . le soleil lui-même, qui s'étant au soir dépouillé de ses rayons regardait par un trou ce qu'on faisait au monde quand il n'y était plus" (p. 31).

Cyrano produces his own verbal fireworks when he gives new life to the ultimate in the already said, to words so borrowed that they fulfill the libertine dream of being beyond origin. Popular language receives the same literal interpretation as other systems in *L'Autre Monde*. Cyrano's literary citations attempt to confirm the "reality" of incidents from various works, by providing eyewitness accounts (either the narrator's or the demon's) that consider them as historical rather than literary facts. The treatment of biblical scenes that Le Bret found dangerous enough to merit expurgation is in fact no more devious or sophisticated. All of the narrator's long conversation with Elie in the Earthly Paradise examines the consequences of the assumption that everything narrated in the Bible literally took place in exactly that manner. Hence, for example, Elie's description of the solution to the dilemma of interplanetary travel devised by Enoch when he, long before the narrator, decided to head for the moon. Jacob's ladder had not yet been invented, so he is forced to resort to his memory of God's words "l'odeur des sacrifices du juste est montée jusqu'à moi." Enoch fills two bottles with the smoke from his next sacrifice, attaches them under his arms, and, like the narrator after him, aspires straight up to Paradise.

When Cyrano extends this same treatment to lexicalized expressions, his game becomes both more complex and more elusive. One indeed begins to suspect, along with Blanchot, that there are metaphors coming to life all over the pages of *L'Autre Monde*, like the solar men who are born when they bubble up out of the warm mud (p. 132). Blanchot's discussion of the scenario devised by Cyrano to act out the implications of formulas such as "mourir de chagrin" and "être dévoré de mouches" provides a model for further explorations of the expressions that lie unnoticed behind Cyrano's words and situations. Not all of them, however, remain hidden. For example, the translation of one proverb from metaphoric to literal status is clearly explained:

> . . . Le chasseur décharge en l'air un coup de feu, et vingt ou trente alouettes churent à nos pieds toutes cuites. Voilà, m'imaginai-je aussitôt, ce qu'on dit par proverbe en notre monde d'un pays où les alouettes tombent toutes rôties! Sans doute quelqu'un était revenu d'ici (p. 64).

With the narrator's lunar experience, terrestial language finally finds a home. Words with only a metaphorical signification are given a new life when what is impossible suddenly takes place. *L'Autre Monde* attempts to reinstate the old, symbiotic relationship between words and things and, in so doing, releases language from the tyranny of the already said and restores to it some of its lost magic. Language is freed, if only briefly, from the context of broken-down communication and displacement of identity, and is portrayed as an all-powerful force. Words can make anything happen. Everything that can be said is possible, if not in this world, at least in another. With his proverb-come-true, Cyrano rejoins D'Assoucy's carnivalistic celebration of the joys of language. Because of its unbroken ties to oral tradition and the spirit of carnival, street language, Boileau's (in)famous "langage des Halles," can remain creatively alive and anti-hierarchical. It can resist confinement through codification, while its connotative suggestiveness simultaneously permits self-conscious explorations. By setting off proverbial language's fireworks, the libertine authors most intimately connected with the burlesque manage to unite Bakhtin and Foucault.

3. THE MUTED BELL

Je suis la cloche qui annonce une aurore nouvelle. (Campanella)

Spink provides a translation of Gassendi's pedagogical goal:

> I always saw to it that my pupils were in a position to defend Aristotle fittingly, but I proposed to them nevertheless by way of appendices the opinions by which Aristotle's dogmatic teaching is weakened. . . . By this means my pupils were warned not to decide too hastily, seeing that they would never meet with an opinion or proposition so admitted and so plausible that its opposite could not be shown to be equally probable, if not more probable still.[51]

The master of relativism's discourse on method provides a succinct résumé of the attraction and the pitfalls of the dialogic. Most evident is its attraction. Such a demonstration that "toutes choses sont vraies" must have seemed a heady philosophy indeed. Gassendi's method was perfectly suited to an age when, for the first time, relativistic writers refused to have their open-endedness counterbalanced by unflinching belief in some untouchable system of values. Even their immediate predecessors were either unwilling or unable to go that far: dialogue in Rabelais, for example, is ultimately broken by his unambiguously reverent attitude toward antiquity. The seventeenth-century libertines, however, are prepared to look to the future without even the comfort of a backward glance. Witness Adam's description of the new attitude toward satire developed by Sorel: "Ce n'est pas au nom de la tradition que Sorel condamne les vices de son temps. . . . Il n'invite pas les hommes à se retourner vers le passé. Il les appelle à se libérer."[52] It might be argued that the liberation Sorel presents is restrained by an almost religious glorification of nature. Yet even if this barrier to the development of seventeenth-century libertinism did exist at one point, it too will eventually disappear. By the time Cyrano comes along, even the religion of nature has been rejected, and most of his commentators would agree with Prévot's judgment: "La cohérence de ses critiques et de sa satire ne donne naissance à aucune sagesse. Thèse et antithèse ne se résolvent pas en synthèse, la dialectique demeure en suspens."[53]

By demonstrating an absence of faith unheard of prior to their appearance, the libertines outdo their sixteenth-century precursors in a manner many have interpreted as a necessary prelude to the explosion of freethinking in the eighteenth century. The libertines of the seventeenth century have often been considered a vital link in an intellectual chain, a life force that succeeded in keeping a movement alive at what could be viewed as its nadir: "C'est eux et non les dogmatistes du dix-septième siècle qui établissent et nous font toucher du doigt la continuité de la chaine, l'union des idées. Sans eux serait inexplicable, au temps de Voltaire, ce retour offensif."[54] Such an attitude is hardly surprising. It can turn for support to no less an authority than Voltaire. In a letter to Chaulieu, the first leader of victorious freethinking imagines a conversation with Chapelle and Bachaumont in which the former tells him:

> Puis à Chaulieu l'épicurien
> Je servis quelque temps de maître:
> Il faut que Chaulieu soit le tien.[55]

The vision is heroic and therefore appealing. It is tempting to accept at face value the romanticism of the young Voltaire and not to question the extensive influence exercised by the seventeenth-century libertine thinkers.

But there is, after all, madness in Gassendi's method. A teaching that aims to demonstrate that no system is airtight—that no system can be used to exclude the possibility of other, even contradictory, ones—such a teaching can only make life very difficult for its adherents. Taken to its extremes, dialogic reasoning leaves nothing to hold on to. A thinker who accepts its tenets must always see that the opposite of any system that attracts him is equally plausible. He must never lose the awareness that any system that gains a following will eventually be overthrown, and, most difficult of all, that even a system of freedom and relativism, a system that pretends to be a non-system or an anti-system, cannot survive the holocaust. Thus, in the *incipit* of *L'Autre Monde*, the narrator and his friends mock the comprehensive systems that pretend to have an explanation for everything (Christianity, Classical mythology), but the loudest laughter of all is reserved for the narrator's system of relativism. Any reader alert to the consequences of the leveling process of *L'Autre Monde*'s juxtapositions cannot but sense that the new scientific openness, allegedly championed by a libertine such as Cyrano, will not stand up to the force of questioning he unleashes.

The signs of the defeat of the libertine experience are inscribed in the libertine life-stories. At key moments, the libertine hero experiences intellectual failure, the failure of knowledge, the impossibility of total freedom, and always under humiliating circumstances. The page is given three vials that represent infinite knowledge and complete liberation, but he lets them fall in a moment of awkwardness. The narrator of *L'Autre Monde* literally crashes into paradise, and ends up in a most ignominious position: "Je me trouvai sous un arbre embarrassé avec trois ou quatre branches assez grosses que j'avais éclatées par ma chute, et le visage mouillé d'une pomme qui s'était écachée contre" (p. 41). He falls not only into the Garden of Eden but also into knowledge, in the form of an apple, but the relationship is not a successful one. He destroys the fruit of wisdom, and ends up with it smeared all over his face, no wiser for the experience. No less humiliating is Dyrcona's encounter with infinite freedom in the beginning of the *Estats et empires.* He acquires his name (when Cussan asks: "Et vous, monsieur Dyrcona, quel a esté le vostre?") in the episode when the three friends tell each other their dreams. Dyrcona had seen himself pursued by assassins, and escaping them, when "dans un Ciel libre et fort éclairé, mon corps soulagé de toute pesanteur, j'ay poursuivy mon voyage jusques dans un Palais où se composent la chaleur et la lumière." The dream of liberation, however, ends just as abruptly as the page's possession of the vials: "J'y aurois sans doute remarqué bien d'autres choses, mais mon agitation pour voler m'avoit tellement approché du bord du lit que je suis tombé dans la ruelle, le ventre tout nu sur le plastre, et les yeux fort ouverts" (p. 106). Dyrcona is agitated; the page opens his hand; both are afraid of the experience of knowledge. The humiliating positions in which they find themselves serve to burlesque the great dream of freethinking.

The fact that the narrator's dream comes to a bad end just after he arrives in a place that evidently represents the sun is a premonition of failure for the work in which his dream is inscribed. In any libertine system, and especially in one with a Promethean vocabulary like Cyrano's, the sun, the home of light, enjoys a privileged position. It is on the sun, for example, that the demon is born, and from there that he brings the books of total philosophy. But for a libertine who has taken the dialogue of freethinking so far that he is afraid of a world in which it would find perfect realization, the sight of the sun can only bring about a sensation of vertigo. Indeed, as Dyrcona approaches the sun for the second time (this time in "reality," not in dream), the normally stoic traveler registers the strongest emotional reaction of his life. It is with "horreur" that he realizes that his body has become transparent (p. 134). In his commentary on this passage, Blanchot concludes: "Il ne supporte pas ce regard suprême qui le rend invisible à force de le voir. Cette chute angoissée dans le jour, cet attachement instinctif au corps obscur et impénétrable représente beaucoup plus que les idées physiques qui tournent autour de l'episode."[56] Much more indeed. When Dyrcona continues to the land of perfect light, he disappears. He disappears because he is seen too well. He also disappears because he is no longer able to be seen. The sun blinds all those who get too close to it, all those who try to look at it without mediation. If you choose to see the sun, you will never again see anything else. The same analogy holds true in the realm of questioning. In the home of total dialogue, your book, too, becomes invisible, loses its importance. When too clearly seen, its ideas disappear like Dyrcona's body.

It is logical, therefore, that Dyrcona's solar explorations mark the apex of monologic systems. Cyrano, the most daring of the libertine novelists, the man with "une imagination de feu," ends his novelistic enterprise by constructing a monument to (his fear of) the impossibility of the libertine enterprise. Once Dyrcona reaches the sun, the entire form of his story is irrevocably altered. He finds fewer interlocutors; he no longer dialogues with himself; dialogue is generally replaced by description and narrative; a series of interpolated stories acquires an inordinate importance; the "corps obscur" of intertextuality to which he had clung almost disappears; there are few references to illustrious predecessors. In general, the question of self-consciousness vanishes from the pages of the *Estats et empires*. Dyrcona learns that the perfect language exists, the "langue matrice," in which there is no gap between thought and expression: "Cet idiome est l'instinct ou la voix de la Nature." The "langue matrice" is comprehensible to all beings, human and animal, because it is so logical: "Le premier homme de nostre monde s'estoit indubitablement servy de cette langue matrice, parce que chaque nom qu'il avoit imposé à chaque chose déclaroit son essence."[57] He also learns that in science there is "un Vray, hors lequel on estoit toûjours éloigné du facile" (p. 129). Such theories of language and scientific truth are perfectly suited to make the last master who appears to guide Dyrcona feel at home: when the *Estats et empires* breaks off, Descartes has just entered the scene. Furthermore, allegory, the monologic's best friend, rears its ugly head on the sun, first in the battle between the "beste à Feu" and the "animal Glaçon," the *Salamandre* and the *Remore*, and then in Campanella's long description of solar topology, especially the rivers and fountains of the five senses. In this context, the outcome of the combat between fire and ice comes as no surprise: "Ainsi mourut la beste à Feu sous la paresseuse résistance de l'animal Glaçon" (p. 180). In the long run, the Promethean complex does not even die a glorious death—it simply has its energy "lazily" pushed out of it. The demon may distribute solar books, but he had to leave the sun before he could begin giving out inspiration.

In a sense, this less-than-glorious culmination of the libertine quest was inscribed in its beginning. The descriptive, allegorical passage at the end of the *Estats et empires* serves as a structural counterpart to *L'Autre Monde*'s (false) utopia. Both are concerned with the gratification of the five senses. Unlike Rabelais and Voltaire, Cyrano situates his utopia at the beginning of his text. And he has his narrator speedily evicted from this monologic, borrowed, and (for a libertine) empty anti-paradise, never again to find his way back—not that he wants to. It seems odd that he, like Candide, never attempts to regain "paradise," until it becomes clear that "paradise" is exactly where he was heading all along. Dyrcona builds machine after machine and makes countless voyages, just to end up where he started, in the midst of allegory, this time in the company of Descartes.

Hardly a glorious end for the libertines' most unrelenting questioner and most skillful practitioner of the art of dialogue. But as the page knew from the moment he began to put his story in writing, only disgrace(s) can await those who adopt this life style. As to whether their books served a useful function, kept a chain unbroken, were listened to in an age that saw the triumph of freethinking's vertiginous spiral, well, Sade, the most superb of the "hommes noirs," said there was no seventeenth-century novel before Madame de Lafayette. Diderot told his daughter to read *Le Roman comique*, but no *Histoires comiques*. Rousseau had surely never heard of his less than illustrious predecessor in the discovery of persecution's joys. The libertine novelists would almost certainly not have been surprised at this outcome. They made no great promises, and would have agreed with Galileo that, without them, they would have no following: "Grandiose promises attract the natural curiosity of men and hold them forever involved in fantasies and chimeras."[58] They never pretended to be of the race of Campanella, capable of ringing in a new dawn. Hence their disgrace. Unless, of course, they somehow agreed with the judgment of the *Fragments*' libertinely anonymous narrator: "Cette disgrace n'est que paroles qui ne sont que vent" (p. 7).

1. Paul Hazard, *La Crise de la conscience européenne*, p. v.

2. In "Ideas or Epistemes: Hazard versus Foucault," Jan Miel contrasts these two important schemas, and argues for the usefulness of supplementing Hazard's *crise de conscience* with a second period of crisis that he situates at the end of the sixteenth century.

3. Spink, p. 6.

4. Pintard, pp. 75–76.

5. *Degré zéro*, pp. 49–50.

6. In Foucault's terminology, an episteme is the basis structure of knowledge of a given period.

7. *Les Mots et les choses*, p. 70.

8. The two visions of modernity sometimes coincide, and the same work is interpreted on the one hand as a meditation on the arbitrariness of language and on the other as an attempt to shatter that arbitrariness.

9. In this section, I will follow the practice adopted by Roman Jakobson in his preface to the French edition of *Marxism and the Philosophy of Language* (Editions de Minuit, 1977) of attributing this work to Bakhtin. Jakobson states that Vološinov, the critic to whom this work was previously attributed, merely revised certain sections to meet the demands of censorship and allowed his name to be used as a pseudonym for Bakhtin. This change in attribution remains problematic, and many critics now refer to the author of *Marxism* as Bakhtin/Vološinov.

10. *Marxism and the Philosophy of Language* and the first edition of *Dostoevsky's Poetics* both appeared in 1929, a second edition of *Dostoevsky's Poetics* in 1963, and *Rabelais and His World* was finally published in 1965, even though the work's composition dates from 1940. In quoting from these works, I will refer to the recent English translations of them.

11. *Rabelais and His World*, pp. 11, 34.

12. Ibid., p. 26. The link Bakhtin establishes between the carnival and the grotesque recalls Wolfgang Kayser's concept of the grotesque. Indeed, Kayser, like all the theoreticians mentioned here, describes the mid-seventeenth century as an important period of transformation and, like Bakhtin, feels that the *grand siècle*'s work is a negative force, responsible for a "loss of substance" as far as the grotesque is concerned. "Here the grotesque had lost all its sinister overtones and merely elicits a carefree smile." According to Kayser, the grotesque loses its energy because of "the tendency to equate it with the burlesque," and he mentions Cyrano and Scarron as two of the writers who share an important responsibility for this "crime" (*The Grotesque in Art and Literature*, p. 27). Bakhtin realizes that surface similarities appear to link his system with Kayser's, and is quick to stress their differences. He feels that Kayser errs in separating the gro-

tesque from carnival and folk humor and in privileging Romantic theories of the grotesque at the expense of ancient, medieval, or Renaissance ones. These fundamental errors lead Kayser to view the grotesque only as a principle of terror, and the world of the grotesque not as a world upside down but a world become alien to men. Kayser's shortcomings culminate in what is for Bakhtin a completely false definition of the grotesque: "The Grotesque is the estranged world" (Kayser, p. 184; *Rabelais*, pp. 39, 46–47).

13. *Rabelais*, pp. 33–34.

14. Thus, Kristeva interprets him as a precursor for her own theories of intertextuality in "Le Mot, le dialogue, et le roman."

15. Pp. 57–58. (The English edition is attributed to Vološinov.) It is interesting to read Bakhtin's attack in conjunction with Louis Marin's study of the irrationality behind Port-Royal's rationality, of the anti-representational drive behind its theory of representation (*La Critique du discours*).

16. *Marxism*, p. 11.

17. These are the formal characteristics I ascribe to the libertine novel in chapter three. Bakhtin's study of the menippea makes it possible to situate this novel in a long "tradition."

18. Hirzel, *Der Dialog: Ein Literarhistorischer Versuch*, 2:443–44; Consentini, *Fontenelle's Art of Dialogue*.

19. Although Théophile and Sorel are the first French seventeenth-century novelists to begin their novels in this way, other subsequent *histoires* and *romans comiques* will choose the same type of parodic *incipit* (*Le Romant satyrique*, *Le Gascon extravagant*, *Le Roman comique*, etc.). It eventually comes to constitute one of the distinguishing marks of a comic novel. See my "Scarron's *Roman comique*: The Other Side of Parody."

20. *Traicté de la peste* (J. et C. Périer, 1623), quoted by Pintard, p. 196.

21. In *Francion*, the functions of writing and reading are partially divided between the two narrators. The anonymous voice that first assumes responsibility for the narration is a reader so familiar with heroic texts that he is able to parody them. This initial narrative voice does not lay claim to the composition of *Francion*, but Francion himself does.

22. The older page is capable of joining the narrators of the *Fragments* and *Francion* in their mockery of the clichés he favored in his youth. He sees the ridiculous aspect of the narrative inflation in his performance for his mistress and her cousin: "Je leur fis une description des beautés d'Amour, qu'elles trouvèrent merveilleuse, pour ce que je pris un style poétique. Je ne me contentai pas de leur représenter tout le corps de Cupidon comme une belle statue d'albâtre qu'on aurait couchée sur un lit, et de faire ses cheveux d'une agréable confusion de filets d'or. Je leur voulus encore dépeindre en ce sujet des choses qu'on ne voyait pas. . . . Je leur représentai sa bouche . . . et leur dis que le vif corail de ses lèvres couvrait encore deux rangs de perles plus blanches et plus précieuses que toutes celles que donne la mer" (pp. 124–25).

23. *Narcisse romancier*, p. 66.

24. In *Imitation and Illusion in the French Memoir Novel*, Philip Steward discusses many different variants on the use of historical figures as characters in the eighteenth-century novel: as title characters in pseudo memoirs, as minor characters who function almost as elements of local color. He also documents

cases in which only a name is borrowed to be given to a completely fictional character, and examples of characters whose names resemble those of historical figures. The only moment in this movement toward realism in naming that could be related to Cyrano's creation of a fictional past for his characters concerns the choice of names that are similar to those of other novelistic characters (Mouhy's *Melicourt* and Crebillon's *Meilcourt*, for example) (pp. 217, 221, 264, 270).

25. "Cyrano: mise à l'envers du vieil univers d'Aristote," p. 64.

26. Many of whom, Agrippa de Nettesheim and César, for example, did in fact claim to have acted or written under the influence of some sort of guiding spirit, so the demon's claims can be easily "verified."

27. Otherwise known as "or potable." Although it is difficult to imagine why he made such a change, Cyrano merely substitutes a synonym for the alchemist's substance.

28. Note to letter 58 (Flammarion, 1964), p. 121.

29. A slightly different vision of this problem is presented by D'Assoucy in the *Combat de Cirano de Bergerac avec le singe de Brioché* in which he describes Cyrano's reaction when he is put on trial for the murder of Brioché: "Bergerac se deffendit en Bergerac; c'est-à-dire avec des écrits facétieux et des paroles grotesques: Il dit au Juge qu'il payerait Brioché en Poëte, ou en monnoye de Singe; que les especes étoient un meuble que Phébus ne connoissoit point" (p. 14).

30. *La Vie et les oeuvres de Charles Sorel*, pp. 386–87.

31. *La Pensée philosophique et scientifique de Cyrano de Bergerac*, p. 77.

32. Alcover devotes most of her study to this question. In her *Cyrano de Bergerac and the Polemics of Modernity*, Erica Harth never discusses themes, events, and descriptions in Cyrano without detailing their similarities with contemporary and earlier works. Prévot finds fault with critics (he mentions Alcover) who see copying everywhere in *L'Autre Monde*. He rightly feels that the question to be discussed is not that of plagiarism but those of reference and parody, yet he gives only a faint hint of the playfulness that guides Cyrano's use of borrowed material (pp. 15, 105–6, 124–25). Many of his analyses are in fact concerned with tracing the systems for which various characters serve as mouthpieces, and he thereby rejoins the type of source study he claims to repudiate.

33. *Sceptiques ou libertins dans la première moitié du dix-septième siècle*, pp. 5–6.

34. "Cyrano de Bergerac," p. 559.

35. Meyer, p. 6.

36. The literary phenomena that result from partial reproduction and/or deformation of language or content, such as allusion, stylization, pastiche, parody, and plagiarism, are discussed by Meyer and examined by Bakhtin in the section of *Dostoevsky's Poetics* devoted to the various forms of what he calls "double-voiced" discourse.

37. *The Poetics of Quotation*, p. 8.

38. Which he calls "cužaja reč," "foreign speech," "another's speech," or "reported speech" (*Marxism*, p. 115).

39. The other means are stylization, parody, and *skaz* (the "oral" narration of a narrator), the forms of double-voiced discourse or the dialogic. Bakhtin actually traces the emergence of the new form of the dialogic (the movement from Rabelais to Dostoevsky) to the libertine period. He describes the sharply defined

boundaries of hierarchical literature, which does not allow itself to be penetrated by foreign styles, and chooses as his example French classicism. During its reign, only so-called low genres display noteworthy deviations from its linear style of speech reporting, and Bakhtin notes that "quasi-direct discourse achieves its first powerful development in the fables and tales of La Fontaine" (p. 123).

40. The "second generation" of dialogical texts, which for Bakhtin culminates in Dostoevsky, will attain linguistic and literary dialogism. This later generation's links to carnival and folk tradition are purely artificial. At this point in his schema, Bakhtin's theory of modernity may be said to rejoin Foucault's. Quotation plays an essential role for Foucault as well: "C'est que le dix-neuvième siècle a découvert un espace d'imagination dont les âges précédents n'avaient sans doute pas soupçonné la puissance. . . . L'imaginaire ne se constitue pas contre le réel pour le nier et le compenser; il s'étend entre les signes, de livre à livre, dans l'interstice des redites et des commentaires; il naît et se forme dans l'entre-deux des textes. C'est un phénomène de bibliothèque" ("Un fantastique de bibliothèque," pp. 10–11).

41. From this example and others in *L'Autre Monde*, a relationship between the obsessive movement toward dialogue and libertine paranoia is suggested.

42. Miel, p. 243.

43. Cervantes, pp. 421, 525.

44. Although this passage is not in the first edition of *Francion*, I include it because it represents one of the few instances of self-citation similar to Cervantes's in seventeenth-century French fiction.

45. *Beginnings*, p. 22.

46. Lachèvre partially reproduces the letter under the title "Le Campagnard" (2:205–6). The complete text may be found in the *Oeuvres diverses* (Charles de Sercy, 1654), pp. 59–65, or in the Prévot edition of the *Oeuvres complètes*, pp. 54–56. Critical opinion generally holds (Lachèvre, Erba, Laugaa) that the passage was used in the letter before finding a place in *L'Autre Monde*. Prévot disagrees with this view: "Nous pensons au contraire que le texte de la lettre, plus élaboré, mieux équilibré, plus riche de sens métaphorique, en est un état postérieur" (p. 142). However, the stylistic differences between the two "versions" (if indeed they are different enough to deserve this appellation) are not as important as Prévot contends. Furthermore, his theory completely ignores the signals of difference emitted by this passage in the context of *L'Autre Monde*, signals that designate it as foreign discourse.

47. Besides the catalogue, the *Avantures* presents other ways of performing the alchemical trick of turning linguistic poverty into riches; for example, the so-called burlesque repetitions, in which different forms of the same root are accumulated in a passage. At one point, a midnight encounter with a mysterious stranger inspires an exploration of "lanterne," which culminates in "j'avois beau contempler la lanterne, je ne voyais pas le lanternier. Ce qui me fit juger que c'estoit un homme qui portoit une lanterne sourde . . . car cette honnete lanterne, qui sans doute devoit estre la Reyne des lanternes de tous les pays lanternois" (p. 66).

48. One such image in *Francion* involves Catherine, the ladies' maid who is really a man. In the course of a thwarted robbery attempt, she/he is found dangling upside down from the façade of Valentin's château with his/her long skirts over his/her head: "Tous les habitants du village s'assemblerent devant le Chas-

teau, pour voir le soudain changement d'une fille en garçon," and one woman says: "Cela seroit plus à propos à Caresme Prenant" (p. 83). By making a thief the figure of carnival, Sorel prefigures D'Assoucy.

49. Meyer, p. 69.

50. Blanchot, p. 560.

51. From the preface to his *Exercitationum paradoxicarum adversus Aristoteleos libri septem* (1624); Spink, p. 15.

52. *Romanciers*, p. 32.

53. Prévot, p. 109.

54. Perrens, p. 52. This historical vision is echoed by Adam in *Les Libertins au dix-septième siècle*: "Mais les philosophes, les écrivains ont joué leur rôle dans cette évolution. Ils ont sauvegardé à une époque où le parti religieux dominait le pays, certaines traditions que l'orthodoxie prétendait étouffer. Quand le matérialisme commence à s'affirmer de nouveau dans les premières décades du dix-huitième siècle, nous découvrons qu'il se relie très exactement à celui . . . de Cyrano, de Denis Veiras, et, au delà d'eux mais aussi grâce à eux, à celui des grands naturalistes italiens de la Renaissance" (p. 30).

55. 11 July 1716. *Correspondance*, ed. Theodore Besterman (Geneva: Institut et musée Voltaire, 1953), vol. 1.

56. Blanchot, p. 560.

57. The dreaded name thus enters a libertine text, as well as the glory of classical discourse, the act of naming. For Foucault, classical discourse becomes as transparent as Dyrcona's body in order to name more successfully: "La tâche fondamentale du 'discours' classique, c'est d'attribuer un nom aux choses, et en ce nom de nommer leur être. Pendant deux siècles, le discours occidental fut le lieu de l'ontologie" (*Les Mots et les Choses*, p. 136).

58. Cited by Stillman Drake, p. 26.

NEIGHBORING TRENDS

In the preceding pages, I have attempted to show that the category of the libertine novel possesses a fundamental unity. I would not claim, however, that none of its characteristic marks can be noted elsewhere. A certain number of seventeenth-century novels share some degree of similarity with the works I call libertine. Nevertheless, in every case the distinguishing traits outweigh the resemblances.

For example, three early seventeenth-century novels have much in common with the libertine novels: John Barclay's *Euphormionis Lusinini Satyricon*, Agrippa d'Aubigné's *Baron de Faeneste*, and Jean de Lannel's *Romant satyrique*. Of the three, Barclay's *Euphormio* is certainly closest to the libertine texts, since it is a first-person account of the *disgraces à la page* of an "oppressed" hero, once a freeman, now a slave, who feigns madness in order to gain a certain degree of freedom. Besides its presentation of madness, the work's treatment of the occult, complete with a witchcraft scene reminiscent of the opening of *Francion*, provides an additional thematic similarity. Finally, its occasional verse interludes, obviously influenced by the classical tradition of Menippean satire, link it compositionally with certain representatives of the libertine tradition. Such resemblances are, however, more than counterbalanced by the absence of a breakdown into shorter units, by the lack of a sense of tradition, and above all by the novel's complex relationship to antiquity. It is written in Latin rather than the French chosen by the libertine authors, their decision being in a sense parallel to Descartes's composition of the *Discours de la méthode* in French instead of in Latin. *Euphormio* is also packed with allusions to antiquity, classical literature, and mythology, closer to a sort of libertine *roman héroïque* than to a comic novel. As a result of its classical flavor, the work's alleged autobiographical content is difficult to discern, if indeed it does exist. The final barrier between Barclay and the future libertine tradition is his work's rejection of the dialogic. *Euphormio*'s end is doubly happy, with a stable system provided, first, by a continued faith in the values of Antiquity and, second, by the ultimate financial and political security assured for Euphormio at the home of Tessa Ranactus, whose eulogy provides the closing passage of the novel. *Euphormionis Lusinini Satyricon* is clearly a daring book and one that has no place in the world of the sentimental romances that dominated the novelistic horizon at the time of its appearance, but it remains a far cry from a work of libertine contestation.

Despite such obvious links to the libertine mode in Agrippa d'Aubigné's *Baron de Faeneste* as its use of dialogue form, it is impossible to qualify as libertine a text composed precisely in order to defend a particular stand on a religious issue. The work is marked from one end to the other by its author's convictions, and these, rooted in the belief in one true system, are eminently monologic. *Le Romant satyrique* keeps its distance from libertine fiction. If the Ayme-Dieu passage is interpreted as a reference to Théophile, it could be described as a novel with a sense of tradition. But this tradition cannot be termed libertine, for Théophile is defended only if he is not guilty of the crime of atheism. Lannel's novel remains at the stage of the *roman à clef*, rejecting autobiographical impulses. With its third-person narration and its lack of fragmentation, it stays within contemporary norms.

The second category of works to merit comparison in this context is vaster, composed of novels of other writers who were intimately connected in some capacity with the movement of *libertinage érudit*. These texts are so varied that they are best examined in chronological order. The *Confessions* of J.-J. Bouchard are libertine only in the eighteenth-century sense of the word, a unique case in the milieu from which they originated. Editors[1] of this third-person account of the sexual exploits of the young hero Oreste generally assume it is autobiographical, although in addition to the veil of the third person, the *roman à clef* technique is also employed. Since extremely little is known about

Bouchard's youth, the importance of the autobiographical component cannot be measured with any degree of precision. The only real similarity between the *Confessions* and the libertine novels is evident when Bouchard occasionally deviates from the use of Greek pseudonyms to refer directly to his closest contacts in the world of *libertinage érudit*, Luillier and Gassendi.

The next two examples, works by members of the Tétrade, provide even more convincing evidence that this milieu was simultaneously producing very different types of prose fiction. Naudé's *Jugement de tout ce qui a esté imprimé contre le cardinal Mazarin depuis le sixième janvier, jusques à la Declaration du premier avril mil six cens quarante neuf*, more familiarly known as the *Mascurat*,[2] takes the form of a dialogue between the *libraire* Saint-Ange and the printer Mascurat. It shares evident formal similarities with the libertine novels, but despite this and the occasional presence of references to such figures as Peiresc and Gassendi, the *Mascurat* remains too much the story of Mazarin—his "true" genealogy, and so on—and is insufficiently preoccupied with the "novelistic" to get beyond the stage of polemical literature.[3] It is clearly not the story that matters here, but the defense. *Le Parasite Mormon* (1650), a coproduction of La Mothe Le Vayer and Sorel, has absolutely nothing of the libertine about it, other than the subtitle *histoire comique* it shares with several of these novels. It is a more than predictable third-person adaptation of a story by Zayas, of a type better known through the work of the only novelist in Gassendi's little clan not to have produced a libertine novel, Scarron.

Scarron's *Roman comique* is close to the works of the libertine tradition because of its reflections on language and the self-consciousness that results from Scarron's long association with the burlesque style. Other similarities are its formal division into short chapters, its juxtaposition of disparate fragments, its rejection of closure, and its ultimate defense of relativism and the dia-logic.[4] But Scarron's choice of the third person and his refusal to throw off the mask of the burlesque to let in either a sense of a libertine past or autobiographical elements firmly ground his novel in the tradition of comic fiction. This is also the category to which the novel of Scarron's first imitator, the known libertine Claude Le Petit, must be assigned. *L'Heure du berger* (1662) makes its reference to the *Roman comique* clear with its subtitle, "demy-roman comique ou roman demy-comique," but true affinities with either Scarron or especially with libertine fiction are nonexistent in this rather colorless, third-person pseudo *nouvelle espagnole*. It is evidently not sufficient to be a libertine to produce libertine fiction.

Cyrano's fantastic voyages left a heritage in the form of what Lachèvre terms the libertine utopias of the late seventeenth century: *La Terre australe connue* (1676), by the defrocked *cordelier* Gabriel de Foigny, and Denis Veiras's (or Vairasse) *L'Histoire des Sévarambes* (1677–79). Both these texts are no more than pale heirs of Cyrano's explosive prototype, and they must be situated completely outside French libertine tradition, with which, furthermore, they make no attempt to identify themselves, either through libertine naming or defending. Foigny's utopia is the more interesting of the two, but even he makes relatively little use of the potential of the philosophical dialogue. The first person and the dialogic disappear progressively from *La Terre australe connue*, to be replaced by description of the Australiens and their customs. The only passage that could be identified as autobiographical is the closing one describing the hero Sadeur's trial. This may serve as a reference to Foigny's own trial in Geneva by the Vénérable Compagnie. But even this allusion cannot be compared to the libertine evocations of intellectual repression. Sadeur's trial and condemnation do not occur as a result of his daring pronouncements, but because, during a war between the Australiens and the Fondins, he had refused to fight. Such an account could more accurately be described as a parody of the dangers of the libertine condition. *La Terre australe connue* is a text that conforms to Lachèvre's most negative interpretation of the libertine tradition in its desire to treat "forbidden" religious and sexual matters simply to scandalize, not to arrive at a coherent philosophy. Veiras's utopia has no link with libertine tradition other than its rejection of organized religion as embodied in the Christ-like figure, the imposter and false prophet Omigas. *L'Histoire des Sévarambes* is narrated in the third person and makes no attempt to integrate autobiographical elements.

After Cyrano, a second libertine writer is generally given credit for inaugurating a genre with an important future. Chapelle's

Voyage à Encausse is situated near the beginning of a trail of little-known works by major authors: Racine's *Voyage en Languedoc* (1661–2), La Fontaine's *Voyage de Paris en Limousin* (1663), and Regnard's *Voyage de Normandie* (1689), to mention the major representatives in the seventeenth century alone. The fact that Racine's *Voyage* precedes his would seem to indicate that paternity of the genre should not be attributed to Chapelle. In fact, Chapelle's manipulation of the form first used by Racine demonstrates his choice of an outsider's role within the confines of this particular type of voyage literature. Both Sainte-Beuve and Neubert grant an identical status to all these works, undoubtedly because of their formal similarities: all mix verse and prose, and all are presented as one or a series of letters. Such a comparison does a great injustice to Chapelle, who realizes far more fully than other practitioners the potential of the supple form he employs. He often goes beyond the frivolty of the *récit de voyage* of the well-bred traveler who never ventures very far from home and certainly never knows dangerous or exotic encounters to acknowledge his role in the libertine experience. In Racine's view of Languedoc, preciosity reigns. The threatening unknown and even travelogue concreteness are replaced by graceful mythological references. La Fontaine's text is largely of guidebook quality, with its descriptions of churches, châteaux and their gardens, paintings, and statues. The only names that occur in this voyage are those of artists. At times, in the fifth letter for example, the *Voyage de Paris en Limousin* reads like a museum catalogue. In the *Voyage de Normandie*, Regnard is more attentive to details and above all to details of a "realistic" nature (food, lodging) than either Racine or La Fontaine; but he remains, like them, completely removed from the type of voyage composed by Chapelle. In fact, his text in the form of a letter to a woman with a fictional name (Artémise), with its obsessional vision of women babbling in the coach, completes the reduction to a polite society game of a form that once served as a contribution to the libertine dialogue. The *Voyages* of Racine, La Fontaine, and Regnard may be described as charming bagatelles of famous men, meant, according to Neubert's play on one of the seventeenth-century's most quoted slogans, to entertain but not to instruct.[5] They are clearly of a different tissue from the text they allegedly imitate.

There are certain other seventeenth-century French novels possessing some of the characteristics of the novels I have identified as libertine, but the cross-section of texts just examined here, from Barclay to Regnard, provides a fair estimate of the limits of the incursion of other narrative trends into the territory measured out for this study. It is my hope that even this short review can provide some sense of the libertine novel's unique position in the history of seventeenth-century French prose narrative.

1. They prefer to remain anonymous, undoubtedly because of the rather scandalous content of the *Confessions* for a work of seventeenth-century prose. The *Confessions* probably dates from 1630, the date of the *Voyage de Paris à Rome* with which it composes a single manuscript, but it was not published until 1881.

2. Published anonymously, without date or place of publication. Philippe Wolfe in his article "*Le Mascurat* de Gabriel Naudé" demonstrates that the first edition was published in Paris by Cramoisy in late 1649.

3. On this point, I disagree with Wolfe, p. 115, and with Sainte-Beuve's statement that the *Mascurat* was the seventeenth-century's *Neveu de Rameau* (quoted by Wolfe, p. 103).

4. On this interpretation of the *Roman comique*, see my *Scarron's "Roman comique:" A Novel of Comedy, A Comedy of the Novel*.

5. Neubert, p. 124.

BIBLIOGRAPHY

EDITIONS OF LIBERTINE NOVELS

Assoucy, Charles Coypeau d'. *Avantures* and *Avantures d'Italie*. Ed. Emile Colombey. A. Delahays, 1858.*

Chapelle and Bachaumont. *Voyage à Encausse*. Ed. Charles Nodier. Didot, 1824.

———. *Voyage à Encausse. Oeuvres de Chapelle et Bachaumont*. Ed. Louis Tenant de Latour. P. Jannet, 1854.

———. *Voyage d'Encausse*. Ed. Maurice Souriau. Caen: L. Jouan, 1901.

Cyrano de Bergerac. *Histoire comique*. Ed. H. Le Bret. Charles de Sercy, 1657.

———. *Les Oeuvres libertines de Cyrano de Bergerac*. Ed. Frédéric Lachèvre. 2 vols. Champion, 1921.

———. *Voyage dans la lune*. Ed. Maurice Laugaa. Flammarion, 1970.

———. *L'Autre Monde*. Ed. Madeleine Alcover. H. Champion, 1977.

———. *Oeuvres complètes*. Ed. Jacques Prévot. Belin, 1977.

Sorel, Charles. *Histoire comique de Francion. Romanciers du dix-septième siècle*. Ed. Antoine Adam. Gallimard, 1958.

Tristan L'Hermite. *Le Page disgracié*. Toussainct Quinet, 1643.

———. *Le Page disgracié*. Ed. Auguste Dietrich. Plon, 1898.

———. *Le Page disgracié*. Ed. Jacques Savarin. Les Coulisses du passé, 1924.

———. *Le Page disgracié*. Ed. Marcel Arland. Stock, 1946.

Viau, Théophile de. *Les Oeuvres du sieur Théophile, seconde partie*. P. Billaine, 1626.

———. *Les Oeuvres du sieur Théophile, seconde partie*. Lyon: Jean Michon, 1630.

———. *Prose*. Ed. Guido Saba. Turin: Bottega d'Erasmo, 1965.

* Unless otherwise stated, all books were published in Paris.

CONTEMPORARY TEXTS

Arnauld, Antoine, and Claude Lancelot. *Grammaire générale et raisonnée.* P. Le Petit, 1664.

————, and Pierre Nicole. *La Logique ou l'art de penser.* Ed. Louis Marin. Flammarion, 1970.

Assoucy, Charles Coypeau d'. (Attributed). *Combat de Cirano de Bergerac avec le singe de Brioché au bout du Pont-neuf.* M. Rebuffé, 1704.

Aubigné, Agrippa de. *Les Avantures du Baron de Faeneste.* A. Maille, 1617.

————. *Les Avantures du Baron de Faeneste.* Au Dézert, 1630.

Barclay, John. *Euphormionis Lusinini Satyricon.* Tr. David Fleming, S.M. Nieuwkoop: B. De Graaf, 1973.

Bouchard, Jean-Jacques. *Confessions.* Gallimard, 1930.

Descartes, René. *Entretien avec Burman.* Ed. Charles Adam. Boivin, 1937.

Du Bail, Louis. (Attributed). *Le Gascon extravagant, histoire comique.* Cardin Besogne, 1637.

Foigny, Gabriel de. *La Terre australe connue.* Ed. Frédéric Lachèvre. H. Champion, 1922.

Garasse, François. *La Doctrine curieuse des beaux esprits de ce temps ou pretendus tels.* 2 vols. Sebastien Chappelet, 1623.

La Fontaine, Jean de. *Voyage de Paris en Limousin.* Vialetay, 1969.

Lannel, Jean de. *Le Romant satyrique.* T. Du Bray, 1624.

Le Petit, Claude. *Les Oeuvres libertines de Claude Le Petit.* Ed. Frédéric Lachèvre, 1918.

Ménage, Gilles. *Menagiana.* F. and P. Delaune, 1693.

Naudé, Gabriel. *Apologie pour tous les grands personnages qui ont esté faussement soupçonnez de magie.* Fr. Targa, 1625.

Peiresc, Nicolas-Claude Fabri de. *Lettres.* 7 vols. Imprimerie Nationale, 1888–98.

Regnard, Jean-François. *Voyage de Normandie. Oeuvres.* F. Didot, 1801.

Scarron, Paul. *Oeuvres comiques* (7 vols.; J. F. Bastien, 1786).

Sorbière, Samuel. *Sorberiana.* Vve. Cramoisy, 1694.

Sorel, Charles. *La Bibliothèque françoise.* Compagnie des libraries du Palais, 1664.

————, and François de La Mothe Le Vayer. (Attributed). *Le Parasite Mormon, histoire comique.* 1650.

————. (Attributed). *Les Avantures satyriques de Florinde, habitant de la basse region de la lune.* 1625.

Veiras, Denis. *Histoire des Sévarambes*. Ed. Frédéric Lachèvre. H. Champion, 1922.

Villars, Montfaucon de. *Le Comte de Gabalis*. Claude Barbin, 1670.

CRITICISM ON LIBERTINE NOVELS

Abraham, Claude K. *The Strangers: The Tragic World of Tristan L'Hermite*. Gainesville: University of Florida Press, 1966.

Adam, Antoine. *Théophile de Viau et la libre pensée française en 1620*. Droz, 1935.

_____. *Romanciers du dix-septième siècle*. Pléiade, 1958.

_____. *Histoire de la littérature française au dix-septième siècle*. 5 vols. Del Duca, 1962.

_____. *Les Libertins au dix-septième siècle*. Buchet/Chastel, 1964.

Alcover, Madeleine. *La Pensée philosophique et scientifique de Cyrano de Bergerac*. Droz, 1970.

Alter, Jean. "La Bande à Francion." *L'Esprit Créateur*, Spring 1979, pp. 3–13.

Barbe, Christian. "Cyrano de Bergerac: mise à l'envers du vieil univers d'Aristote." *Baroque*, No. 7 (1974), pp. 49–70.

Bernardin, N. M. *Un Précurseur de Racine, Tristan L'Hermite*. A. Picard, 1895.

Blanchot, Maurice. "Cyrano de Bergerac." *Tableau de la littérature française*. Vol. I. *De Rutebeuf à Descartes*. Gallimard, 1962, pp. 558–65.

Brun, Pierre. *Savinien de Cyrano Bergerac: sa vie et ses oeuvres*. A. Colin, 1893.

Carriat, Amédée. *Bibliographie des oeuvres de Tristan L'Hermite*. Limoges: Rougerie, 1955.

Chambers, Ross. "*L'Autre Monde*, ou le mythe du libertin." *Essays in French Literature*, No. 8 (1971), pp. 29–46.

Charbonnel, J.-L. *La Pensée italienne et le courant libertin*. H. Champion, 1919.

Coulet, Henri. *Le Roman jusqu'à la révolution*. 2 vols. A. Colin, 1967.

DeJean, Joan. "Method and Madness in Cyrano de Bergerac's *Voyage dans la lune*." *French Forum*, September 1977, pp. 224–37.

_____. "The Case of Théophile de Viau: Autobiography on Trial." *Poétique* (forthcoming).

Denis, Jacques. *Sceptiques ou libertins dans la première moitié du dix-septième siècle*. Caen: 1844.

Erba, Luciano. *Magia e invenzione: Note e ricerche su Cyrano de Bergerac e altri autori del primo Seicento francese*. Milan: All'Insegna del Pesce d'Oro, 1967.

Fournel, Victor. *La Littérature indépendante et les écrivains oubliés.* Didier, 1862.

Gaiffe, Félix. *L'Envers du grand siècle.* A. Michel, 1924.

Garavini, Fausta. "*Francion* rivisitato: Diacronia di una struttura." *Sagi e Ricerche di Letteratura Francese,* 14:39–107.

Gautier, Théophile. *Les Grotesques.* Charpentier, 1882.

Grisé, Catherine. "Toward a New Biography of Tristan L'Hermite." *Revue de l'Université d'Ottowa* 36 (1966): 295–316.

Gude, Mary Louise. "*Le Page disgracié*: The Text as Confession." Ph.D. dissertation, University of Pennsylvania, 1976.

Guillumette, Doris. *La Libre pensée dans l'oeuvre de Tristan L'Hermite.* Nizet. 1972.

Guthrie, J. Richard Jr. "An Analysis of Style and Purpose in the First Episode of the *Histoire comique de Francion.*" *Romance Notes* 15 (1973): 99–103.

Harth, Erica. *Cyrano de Bergerac and the Polemics of Modernity.* New York: Columbia University Press, 1970.

Harvey, Howard. "Cyrano de Bergerac and the Question of Human Liberties." *Symposium,* No. 4 (May-November 1950), pp. 120–30.

Ivker, Barry. *An Anthology and Analysis of Seventeenth and Eighteenth-Century French Libertine Fiction.* Ann Arbor, Mich.: University Microfilms International, 1977.

Lachèvre, Frédéric. *Le Libertinage devant le Parlement de Paris: le procès du poète Théophile de Viau.* 2 vols. H. Champion, 1909.

————. *Une réparation posthume due au "Précurseur de Racine": Tristan L'Hermite, sieur du Solier, poète chrétien et catholique.* Margraff, 1941.

Lanius, Edward. *Cyrano de Bergerac and the Universe of the Imagination.* Droz, 1967.

Lapp, John. "Tristan L'Hermite and the Secret Myths." In *La Cohérence intérieure.* Ed. J. Van Baelen and D. Rubin. Editions J.-M. Place, 1977.

Laugaa, Maurice. "Lune ou L'Autre." *Poétique,* No. 3 (1970), pp. 282–96.

Lavers, A. "La Croyance à l'unité de la science dans *L'Autre Monde* de Cyrano de Bergerac." *Cahiers du Sud,* January 1959, pp. 406–16.

Leiner, Wolfgang, and Michael Griffiths. "Names in *Francion.*" *Romance Notes,* Vol. 15, No. 1 (1973), pp. 445–53.

————. "Le Rêve de Francion: considérations sur la cohésion intérieure de l'*Histoire comique de Francion* de Sorel." In *La Cohérence intérieure.* Ed. J. Van Baelen and D. Rubin. Editions J.-M. Place, 1977. Pp. 157–76.

Lemke, Walter. " 'Libertin': From Calvin to Cyrano." *Studi francese,* No. 58 (April 1976), pp. 58–60.

Mandrou, Robert. *Des humanistes aux hommes de science.* Editions du Seuil, 1973.

Maubon, Catherine. *"Le Page disgracié:* à propos du titre." *Saggi e Ricerche di litteratura francese* 16 (1977): 169–95.

Mongrédien, Georges. *Le Dix-Septième Siècle galant: libertins et précieuses.* Perrin, 1929.

_____. *Cyrano de Bergerac.* Editions Berger-Levrault, 1964.

Neubert, Fritz. *Die französischen Versprosa-Reisebrieferzählungen und der Kleine Reiseroman des 17. und 18. Jahrhunderts.* Leipzig: W. Gronau, 1923.

Nicolson, M.-H. *Voyages to the Moon.* New York: Macmillan Co., 1948.

Nodier, Charles. *Bibliographie des fous.* Techener, 1835.

_____. *Bonaventure Desperiers et Cirano de Bergerac.* Techener, 1841.

Perrens, F. T. *Les Libertins en France au dix-septième siècle.* L. Chailley, 1896.

Pintard, René. *Le Libertinage érudit dans la première moitié du dix-septième siècle.* Boivin, 1943.

_____. "L'Autre Tristan L'Hermite." *RHLF* 55 (1955): 492–95.

Prévot, Jacques. *Cyrano de Bergerac romancier.* Belin, 1977.

Rathje, Jürgen. "Théophile héros des *Fragments.*" In *Sprache, Literatur, Kultur.* Bern, 1974.

Reynier, Gustave. *Le Roman réaliste au dix-septième siècle.* Hachette, 1914.

Rizza, Cecilia. "Théophile de Viau: libertinage e libertà." *Studi francese,* September-December 1976, pp. 430–62.

Roy, Emile. *La Vie et les oeuvres de Charles Sorel.* Hachette, 1891.

Saba, Guido, "Aspetti di Théophile de Viau prosatore." *Saggi e ricerche di letteratura francese.* Vol. 9 (1975):107–86.

Sainte-Beuve. *Causeries du lundi.* Garnier, 1868. Book 2.

Serroy, Jean. "D'un roman à métamorphoses: la composition du *Francion* de Charles Sorel." *Baroque* (1973), pp. 97–103.

_____. "Le Monstre anthropomorphe: image de l'homme dans *L'Autre Monde* de Cyrano de Bergerac." *Circé,* No. 4 (1975), pp. 59–68.

Spink, J. S. *French Free Thought from Gassendi to Voltaire.* London: Athlone Press, 1960.

Sutcliffe, F. E. *Le Réalisme de Charles Sorel: problèmes humains du dix-septième siècle.* Nizet, 1965.

Toldo, Pietro. "Les Voyages merveilleux de Cyrano de Bergerac et de

Swift et leurs rapports avec l'oeuvre de Rabelais. *Revue des Etudes Rabelaisiennes* 4 (1906): 302–22.

Van Baelen, Jacqueline. "Reality and Illusion in *L'Autre Monde*: The Narrative Voyage." *Yale French Studies*, No. 49 (1973), pp. 178–84.

Verdier, Gabrielle. "Théophile's *Fragments*: discours amoureux?" *Papers on French 17th-Century Literature*, No. 12, pp. 137–57.

Wolfe, Philippe. "Le *Mascurat* de Gabriel Naudé." *Revue du Pacifique*, Vol. 2, No. 2 (1976), pp. 103–16.

OTHER CRITICISM AND NOVELS CITED

Alter, Robert. *Partial Magic: The Novel as a Self-Conscious Genre.* Berkeley: University of California Press, 1975.

Bachelard, Gaston. *La Formation de l'esprit scientifique.* Vrin, 1938.

———. *La Psychanalyse du feu.* Gallimard, 1938.

Bakhtin, Mikhail. *Rabelais and His World.* Tr. Hélène Iswolsky. Cambridge, Mass.: MIT Press, 1968.

———. *Dostoevsky's Poetics.* Ann Arbor, Mich.: Ardis, 1973.

———. (Vološinov, V. N.) *Marxism and the Philosophy of Language.* New York: Seminar Press, 1973.

Barthes, Roland. *Le Degré zéro de l'écriture.* Editions du Seuil, 1953.

———. *S/Z.* Editions du Seuil, 1970.

———. *Le Plaisir du texte.* Editions du Seuil, 1973.

———. *Fragments d'un discours amoureux.* Editions du Seuil, 1977.

Benjamin, Walter. *Illuminations.* New York: Harcourt, Brace & World, 1968.

———. *Mythe et violence.* Denoël, 1971.

Benveniste, Emile. *Problèmes de linguistique générale.* Gallimard, 1966.

Beugnot, Bernard. "Dialogue, entretien et citation à l'époque classique." *Canadian Review of Comparative Literature.* Special Issue (Winter 1976), pp. 39–50.

Blanc, Henri. "Sur le statut du dialogue dans l'oeuvre de Sade." *Dix-huitième Siècle*, No. 4 (1972), pp. 301–14.

Brunetière, Ferdinand. "Le Maladie du burlesque." *Revue des Deux Mondes*, 1906, pp. 667–91.

Bruss, Elisabeth. "L'Autobiographie considérée comme acte littéraire." *Poétique* 17 (1974): 14–26.

Busson, Henri. *Le Rationalisme dans la littérature française de la Renaissance (1533–1601).* J. Vrin, 1957.

Cardano, Girolamo. *Les Livres de H. Cardanus medecin Milannois intitulez de la subtilité, et subtiles inventions, ensemble les causes occultes, et raisons d'icelles.* Pierre Cavelat, 1584.

———. *De Vita Propria Liber.* Tr. J. Stoner. New York: Dutton, 1930.

Cervantes, Miguel de. *The Ingenious Gentleman Don Quixote de la Mancha*. Tr. Samuel Putnam. New York: Modern Library, 1949.

Cosentini, John. *Fontenelle's Art of Dialogue*. New York: King's Crown Press, 1952.

DeJean, Joan. *Scarron's 'Roman comique': A Comedy of the Novel, A Novel of Comedy*. Bern: Lang, 1977.

————. "Scarron's *Roman comique*: The Other Side of Parody." *Papers on French Seventeenth-Century Literature*, Winter 1978, pp. 51–63.

Démoris, René. *Le Roman à la première personne*. A. Colin, 1975.

Drake, Stillman. "Galileo's Language: Mathematics and Poetry in a New Science." *Yale French Studies*, No. 49 (1973), pp. 13–27.

Drujon, Fernand. *Les Livres à clef: étude de bibliographie*. 3 vols. Rouveyre: 1885–88.

Foucault, Michel. *Les Mots et les choses*. Gallimard, 1966.

————. "Un fantastique de bibliothèque." *Cahiers Renaud-Barrault* 59 (March 1967): 9–20.

————. "Qu'est-ce qu'un auteur?" *Bulletin de la Société française de philosophie* 64 (1969): 73–104.

————. *Histoire de la folie à l'âge classique*. Gallimard, 1972.

————. *Surveiller et punir*. Gallimard, 1975.

Freud, Sigmund. *Character and Culture*. New York: Collier Books, 1963.

Gardiner, Alan. *The Use of Proper Names*. London: Oxford University Press, 1954.

Gossman, Lionel. *Men and Masks: A Study of Molière*. Baltimore: Johns Hopkins Press, 1963.

Gusdorf, Georges. "De l'autobiographie initiatique à l'autobiographie genre littéraire." *RHLF* 75 (1975): 957–94.

Hardee, A. M. *Jean de Lannel and the Pre-Classical French Novel*. Droz, 1967.

Hazard, Paul. *La Crise de la conscience européenne*. Boivin, 1935.

Hirzel, Rudolf. *Der Dialog: Ein Literarhistorischer Versuch*. 2 vols. Leipzig: S. Hirzel, 1895.

Ivker, Barry. "Towards a Definition of Libertinism in Eighteenth-Century French Fiction." *SVEC* 73 (1970):221–39.

Josephs, Herbert. "Diderot's *La Religieuse*: Libertinism and the Dark Cave of the Soul." *MLN* 91 (1976): 734–55.

Kayser, Wolfgang. *The Grotesque in Art and Literature*. New York: McGraw-Hill, 1966.

Koyré, Alexandre. *Du monde clos à l'univers infini*. Gallimard, 1973.

Kristeva, Julia. "Le Mot, le dialogue, et le roman." In *Recherches pour une sémanalyse*. Editions du Seuil, 1969.

Laufer, Roger. *Style rococo, style des "Lumières."* Corti, 1963.

Lejeune, Philippe. *L'Autobiographie en France.* A. Colin, 1971.

———. *Le Pacte autobiographique.* Editions du Seuil, 1975.

———. "Autobiographie et histoire littéraire." *RHLF* 75 (1975): 903–36.

Lever, Maurice. "Sorcellerie et littérature au dix-septième siècle." *Les Nouvelles Littéraires*, 5 February 1973, p. 14.

———. *La Fiction narrative en prose au dix-septième siècle.* Editions du CNRS, 1976.

Lévi-Strauss, Claude. *Tristes tropiques.* Plon, 1955.

Marchand, Jacqueline. *Les Romanciers libertins du dix-huitième siècle.* Editions Rationalistes, 1971.

Marin, Louis. *La Critique du discours.* Editions de Minuit, 1975.

Martin, H.-J. *Livre, pouvoirs, et société à Paris au dix-septième siècle.* 2 vols. Droz, 1969.

Matejka, Ladislav, and Krystyna Pomorska. *Readings in Russian Poetics.* Cambridge, Mass.: MIT Press, 1971.

Meyer, Herman. *The Poetics of Quotation in the European Novel.* Princeton, N.J.: Princeton University Press, 1968.

Michaud, Gustave. *La Jeunesse de Molière.* Hachette, 1922.

Miel, Jan. "Ideas or Epistemes: Hazard versus Foucault," *Yale French Studies*, No. 49 (1973), pp. 231–45.

Morris, John. *Versions of the Self.* New York: Basic Books, 1966.

Nodier, Charles (ed.). *Satyre ménipée.* 2 vols. N. Delangle, 1824.

———. *De quelques livres satiriques et de leurs clefs.* Techener, 1834.

Olney, James. *Metaphors of Self.* Princeton, N.J.: Princeton University Press, 1972.

Perry, Ben. *The Ancient Romances.* Berkeley: University of California Press, 1967.

Rigolot, François. *Poétique et onomastique.* Geneva: Droz, 1977.

Rousseau, Jean-Jacques. *Oeuvres complètes.* Gallimard, 1959. Vol. 1.

Rousset, Jean. *La Littérature de l'âge baroque en France.* Corti, 1954.

———. *Narcisse romancier.* Corti, 1973.

Said, Edward. *Beginnings.* New York: Basic Books, 1975.

Secret, François. "Littérature et alchimie à la fin du seizième siècle et au début du dix-septième siècle." *Bibliothèque d'Humanisme et de Renaissance* 35 (1973): 103–16.

Sherman, Carol. *Diderot and the Art of Dialogue.* Droz, 1976.

Shklovsky, Viktor. *Zoo, or Letters Not about Love.* Ithaca, N.Y.: Cornell University Press, 1971.

Starobinski, Jean. *L'Oeil vivant.* Gallimard, 1961.

_____. "Le Style de l'autobiographie." *Poétique* 3 (1970): 257–65.

Stevick, Philip. *The Chapter in Fiction.* Syracuse, N.Y.: Syracuse University Press, 1970.

Stewart, Philip. *Imitation and Illusion in the French Memoir-Novel (1700–50).* New Haven, Conn.: Yale University Press, 1969.

Strauss, Leo. *Persecution and the Art of Writing.* Glencoe, Ill.: Free Press, 1952.

Sturm, Ernest. *Crébillon fils et le libertinage au dix-huitième siècle.* Nizet, 1970.

Vance, Eugene. "Désir, rhétorique, et texte." *Poétique* 42 (1980): 137–55.

Zumthor, Paul. *Langue, texte, énigme.* Editions du Seuil, 1975.

INDEX

Adam, Antoine, 9, 12, 22, 82, 137, 193, 202 n. 54; and definition of "libertine," 24; *Histoire de la littérature française au dix-septième siècle*, 27 n. 3; *Théophile de Viau*, 13, 71 n. 2, 73 n. 19

Alchemy/alchemist, 67, 110, 112, 137, 143, 145

Alcover, Madeleine, 30 n. 43, 111, 200 n. 32

Alienation, 24, 123, 132, 134, 144, 184; the limits of, 122, 146, 148

Allegory, 62, 71, 196, 197

Anagram, 31 n. 44; Ariston as, 74 n. 47; Dyrcona as, 6, 44, 45, 46, 64; Soucidas as, 20, 44, 146; Ronscar as, 44; Voltaire as, 44

Arland, Marcel, 12, 38, 39, 81

Arnauld, Antoine, 69

Artefius/Artephius, 17, 30 n. 42, 39, 61, 67, 86, 113, 173, 182

Atheism/atheist, 21, 108–10, 139; of libertine novelists, 12, 204

Aubigné, Théodore Agrippa d', 203, 204

Autobiography, 26, 40, 133; fictionalized, 43; partial, 52, 72 n. 8; theory of, 48–49

Bachaumont, François le Coigneux, sieur de, 13, 14, 20, 140

Bachelard, Gaston, 137

Bakhtin, Mikhail, 160–63, 176–77, 183, 192, 198 nn. 9, 10, 12, 200 n. 36

Barclay, John, 203–4

Barthes, Roland, 71, 97 n. 9, 154 n. 19, 159, 160

Baudelaire, Charles, 80

Benjamin, Walter, 70, 77–80, 85, 96, 125

Bernardin, N. M., 38, 73 n. 21

Blanchot, Maurice, 176, 190, 191, 195

Boileau, Nicolas, 143, 192

Borges, Jorge, 33, 42–43, 71, 181

Bouchard, Jean-Jacques, 204–5, 208 n. 1

Brosse, Guy de la, 16, 166

Brown, Norman O., 143

Brunetière, Ferdinand, 156 n. 43

Burlesque, the, 19, 54, 55, 57, 67, 88, 129; attacks on, 142, 143; libertine novelists relationship to, 165, 166

Burlesque etymologies, 47, 73 n. 30, 75 n. 49, 118–19

Camera lucida, 103, 143

Camera obscura, 102, 103, 135, 152, 153 n. 3, 154 n. 13

Campanella, Tommaso, 16, 17, 20, 88, 132, 170, 182, 192, 198; as character in *Estats et empires*, 94, 155 n. 27, 196

Cannibalism, 135, 136, 145, 155 n. 33

Cardano, Girolamo, 16, 24, 30 n. 42, 48, 92, 158; and autobiography, 53, 99 n. 22, 169–70, 182, 183

Carnival, 42, 190, 192, 202 n. 48; Bakhtin's theory of, 160–61, 177, 198 n. 12

Carriat, Amédée, 27 n. 5, 72 n. 11

Castration, 144, 146, 148, 149, 150, 156 n. 45, 187

Censorship, 5, 104

Cervantes Saavedra, Miguel de, 73 n. 25, 103, 201 n. 44; *Don Quixote*, 45, 54, 55, 106, 179–81; *Exemplary Novels*, 179, 181

Childhood, 52, 66, 75 n. 54, 114, 115–17, 154 nn. 14–15

Citation, 43, 169, 174–77, 183, 184, 201 n. 40; characters as, 170–73; self-citation, 95, 184, 186, 187, 188, 201 n. 44

Cliché, 108, 114, 165, 166, 187, 188, 199 n. 22

Closure, 95, 96, 205

Colombey, Emile, 7, 34, 74 n. 46, 136

Combat de Cirano de Bergerac avec le singe de Brioché, 31 n. 45, 75 n. 30, 118, 133, 200 n. 29

Copernicus, Nicolaus, 16, 88, 164, 186

Coulet, Henri, 22

DeJean, Joan, 74 n. 38, 208 n. 4

Demon of Socrates, 137, 170–71, 181–83; as *porte parole*, 19

Démoris, René, 13, 25, 40, 71, 136–37, 138; on *Fragments d'une histoire comique*, 52; on *Francion*, 72 n. 8; on *Page disgracié*, 56, 102, 111, 112, 124

Descartes, René, 12, 15, 197, 203; Cartesian linguistics, 160, 162, 163

Dialogic, the, 26, 66, 96, 178, 186, 205; limits of, 182, 193, 194; theory of, 163, 200 n. 39

Dialogue, 83, 160, 164, 177–79, 193, 196, 201 n. 41; *see also* Dialogic, the; Intertextuality

Diderot, Denis, 57, 77, 197; *La Religieuse*, 37, 186; *Le Neveu de Rameau*, 122

Dietrich, Auguste, 12, 37, 38

Drake, Stillman, 97

Dream, 26, 124, 146, 195; of Francion, 144, 146–52, 155 n. 37

Drujon, Fernand, 39–40

Ellipsis, 90, 95

Exile, 18, 74 nn. 43–44

Flaubert, Gustave, 182

Foucault, Michel, 45, 73 n. 27, 107, 159, 160–63, 192, 198 n. 6, 201 n. 40, 202 n. 57

Fournel, Victor, 9, 22, 97 n. 8, 105

Fragmentation, 25, 90, 93, 94, 96, 204

Freethinking/freethought, 182, 184, 195; in the eighteenth century, 193, 202 n. 54; persecution for, 87, 110, 121, 123; underground survival of, 11; *see also* Libertinage érudit

Freud, Sigmund, 137, 154 n. 23

Fronde, la, 14, 20

Furetière, Antoine, 24, 74 nn. 43–44, 143; *Roman bourgeois*, 22, 165

Galilei, Galileo, 12, 24, 25, 26, 89, 91, 97, 164, 197

Gambling/gambler, 85, 92, 124–30, 154 n. 23; and cardsharp, 125, 127, 128, 130, 135; and swindling, 125, 126, 128

Garasse, François, 5, 28 n. 9, 29 n. 15, 51

Garavini, Fausta, 147

Gascon extravagant, Le, 42, 108, 120, 199 n. 19

Gassendi, Pierre, 10, 16, 25, 134, 186, 205; as libertine emblem, 17, 19; as teacher, 11, 12, 13, 15, 192, 194

Gautier, Théophile, 3, 33, 157, 188; *Les Grotesques*, 9

Genealogy, 36, 53, 59, 118, 142, 144, 170; family tree, 18, 29 n. 15

Godwin, Francis, 171

Gonzales, Domingo, the Spaniard on the moon, 89, 91, 130, 171–72, 178

Gossman, Lionel, 70

Grammaire générale et raisonnée, 27 n. 2, 69, 160, 162

Harth, Erica, 200 n. 32

Harvey, Howard, 15

Hazard, Paul, 157

Hermaphrodite, 144

Histoire comique, 26, 88, 165, 199 n. 19, 205

Homosexuality, 21, 109, 136–42

Hugo, Victor, 69

Imposter, 56, 73 n. 29, 112, 113, 126, 154 n. 12

Intertextuality, 162, 166, 168–70, 180, 188, 196; and dialogue, 26, 177, 182; *see also* Dialogue

Ivker, Barry, 23

Jakobson, Roman, 198 n. 9

Jansenism, 57, 69, 70

Josephs, Herbert, 23

Kayser, Wolfgang, 198 n. 12

Kepler, Johann, 16, 88, 164

Kristeva, Julia, 84, 98 n. 13, 199 n. 14

Lachèvre, Ferdinand, 12, 156 n. 47, 201 n. 46, 206; and definition of "libertine," 24; *Libertinage en France*, 9

Laclos, Choderlos de, 174

Lafayette (Mme de), Marie Madeleine Pioche de la Vergne, 171, 197

La Fontaine, Jean de, 201 n. 39, 207

La Mothe le Vayer, François de, 10, 17, 146; *Dialogues d'Orasius Tubero*, 18; *Parasite Mormon*, 30 n. 30, 205

Lannel, Jean de, 203, 204

La Tour, Georges de, 125, 126, 127

Laufer, Roger, 14

Laugaa, Maurice, 98 n. 19, 99 nn. 21–22, 201 n. 46

Le Bret, Henri, 5, 28 n. 6, 172, 191

Leiner, Wolfgang, 146, 147
Lejeune, Philippe, 48, 69, 73 nn. 18, 27
Lemke, Walter, 31 n. 51
Le Petit, Claude, 15, 98 n. 15, 205
Lever, Maurice, 30 n. 33, 98 n. 15, 153 n. 7
Lévi-Strauss, Claude, 135, 136
L'Hermite, Jean-Baptiste, 7, 28 n. 11, 36, 37
Libertins/libertinage érudit, 10, 11, 14, 17, 204, 205; *see also* Freethinking/freethought
Loret, Jean, 68, 86, 124, 178

Madman/madness, 6, 10, 26, 107, 121, 154 n. 19, 203; *avoir un quartier dans la tête*, 5, 96, 120; baroque madman, 108, 119, 120, 153 n. 8; *extravagant*, 120, 126, 127; *lunaire*, 104; lunatic, 104, 119, 120, 154 n. 18, 174
Magic/magician, 26, 110, 111, 114, 119, 154 n. 14; in *Page disgracié*, 41, 62, 73 n. 21
Manifesto: literary, 165, 166, 187, 188; political, 13, 15
Marchand, Jaqueline, 23
Marin, Louis, 199 n. 15
Martin, H.-J., 72 n. 10
Memoirs, 65, 66, 107
Ménage, Gilles, 5, 27 n. 6, 96
Metaphor, 79, 142, 171, 190–92; *see also* Narration: "metaphorical"
Metonymy, 20, 81
Meyer, Herman, 176, 190, 200 n. 36
Michaud, Gustave, 11
Miel, Jan, 179, 198 n. 2
Mise en abyme, 167, 183
Molière, Jean-Baptiste Poquelin, 12, 168
Mongrédien, Georges, 28 n. 6, 154 n. 10
Monkey/monkey business, 114, 130–34, 155 n. 26, 200 n. 29; *singer*, 132, 146, 184, 190
Monster/monstrosity, 124, 149

Naming, act of, 6, 62, 75 nn. 50–51, 195, 202 n 57; *see also* Proper name
Narration: first-person, 35, 55, 58, 68, 77, 79, 166; "metaphorical," 86, 87, 90, 92, 97; paratactical, 86; third-person, 25, 55, 58
Naudé, Gabriel, 10, 111, 112, 113, 205
Nerval, Gerard de, 6, 81, 153 n. 8
Neubert, Fritz, 14, 136, 207
Nicole, Pierre, 41
Nodier, Charles, 39
Nom d'auteur, 44, 45–47, 73 n. 27

Onomastics, 4, 41

Paranoia, 68, 123, 124, 127, 134, 151, 188, 201 n. 41
Parataxis, 55, 81, 86, 94, 95, 96, 146, 163
Parody, 89, 107, 165, 166, 199 nn. 19–20, 200 nn. 32, 36
Pascal, Blaise, 41, 70
Pedant/pedantry, 56, 107, 109, 110, 154 n. 18; Hortensius as, 106, 174; Sidias as, 106, 188
Peiresc, Nicolas Claude Fabri de, 11, 16, 25, 205
Perry, Ben, 97 n. 1
Phoenix, 133, 144, 145
Picaresque, 49, 65
Pintard, René, 10, 11, 13, 15, 16, 17, 158; and definition of "libertine," 23, 24
Plagiarism, 21, 73 n. 31, 175, 184, 200 nn. 32, 36; Cyrano's fear of, 146, 156 n. 48, 187
Pontis, Louis de, 70, 75 n. 60
Porta, Jean-Baptiste, 16, 115, 154 n. 13
Portrait, 153 n. 4; self-portrait, 58, 68
Prévot, Jacques, 28 n. 6, 30 n. 41, 72 n. 9, 153 n. 6, 200 n. 32, 201 n. 46
Prison/imprisonment, 3, 102–7, 121, 129
Prometheus, 57, 63, 91, 156 n. 45, 190, 195
Proper name, 4, 6, 8, 20, 62; absence of, in libertine texts, 34, 35, 43, 69; "Cyrano de Bergerac" as, 6; "Dassoucy" as, 7, 46–47; first name as, 28 n. 9; "Galileo" as, 28 n. 9; names of characters as, 60–61, 62, 200 n. 24; "Théophile de Viau" as, 4; "Tristan L'Hermite" as, 7; *see also* Naming
Proverb, 190, 192
Public letter, 111, 134, 146, 185–86, 201 n. 46

Quotation; *see* Citation

Rabelais, François, 143, 146, 163, 193, 197, 200 n. 39
Racine, Jean, 207
Realism, 43
Relativism, 86, 162, 179, 193, 194, 205; and the novel, 164, 169, 190
Reynier, Gustave, 22
Rigolot, François, 74 n. 39
Robbery, 47, 73 n. 31, 124, 145, 146, 188–90, 202 n. 48; *see also* Plagiarism
Roman à clef, 17, 39, 40, 44, 177, 204; libertine rejection of, 18, 20
Roman héroïque, 22, 25, 57, 79, 81, 82, 96, 165

Rostand, Edmond, 143
Rousseau, Jean-Jacques, 6, 28 n. 8, 48, 70, 93, 123, 135, 174, 197
Rousset, Jean, 31 n. 54, 45, 68, 153 n. 8, 168

Sade, Donatien Alphonse François, comte, called marquis de, 23, 197
Said, Edward, 184
Sainte-Beuve, Charles, 14, 207
Satire, 44, 193; Menippean, 26, 94, 160, 163, 199 n. 17, 203
Scarron, Paul, 12, 79, 146, 156 n. 48, 184, 198 n. 12; *Roman comique*, 22, 55, 57, 98 nn. 11, 15, 165, 197, 199 n. 19, 205–6, 208 n. 4
Scheherazade, 79, 86, 167, 168
Scudéry, Madeleine de, 31 n. 54, 40, 68, 186; *Clélie*, 96, 168
Self-consciousness, 26, 142, 167, 174, 187, 192, 196, 205; techniques of, 45, 179
Serroy, Jean, 44, 147
Shklovsky, Viktor, 43
Socrates, 89, 182
Sorcery/sorcerer, 110–18, 141; *see also* Magic

Spink, J. S., 10, 15, 158, 192
Starobinski, Jean, 49, 65, 152
Stevick, Philip, 95
Stewart, Philip, 84, 199 n. 24
Storyteller/storytelling, 74 n. 48, 79, 80, 86, 167, 178
Sublimation, 110, 143, 144

Thief; *see* Robbery
Trial, 91, 92, 111, 131, 206; Théophile's, 8, 30 n. 31, 74 n. 36

Utopia, 44, 145, 187, 197, 206; *paradis terrestre*, 57, 67, 83, 90, 185–87, 191, 194–95

Van Baelen, Jaqueline, 98 n. 21
Vance, Eugene, 141–42
Voltaire, François Marie Arouet de, 84, 193–94, 197

Wolfe, Phillip, 208 nn. 2–3

Zamiatin, Evgeny, 1, 26
Zumthor, Paul, 73 n. 32